W9-DGT-221

OUTLINES OF SOCIOLOGY

PAINE-WHITMAN STUDIES IN
SOCIAL SCIENCE AND SOCIAL THEORY

LUDWIG GUMPLOWICZ

OUTLINES
OF
SOCIOLOGY

EDITED WITH AN
INTRODUCTION AND NOTES
BY
IRVING L. HOROWITZ

NEW YORK
PAINE-WHITMAN PUBLISHERS
1963

Paine-Whitman Publishers, 1182 Broadway, New
York City 1, New York.

Library of Congress Catalog Card No. 63-7232

First German language edition, 1885
First English language edition, 1899
Second German language edition, 1905
Reprinted, *Ausgewaehlte Werke*, 1926
Second English language edition, 1963

Contents

EDITOR'S PREFACE

THE EMINENCE OF LUDWIG GUMPLOWICZ as a sociologist has long been acknowledged. His specific ideas, on the other hand, have rarely been seriously considered. While many of his theoretical formulations are no longer acceptable, no responsible historian of sociology fails to give a mention, or an analysis, of Gumplowicz' *Grundriss der Soziologie*. Yet no critical edition of this pivotal work has been published since its original publication in English in 1899, and then in a very limited (and unfortunately crude) edition. Without exaggerating the wisdom of the *Soziologie*, it must be ranked among the most important statements of sociology in its formative period, a work clearly on a par with Durkheim's *Rules of Sociological Method*.

The introductory essay offers, in addition to the main contours of the *Soziologie*, an overview of Gumplowicz' main ideas in general, particularly those expressed in his other major work, *Der Rassenkampf*, and an examination of the men and movements in sociology he helped to influence. My essay is somewhat longer than originally intended. In part this was a response to a mounting recognition that Gumplowicz is not so much a minor figure in the development of sociology, as a neglected one (*Cf.* Salomon, 1926). As such, I intend my remarks to serve as a basis for a deeper and truer understanding of a pioneer in sociology; and hopefully, as a stimulus to those interested in the problem areas treated, to go further into the sources of our discipline. Work in the history of sociology is very much a task yet to be performed rather than a goal realized. The absence of any full scale analysis of the intimate interrelation and interpenetration of German and American sociology makes this plain.

The main editorial tasks with which I have had to grapple were the establishment of a definitive text, which involved a careful check and correction of the original translation of the *Soziologie* (Gumplowicz, 1899), inclusion of the most important additions Gumplowicz made for the second German edition of the *Soziologie* (Gumplowicz, 1905), and to supply the necessary annotation which would make the text more meaningful to a present day audience of teachers and students of the social sciences.

While a presentation of the work of Gumplowicz hardly demands apologies, there is a nagging feeling that those concerned with the history of sociology in the present climate of sociological empiricism are somewhat in the same position as those *virtuosi* interested in the history of British water beetles. Nonetheless, in a profound sense, sociology is its history, which is to say that the present state of sociological research could only have come about by a settlement of questions of theory whose development took a long time, to say nothing of their resolution. Thus a closer scrutiny of sociological history is revealing not just as an insight into the origins of present-day conflicts within the discipline, but more important, as a source of fertile ideas in the overcoming of inherited difficulties

Beyond these pragmatic reasons for paying greater attention to the history of sociology is the intrinsic interest of the field as such. Historical wisdom is one avenue open to consciousness for overcoming that sectarian and anthropomorphic pride in the present. From this height we may explore from where we have come and where we are going. For these reasons, as well as the obvious contemporary relevance of Gumplowicz' *Sociology,* the following is offered. In terms of my own work, I consider this interest in Gumplowicz to be an outcome and convergence of a number of lines of thought— a concern with conflict and problems of conflict resolution (Horowitz, 1957, 1961a, 1961b) and a parallel interest in sociological theory and the sociology of knowledge (Horowitz, 1960, 1962). It is to be hoped that the reader of Gumplowicz' *Outlines of Sociology* will also see its relevance to his own efforts in social science.

I am grateful for the valuable translation assistance of Mrs. Ilse Gotsch (who worked with me on the changes and additions made in the second edition of the *Soziologie*), and Mr. Hans von Brockdorff (who researched the Ward-Gumplowicz correspondence). I want also to record my appreciation to Professor Maynard Smith, who gave this introduction his customarily discerning examination. The tendency to "Platonize" the German language, which H. H. Gerth witnessed in Weber, is no less marked in Gumplowicz. They shared a style of writing that can perhaps best be described as "academic formalism." It became necessary to rethink each paragraph if only to distinguish the sentences (hidden behind a veil of commas and semi-colons) that lurked within. Nonetheless, although the manual work was shared in common (with the heaviest load falling to the original translator F. W. Moore), it should be added that responsibility for the changes and editorial arrangement of the English text is fully assumed by myself.

The need for a new edition of Gumplowicz' work became evident in my course on the history of sociology. As we went fishing for some primary representation of such major tendencies in early sociology as conflict theory, natural history method, and positivist-naturalist philosophic orientation, it became increasingly clear that Gumplowicz fulfilled these requirements better than any other sociologist. It is thus to the students of this thrice-baked course that this introduction owes its inception.

This volume is dedicated to my colleague, Ignacy Aleksandrowicz —a learned man and a courageous man.

Hobart and William Smith Colleges   I.L.H.
Geneva, New York [March 21, 1962]

INTRODUCTION/THE SOCIOLOGY OF
LUDWIG GUMPLOWICZ: 1838-1909

Irving L. Horowitz

A CENTRAL PURPOSE of the history of science is to draw the particular disciplines out of the invariable sectarian pride accompanying the flood of discovery and application. More recently developed social sciences, such as sociology, in part as a justifiable desire to avoid the production of memoirs prior to having produced new insights, are only now becoming aware that any useful history of science is at the same time a source for new discoveries and no less, a fresh view of the past. Who can doubt that Parsons' (1937) investigations of the writings of Durkheim, Weber and Pareto opened wide new sociological channels? It is likewise clear that Sabine's (1937) work in the history of political theory, particularly his efforts on behalf of the English forerunners to political science—Hobbes, Winstanley, Harrington, and Sidney—performed a similar role of cutting new pathways. Examples of this can be multiplied indefinitely: Wolff's efforts on behalf of Simmel (1950, 1959); Gerth on Weber (1946, 1951, 1952, 1958), Merton on LeBon (1960), Kecskemeti on Mannheim (1952, 1953, 1956). The point is a simple one. A true accounting of the history of any given science is often a useful handmaiden to problems of current research.

Nonetheless, despite the ready accessibility of the sociological "classics" there has developed a powerful animus in present-day American sociology for the historical evolution of the field. A strong "we" and "they" flavour motivates much analysis of differences between American and European styles of doing sociology. So much is made in our sociological generation of the differences and contrasts between "German sociology" (reputed to be philosophy-oriented, rationalistic, impressionistic, individualistic, and historical) and

"American sociology" (reputed to be policy-oriented, empiricist, rigorous, cooperative, and bound by inter-subjective modes of verification) that the close kinship of European and American sociology in historical and philosophical common-soil is all too frequently overlooked. The attempt at typology has too often degenerated into stereotypy (Cf. Bramson, 1961:51-52).

We pair Robert E. Park with Ferdinand Tönnies, W. I. Thomas with Florian Znaniecki, Albion Small with Gustav Ratzenhofer and Adolf Wagner, Lester Ward with Ludwig Gumplowicz, Talcott Parsons with Max Weber, to name but a few. The bonds are so natural and evident in the writings of these scholars that the incessant stress on differences in national styles is not only a disservice to the cause of international science, but a *prima facie* distortion of the actual emergence and character of sociology. The early files of *The American Journal of Sociology*, with articles by Simmel, Höffding, Münsterberg, Ratzenhofer, and Tönnies, not to mention the renewed impact on American sociology of such scholars-in-exile from fascism as Mannheim, Schütz, Neumann, Adorno, Zilsel, and Lazarsfeld, should of itself caution rather than stimulate the nativistic impulse for scientific distinctiveness. The same sociologists who manufacture ethnocentric typologies for the social sciences would be the first to condemn any effort at developing a typology of mathematics or physics along nationalistic or racialistic lines. What is distinguished is not necessarily distinctive, and likewise, what is distinctive is not always distinguished.

1. Gumplowicz, Character and Thought

"After 1848 ideologies spread in Austria like an infectious disease. They emerged from the stagnant waters of discontent which the unfinished revolution had left behind. Unrealized political desires rationalized themselves into bogus systems of political thought, and emotional frustration developed into mental hysteria. Go-getting journalists stirred Austrian *Urgemutlichkeit* into paroxyms of discomfort, and the lower strata of Alpine feeblemindedness worked their way to the surface and became politically conscious. Hungarian pig-breeders and Viennese stockbrokers struggled for an intellectual articulation of their demands for greater profits. From the ethnical hotch-potch of the Sudetan Germans sprang the doctrine of racial purity and racially pure but cosmopolitan Jews became ardent propagandists of the Teutonic mythology of Richard Wagner. In a pandemonium of *Gemutlichkeit* and confused political aspirations, where commercial travellers hobnobbed with *Geist*, priests

with corrupt journalists, bankers with saviours of the people and adver-
tising agents with artists, the last remnants of Austrian culture dissolved."

— Erich Heller, 1952 —

Ludwig Gumplowicz, who has been something of a shadow
without substance in American sociological circles—a man categor-
ized falsely as an advocate of racism and thus consigned to *purga-
torio* with like-minded deviants such as Lombroso, Gobineau, and
H. S. Chamberlain—well illustrates the cost in terms of fresh insights to current sociological problems this impulse to stereotypy
has created. I shall consider Gumplowicz' contributions under the
following headings: *The Group Basis of Human Society; Functionalism and the Natural History of Society; Rassenkampf and Klassenkampf: The Sociology of Conflict; and Belief and Behavior: The
Sociology of Knowledge.* Whatever else these topics are, they most
certainly cannot be classifed as of purely antiquarian concern. Indeed, what makes Gumplowicz a vital intellectual force is his presag-
ing of the rise of small group theory, his appreciation of the function
of power and organization in social structure, and his understanding
of the non-rational basis of mass belief and mass action.

Gumplowicz' public life was as lacking in dramatic content as
his private life pulsated with the stuff of novels. He was born in
Poland in the City of Crackow in 1838, into a middle class Jewish
family of Polish and Russian ancestry. Despite his thorough im-
mersion in the educational and cultural spheres of Austrian and
German life, he is still considered by biographers as a distinctively
Polish product (*Cf.* Posner, 1911; and Mirek, 1929). The basis of
this claim is partially supported by Gumplowicz' participation in
the abortive Polish uprising of 1863 and his editing of a radical
magazine *Kraj* (The Country). Judaism entered into his calculations
and deliberations often (but also elliptically): first through a consideration of the historical and philosophical ground of the *Old
Testament* and later in his social theory of racial types—in which
the Jewish people were referred to as an example of the doctrine of
social distance and social exclusiveness (Gumplowicz, 1883: 327-35).
In nineteenth century Austria, with its dozens of national, ethnic and
linguistic groups, group survival was more than a theory, it was a
political passion.

From a technical and scientific viewpoint, Gumplowicz was completely caught up in the claims and counter-claims of the Germanic *Zeitgeist*. His education at The University of Vienna, where he received his doctorate in 1862, was a center of German currents in the philosophy of history as well as in theological "higher criticism." It was natural, therefore, for his dissertation topic to be a coordination of historical evolution and its relation to the philosophy of the *Testaments*.

In 1875 he became a *Privatdozent* in political science at the University of Graz, a small institute in Austria's southern tier. The character of intellectual life at Graz can be gathered from the following remark of Gumplowicz in his correspondence with Ward. "I am especially thankful to you for sending me your article from *The American Journal of Sociology*, for this article is not available at Graz. Our university library is so poor and so poorly managed that this periodical is not obtainable; especially since German professors of sociology don't really want to know anything about the subject" (Gumplowicz, 1933:11). We may surmise that life at Graz proved anything but pleasant. In this same communication, Gumplowicz takes note of the gossip and complaints of his colleagues. "Gumplowicz isn't a lawyer, instead he turns the heads of the students."

For his own part, although he busied himself with treatises on law (Gumplowicz, 1879, 1897, 1902), Gumplowicz accused critics of a metaphysical view of law and society, what he called an "unproductive scholasticism." This condition, which he found widespread in German speaking universities, formed the initial basis for his belief that the future of sociology would be realized in America, France, Italy, and England—but not in Germany. Some explanation for the sorry state of the discipline in Germany and Austria before the First World War is provided by Becker. "Relatively few chairs were maintained exclusively in the interests of sociology, but the subject was admitted as a *Lehrfach*, and a fairly large number of professors added 'and Sociology' to their titles." He goes on to note that "the vested interests of a professional caste operated against admission of a subject largely cultivated, not only in Germany and Austria, but elsewhere as well by amateurs . . . Moreover, the flaming nationalist, Heinrich von Treitschke, declared war on 'so-called science of society' as early as 1859, even going so

far as to link it with socialism, and the ammunition thus furnished
was ceaselessly discharged by the professors of history, political
science, and philosophy. To cap it all, sociology was declared to be
'Western,' filled with the poison of the Enlightenment. Small wonder,
then, that only the most courageous or foolhardy spirits avowed
sociological interests" (Becker and Barnes, 1938: II, 870-80).

Whether through courage or foolishness, Gumplowicz continued
on at Graz. His life of quiet desperation was punctuated with a few
notable academic promotions. In 1882 he was appointed adjunct
professor in political science, and eleven years later, in 1893, he
received his full professorship. Despite his titular post, which gave
him a relatively free schedule, his work trailed off badly after this.
The last years of his life were spent in lecturing, translating, and in
turn, pursuing his translators. A series of personal calamities took
place commencing with the death in 1894 of his most brilliant son
(who had achieved a high professional status in social statistics)
through suicide.

The death of Gumplowicz' friend and intellectually kindred
spirit, Gustav Ratzenhofer, affected him deeply. Whatever differences the two had, they shared important beliefs first, in the absolute
worth of sociology as an exact descriptive science, and second, the
group basis of social life. "Your letter of November 8th (the date
our unforgettable Ratzenhofer passed away) has arrived. What you
wrote me about the unfortunate Ratzenhofer interested me very
much. I was yearnfully awaiting his return—he had written me of
his impressions of America—and now he is returning a corpse. I
can't tell you how much this loss has affected me. In him I had a
true friend and ally. And what accomplishments he has made to our
discipline! He formulated all problems systematically and was able
to register tremendous sociological advances. He is an irreplaceable
loss" (Gumplowicz, 1933:16).

At the same time that colleagues like Ratzenhofer were passing
on, opposition to empirical sociology, and to sociologists of Jewish
extraction in particular, was mounting. Bismarckian nationalism was
on an incline that was not to be halted short of disaster in World
War One. Official circles, of which the academic was among the
most vociferous, reinterpreted the growth of labor and socialist
politics as a direct consequence of Jewish internationalism. Gum-

plowicz complained of this "witches' Sabbath of nationalism" many times in his correspondence. The impact of anti-Semitism in the world of letters can be gathered from this comment to Ward: "In Germany there today exists a tremendous anti-Semitic tendency that is penetrating into scientific fields, seeking to support such postures with anthropological arguments. These gentlemen (Thompson —- Chamberlain, *Die Grundlagen des XIX Jahrunderts*, Wilser, Woltmann, etc.) wish to prove that mixing the Germanic races with the Semitic races is detrimental, and that it is thus necessary on this count to exclude Jews from civil liberties—forbidding thereby the connection between 'Semites' and 'Aryans.' It seems to me that it is this social tendency which influences current scientific opinion" (Gumplowicz, 1933:15). The loss of Ratzenhofer, who at the time of his death was working on a refutation of such pseudo-science, was thus a direct loss in the struggle of sociology for emancipation from nationalist and racist tyrannies (*Cf.* Weber, 1922:530).

Throughout these last years of life Gumplowicz was plagued with family illnesses. His wife suffered from progressively deteriorating maladies that made Graz as much a prison-house as a school. "I am remaining in Graz," he wrote to Ward. "You know my situation. My wife cannot undertake any trips; she is too weak for this. Nor do I want to leave her alone—we have no family here, and I must therefore renounce the rest of the world and remain at home. For the past ten years I have not left Graz for a single moment" (Gumplowicz, 1933:18). Again, in a letter of August 1907, he writes feelingly of his wife's sickness—this time from an eye cataract. It had the effect of curbing all of Gumplowicz' work, and equally, seriously disturbing his psychological equilibrium. He speaks of "being suddenly robbed of my composure" and being "put in a despairing mood." The seriousness of the situation "has also given me a strong jolt so that I suddenly feel my old age—now I *feel* like a seventy year old man" (Gumplowicz, 1933:26).

The constancy of personal tragedy finally caused Gumplowicz a nervous breakdown. The only work he was permitted was reading and proof-reading. Following his nervous disorders, a cancerous eye condition developed which necessitated an operation. Gumplowicz rejected the diagnosis, and resolved "to depart from life" rather than submit to surgery. By 1909 the incurable nature of the

ailments of Gumplowicz and his wife became manifest. And in his
final letter to America, a note of quiet resolve replaces the former
desperation. "I find my situation in no way tragic, since I have
reached my seventieth birthday. I have had the consolation of seeing
my *Rassenkampf* appear in a second edition—after 26 years—and
I have also willed the world a small work on *Sozialphilosophie* before
my departure. My swan song" (Gumplowicz, 1933:31-32). The actual
"departure" took place later in the year, on August 20th, 1909.
During the day, Gumplowicz and his wife committed suicide.

Gumplowicz' *Schwanengesang* was a return to problems of
social philosophy with which he began his career. The work represented the most sophisticated statement of a positivist and naturalist
social philosophy that had yet to appear. The philosophy of sociology
was itself said to be positivism (Gumplowicz, 1910). But the genuine
continuation of the unity of science tradition in sociology extended
far beyond any last-minute attempt to construct a world view. The
emancipation of social science from metaphysical tradition was not a
one-man undertaking. However, the impulse released by Gumplowicz
was carried forth in the work of Lester Ward in America, Gaetano
Mosca in Italy, and ironically enough, by a young Austrian economist who came to the University of Graz a year after Gumplowicz'
death, Joseph Schumpeter.

2. The Group Basis of Social Life

"As for what is called individual morality, if we understand by that a
totality of duties of which the individual would, at the same time, be
subject and object, and which would link him only to himself, and
which would, consequently, exist even if he were solitary; that is an
abstract conception which has no relation to reality. Morality, in all its
forms, is never met with except in society. It never varies except in
relation to social conditions. To ask what it would be if societies did
not exist is thus to depart from facts and enter the domain of gratuitous
hypotheses and unverifiable flights of the imagination. The duties of the
individual towards himself are, in reality, duties toward society."

—*Emile Durkheim, 1897* —

"The philosophy of individualism ignores the fact that the mental and
moral structure of individuals, the pattern of their desires and purposes,
change with every great change in social constitution. Individuals who
are not bound together in associations, whether domestic, economic,
religious, political, artistic, or educational, are monstrosities. It is absurd

to suppose that the ties which hold them together are merely external
and do not react into mentality and character, producing the framework
of personal disposition."

— John Dewey, 1930 —

The central contribution of Gumplowicz to the development of
empirical sociology is the focus upon human groups. After giving
due credit to all those before him who similarly saw the basis of
human society in group interaction, it remains a paramount fact
of sociological history that to Gumplowicz belongs the credit of
discovering the interpersonal context of sociological study, and its
relationship to those phenomena most closely related to group
existence—the psychological constitution of personality, and at the
other pole, the political constitution of the State. If Gumplowicz was
perhaps too concerned with a description of the formal boundaries
between social science disciplines, he at least distinguished himself
from most colleagues by giving empirical substance for his claims
as to the actual terrain of sociological operations.

Sociology in the late nineteenth century expended itself in
definitional searches. In the main, the three most prominent definitions of the field current in Gumplowicz' time exhibited powerful
national as well as philosophical bias. In Germany, the neo-Hegelian
views of Paul Barth (1897) and Wilhelm Dilthey (1883) held sway.
Sociology was defined as a branch of the philosophy of history—
a "moment" in the *Lebenswelt*. Gumplowicz was totally out of sympathy with such a view since he saw the philosophy of history as a
history of errors, a transcendental superimposition upon social realities. In England, Spencer initiated the empirical study of sociology,
but only at the expense of having it transformed into a human
application of biological principles (Spencer, 1874). Gumplowicz'
severest criticisms of the German Spencerians, particularly Schäffle
(1885), and Lilienfeld (1873), were their uncritical acceptance of
a strictly biological and evolutionary frame of human reference for
the illicit purpose of defending the worst malpractices of the Bismarckian State. Sociology in France, particularly the positions taken
by Quetelet (1835) and Comte (1839), represented for Gumplowicz
the necessary main road of the discipline. The Cartesian spirit of
rational description based on mathematical analysis, especially

evidenced by Quetelet, made possible the pursuit of sociology as a description of social facts (*Cf.* Lazarsfeld, 1961: 164-179). The rationalist search for laws of development, the frank acceptance of a "profane" range of problems in the face of which "sacred" canons of what men "ought" to be like were of little worth, penetrated Gumplowicz' thought directly. Although he retained a skeptical attitude towards the convergence of positive sociology and a humanistic religion, and was equally unconvinced by the statistical proofs of social laws offered by Quetelet, there is little doubt Gumplowicz valued the contributions of his French predecessors above all others. Perhaps this is why, of all German sociologists, Gumplowicz comes closest to the "Durkheim school."

Gumplowicz staked out a claim for sociology in a unique way. If most sociologists up to his time sought proof for sociology by reference to the philosophy of history, biology, or mathematics, he aimed at an internal validation for his claims. This proof he found in the concept of the social group. In presenting sociology as the study of groups interacting, and in forcefully arguing that thought itself is a product of group life in all its forms—of the nuclear family, then of the extended family, of the universe of kinship relations, up to the larger social groups such as formal organizations and community organizations—Gumplowicz contributed decisively in setting forth the actual content and limit of sociology as a scientific pursuit. That his contribution was made in conjunction with the work of like-minded social scientists does not lessen the debt of the present to the past; it only makes the task of assigning priorities of discovery more complex and intriguing.

The main distinction between anthropology and sociology, aside from the conventional carving-up of the human world into "preliterate" and "literate" peoples, hinges upon the terms culture and society. Should the chief interest be on those factors of change which occur through invention and diffusion or on those factors conditioned by the symbolic interaction of people? If the wise scholars of both disciplines have finally overcome the "battle" between ethnography and ethnology, and the host of related dualisms separating the social sciences, the structural and organizational divisions inherited from these earlier controversies have not so easily been transcended. Suspicion of each other's "imperialist designs" and contempt for the methodological bases of the "other" human science still plague relations between anthropology and sociology.

Despite Gumplowicz' wide use of the anthropology of his times, it cannot be said that his emphasis on the social group led to an easing of diplomatic tensions between the two sciences. His definition of culture remained narrow; confined as it was to the physical artifacts produced and transmitted by mankind. The process of transmitting ideas, habits, mores, and customs was held to be exclusively a matter for sociological inquiry. Still more striking was a Lamarckian turn to Gumplowicz' thinking on this question, since even certain biogenic characteristics were viewed as socially conditioned. Throughout, he maintained that the "physiognomical character of a folk or social group is not anthropological but social. On the one hand this explains how it is possible for a foreigner to assume the character of the group into which he goes; while on the other, that transformation of the individual by the group proves that we are dealing with purely social and sociological facts" (Gumplowicz, 1905c:276). In Gumplowicz' view anthropology necessarily assumes the immutability of human characteristics, while sociology alone deals with changing human nature. This follows from his reductionistic conception of anthropology—a view of culture as essentially part of biological structure. While in retrospect it is easy to perceive the partisan shortcomings in his approach, it must be remembered that anthropology prior to the work of Tylor, Malinowski and Kroeber did tend heavily towards a reductionist view of culture.

In Gumplowicz' scheme culture accounts for the psychic types; but in its turn, culture is said to be produed in the cross-fertilization of social groups. His position was a blend of positivism and monism. The idea of complementaristic explanation in the social sciences either did not appeal to him, or what is more likely the case, did not occur to him. However, whether by design or accident, his forceful presentation of the group basis of social life opened wide the gates to empirical sociology. It did this by considering the group as logically including physiology and personality, and yet the integrating force behind them both.

Gumplowicz is properly known as an advocate of conflict theory, of the view that the motor-force in social change is the antagonism between different communities, nations, ethnic groups, and races. However, these hostilities between formal groups occur heterogenously — between groups. What is presupposed is the homogeneity of the individual group as such. In this form, Gumplowicz made room for the role of consensus in the organization of group life. The social type is a product of consensus between the membership of the same group, of an individual's capacity for performing tasks according to both its formal and informal rules in consequence of such binding elements as linguistic and geographical unity. This type of consensus Gumplowicz terms "social influences." The importance of internal homogeneity is to focus upon the inter-group nature of social conflict. Warfare, invasions, and even migrations, are not conducted by individuals, but by the group *en masse*. Even though Gumplowicz' attitude toward consensus does not extend beyond the "we" stage into the "they" stage, this very crystallization of social forces into egoistic forces is presupposed in the contact of heterogenous groups.

Ferdinand Tönnies in his classic study of *Gemeinschaft und Gesellschaft* (1887) states as his main aim to "study the sentiments and motives which draw people to each other, keep them together, and induce them to joint action." The notion of *Gemeinschaft* as a "community of fate" was one which Gumplowicz shared with Tönnies. But Gumplowicz' "natural bonds" in which the group shares in "the same fate" is unrestricted by any one set of social roles or occupational activities (1905c:239). The homogenous group may be based on language, religion, or politics, and hence is not restricted in terms of a prevailing economic structure. Societies, nations and families, no less than *Gemeinschaft* organization, exhibit the closest kind of solidarity. Through this reading of the relationship between the nuclear group and other groups, Gumplowicz was spared Tönnies' idealization of feudal relations that ended up with a nostalgic variety of peasant socialism. The solidarity of the group depends on an internal cohesiveness to be sure, but this very cohesion (which can exist in a delinquent sub-culture no less than in a rural community) is guaranteed by how vigorously it defends and pursues its interests against other groups. In Gumplowicz' view, an adequate theory of social change depends upon the closest attention to the strife which exists between groups of noticeably different mores, customs and habits. That which reinforces social distance, at the same time strengthens the group of which one is a member.

If the group forms the kernel of social structure as well as social process, the next major task is to define the component parts of this central agency in human interaction. There are two differentiated tendencies distinguished by Gumplowicz. The first set includes consanguinity, local association, and common interests, *i.e.*, common religious, political and intellectual standards of conduct. The second set moves vertically rather than on a horizontal plane. In this range the group presupposes material interests (a common geographic location, sociability, and kinship); economic interests (similar and equal possessions, common class and ethnic affiliations); and moral interests, used by Gumplowicz to designate secondary group associations (church membership, political loyalties, occupational ties, etc.). These group-making factors, whether enhancing mobility or reinforcing patterns of stratification, have as their firm core the essential human need for communication—a need which can only be satisfied in common endeavour to secure goals which may in all likelihood be different from those of other groups. The need for social solidarity has many representations, but they are only as strong as the power of the group from which they emerge.

At this point in his discussion, Gumplowicz makes an authentic contribution to the subsequent development of sociology by means of a refined series of bi-variate statements concerning the relationship of the social group and social power.

First: The *power* of the group is not uniquely determined by its size or even its complexity, but rather by the quality of group cohesion and discipline. Power is thus considered to be a consequence of social organization—in the face of which a simple numerical majority is hard-pressed to assert its "right." The theory of elites is thus neither a diabolical hoax perpetrated on an unsuspecting mass, nor a necessarily benevolent force omnipotent in its decision-making prowess. Gumplowicz is particularly severe with those who adopt a sentimental attitude toward the masses or an apologetic view of the elite. He sought to abolish both from sociological consideration, in much the same fashion that Spencer held class feelings to be sociological impediments.

Second: The greater the number of group-producing factors,

the more intimate is the social bond. The cohesive force of the group
depends on the ability of the group to imprint its collective personality on the individual. Left at this point, Gumplowicz' position seems
to be a truism. Its empirical significance comes to the fore when we
consider the last of his bi-variates concerning the group.

Third: The power of the nuclear group diminishes in proportion as language, religion and like factors become common to several
social groups. In Gumplowicz' view, any sociological explanation for
the rise and fall of a given social group is linked to those elements
within it making for (or detracting from) a tighter allegiance between the individual and his group. Deviation from the norms of
the groups are indications of the presence of other group agencies
with either equal or superior attractive qualities. In any case, adhes-
ion to the norms are indicative of the strength of the collectivity,
while disaffiliation or disaffection indicate the presence of counter-
group pressures. This observation brought Gumplowicz to the threshold of reference-group theory.

The "natural history" of society is thus the formation and reformation of group life. This is not a matter of "better or worse,"
"good groups" versus "bad groups," but simply of continuities and
discontinuities in the social careers of men. The group is the main
pillar of a social structure because it contains all necessary elements
of pattern-maintenance: norms, roles and values at the ideational
level, and established institutions having stable relationships at the
social and economic levels. But the group is also the essential agency
of social change, since it is at this level that "creative burst" is to be
found, and it is at this level that the historic contest with contending
social systems is joined in earnest. Thus it is that for Gumplowicz
the group is the master agency in collective dynamics no less than
the cement of social equilibrium.

3. Functionalism and the Natural History of Society

"A full consideration of the problem of historical uniformities would be
very long, and might well end in the cloudland of metaphysics. We shall
have to be content with the crude assertion that the doctrine of the
absolute uniqueness of events in history seems nonsense. History is
essentially an account of the behavior of men, and if the behavior of
men is not subject to any kind of systematizing, this world is even more
cock-eyed than than the seers would have it.

Upon the social scientist there pours the full force of those sentiments we call moral as well as those we call selfish. He can hardly avoid wanting to change what he is studying: not to change it as the chemist changes elements he compounds but to change it as the missionary changes the man he converts. Yet this is just what the social scientist must try to avoid as a better man would avoid the devil."

— *Crane Brinton, 1938* —

If Spencer can be said to be the first sociological functionalist, Gumplowicz can with equal justification be said to be the earliest critic of functionalism. Gumplowicz had a rare gift of philosophic understanding which preserved him from most of the logical implausibilities of early functionalism: its tendency to draw inferences from strictly biological phenomena, its teleological substitutions for causal analysis, and its equation of the operational with the morally worthy. Each of these in the functionalism of Spencer receives Gumplowicz' critical attention; and what is so interesting is how these same criticisms have arisen in connection with current functionalist formulations (*Cf.* Nagel, 1957; and Hempel, 1959).

Early functionalism was greatly concerned with the how and why of social equilibrium. Indeed, functional adaptation very often was used synonomously with high survival possibilities in the face of new or unseen forces. Dysfunctional elements have continued to be viewed as essentially disruptive to the consensual basis of society (*Cf.* Blalock and Blalock, 1959: 84-92). Thus analysis of war, revolution, *anomie*, privatization, etc., tend to be made in terms of how they disturb the functional prerequisites of survival of the social organism. Gumplowicz, with his intense interest in how social structures change, could not take equilibrium models or schemes for functional adaptation as methodological norms. Because he had no pressing need for a functional orientation, he had no need to create a special theory of dysfunctionality to account for change. Change and movement, is the normal condition of a sub-culture or of society in general. The main question is not how the social group functions, but rather how the social group arises, develops, and finally decays or becomes transformed into something totally different. "Periodicity of development is a natural, necessary and universal law." The Spencerian emphasis on how a structure adapts itself to new functional requirements occupies little place in Gumplowicz' sociology.

He takes it for granted that a point is reached when functional adaptation cannot take place. Such a point would be when a social organism is confronted with a more powerful adversary adjacent to it. Gumplowicz' "heterogenous" theory of change is at bottom a view of how social structures are fragmented and reformed through warfare, migration, and other forms of qualitative disruptions in the social system.

The emphasis which Gumplowicz places on "laws of development" marks him apart from functionalism in another decisive sense. Since for Gumplowicz mankind exhibits a "unitary process" one can indeed logically speak of societies as being better or worse, and higher and lower in the scale of social evolution. The functionalist for his part sees mankind as exhibiting a plurality of cultural forms, each of which is judged by its "survival" capacities. Because of this, pluralism becomes the sole universal cultural property, since survival rather than qualities of social organization becomes the major test for judging the social system. Societies are thus viewed as different from one another rather than more advanced and less advanced. The recent efforts by Parsons (1951) and Merton (1957) in sociology, and Kluckhohn (1951; 1959) in anthropology to overcome the serious drawbacks in early functionalist formulations indicates how sophisticated Gumplowicz' thinking was on this matter.

The specific criticisms made by Gumplowicz deserves notice, if only as a gauge for measuring the distance between modern functionalism and its founders. Spencer's lead idea, derived from Darwin, that functional differentiation characterizes more advanced societies, and that the greater the margin of differentiation the greater are the possibilities of the adaptation of a structure to changing conditions, is criticized by Gumplowicz on several counts. He first points out that such a formulation is simply a tautology, saying nothing more than that the motion of social bodies is universal, without disclosing the why and wherefore of such motion. Further, Gumplowicz emphasizes that functionalism is a doctrine of *application* of universal laws of evolution; but in failing to develop specifically social laws it fails to apply itself to the main task of science— explanation and prediction. Gumplowicz' own intense interest in "laws" of sociology led him to make teleological formulations of his own—such as the law of *Lebensfuersorge* ("solicitude for the means of subsistence"). This forces each social aggregate to try to make every other social aggregate coming within its reach to serve a supreme end. But if his doctrine of social laws harbored its own form of metaphysical importation, it is important to see that his search was in the correct direction, for a general theory of social change that would not limit itself arbitrarily to problems of differentiation and integration (Gumplowicz, 1905c:164-165).

Another criticism of Spencerian sociology was its built-in justification for the *status quo*, the assumption that the present somehow sums up the past by virtue of its greater adaptability. Gumplowicz notes that this sort of theorizing is as inviting to conservative thought as the Hegelian doctrine of a world history which demands loyalty for its own sake, and that exhibits a terminal point in the Germanic present (Gumplowicz, 1926:296-297). Functionalist empiricism thus shares with dialectical historicism a total commitment to society as it may be presently constituted. Gumplowicz adds to this that there is a powerful anthropomorphism in functionalist thought, making it anything but neutral with respect to sociological issues. Functionalism confuses the development of a social institution by identifying it with the imagined development of mankind as a whole. In so doing, it smuggles in a moralistic standpoint in place of objective and scientific criteria.

It is not altogether evident that functionalist sociology has come to grips with the sort of issues raised by a "conflict theorist" such as Gumplowicz. He anticipated by a good half century the charge that functionalism in sociology is really an illegitimate argument by analogy, utilizing principles of biology and physiology which may or may not be applicable to these more elementary forms of organic life. "Social communities are the sociological units or elements, and it is not possible to ascertain their mutual relations from the properties of their constituent parts, *i.e.*, from the properties of individuals. No one starting from the latter can reach the nature of the group. Hence, biological analogies are worthless in sociology except as illustrations" (Gumplowicz, 1885:28-29).

Despite the severity of Gumplowicz' critical assault on Spencer's functionalism, he retained an enduring and sincere respect for the English writer. This respect was based on Spencer's capacity to avoid the worst aspects of biologism by not confusing his illustrations from biology with properly social facts and social laws. Gumplowicz could not say the same for his colleagues, Schäffle and Lilienfeld. For them, *Darwinismus* as an ideology became the touchstone for all sociological investigation. Organisms of individual species were converted into organisms of the State and ultimately of the social system itself. In this way, sociology was translated into a system for the preservation of the organism, or in truth, for the preservation of those social institutions that comprised the social system. Evolution was thus converted, not so much into a theory of social change, as it was into a doctrine of social preservation. Social facts no longer were granted accreditation on their own merits. All things were seen as related to the organism as a whole. Thus, in Gumplowicz' view, the outcome of organicism was not a truly scientific sociology, so much as an oracular demand for seeing the whole as whole, and of preserving the whole from any defects of the parts.

Gumplowicz countered organicist claims with a demand that life be seen as organized into logically distinct levels of complexity, and hence, as necessitating different sorts of laws. His "domains of knowledge" was a first step in the direction of a sociological theory of integrative levels, in which each level of existence—physical, biological, and social—exhibits independent laws of development as well as distinctive principles of organization. Laws at each level must be discovered on their own terms and at their own levels. By assuming this stance, Gumplowicz believed that the false alternatives of atomism and organicism could be satisfactorily resolved. His fine distinction between attacking social problems directly, at the level at which they are encountered, rather than deducing sociological laws from either physics or biology, helped to place sociology on an independent footing. In so doing, he further compelled social scientists to take an integrative and empirical approach to their work by drawing attention to "social acts" and "actors" and away from the vagaries of apriori systems in which society is inferred from "the general will," "the social organism," or "natural rights" (Gumplowicz, 1905c:52). The method of sociology must start and end with the proper subject matter of the discipline—the group life and interaction of human beings. If seriously and conscientiously applied this remains the best safeguard against physicalism and organicism alike.

Gumplowicz did not entirely escape the language of biological functionalism. The constant references to "ends" . . . "purpose" and "inherent reasonableness" are nowhere defined. Nonetheless, he did move beyond the thoughtless employment of functionalism as the exclusive method of sociological research. Functional prerequisites meant for Gumplowicz adaptation to ends through human planning and foresight, a form for meeting expected contingencies. He did not rule out other methods of problem solving in sociology. In this, he differed radically from the liberal uses of functionalism made by his contemporaries.

Thus far, we have attempted an explanation of Gumplowicz' attitude to the functionalist method. His own method, that which he saw as properly fitting sociological research, can best be described as a forerunner to the natural history of society technique. Such an approach suited his work well; offering a positive approach to historical sociology without any implication of ideological commitment to any one direction of social life. It also offered a complementary methodology to his theory of the group basis of social life (and all that this implied in terms of racial, ethnic and class conflict among heterogenous groups).

History is a record of social actions for Gumplowicz. As such it is really the foundation for developing sociological laws. As he says, if man is a determinate animal subject to "blind natural forces" and "following eternal laws" history could no longer be seen as something apart from sociology. Nor could historical determinism be capriciously overturned to suit individual thought patterns or free wills. His radical determinism considers man as an agent of history rather than a maker of history. Since all historical phenomena are combinations of group phenomena, the group provides the source and genesis of social existence and human thought. It follows then that the method of sociology is properly an account of the natural history of social groups.

The attitude of Gumplowicz toward history was strongly influenced by the cyclical philosophies. History does not so much present mandates or guides to action, as it serves as a basis for placing the present in cultural perspective. He was deeply influenced by the theory of *ricorso*, first developed by Ibn Khaldun in the fourteenth century and independently rediscovered by Vico (Gumplowicz, 1926:

124-126). History, in the sense of the evolution of morals, intellect, politics, does not so much reveal progressions as it does simple changes of state. Thus intellectual history is a series of cyclical changes to meet immediate societal responses. Material history, in the sense of science and technology, does show progress. However, such developments are cumulative, evolutionary, and beyond the whims of man to order about. Since this is the case, men are the agencies of change, rather than the conscious promoters of change. Even "the most cruel and barbarous conquerors are the blind instruments of human progress." Gumplowicz adds that the founding of civilizations is itself a consequence of objective social laws, over which men preside rather than prescribe (1905c:57).

So firm was Gumplowicz in his insistence on the monistic and objective character of historical events, that he never doubted "that sociological laws prevail unchanged whether we have historical evidence of the fact or not" (1905c:60-61). Sociological laws are considered to be as binding as logical propositions—a realm of universals rather than probabilities. Thus the functionalist orientation toward cultural relativity, historical specificity, and social limits on the range of applicability of sociological statements—none of these found their way into Gumplowicz' sociology. He was still profoundly attached to a Newtonian world in which explanation was sought in terms of simple propositions having universal validity. It was this aspect of natural sciences such as physics and geology that Gumplowicz ranked highest and most in need of emulation by the sociologist.

Gumplowicz' lifelong search for "a single simple principle" gives to his positivism a more dogmatic turn than any of his sociological investigations warranted. Sociology, while held to be an autonomous scientific enterprise, was at the same time discussed as if its very survival hinged on a philosophical monism (1905c:121). And while Gumplowicz disclaims any apriori elements in his position, his metaphysical substructure reveals an unwillingness even to entertain philosophic alternatives to the "unitary principle" of human and natural development. For example, while it is true, as he says, that some civilizations fall under the ethnic and cultural sway of other more dynamic civilizations, e.g., the collapse of indigenous populations in Central and South America in the face of the Spanish and Portuguese conquerors, this is hardly a proof of the unitary principle. There are numerous cases in recorded history in which foreign domination does not lead to submission and/or absorption in the higher culture; for example, the Swedish and German impact on Russian culture is negligible, despite their overwhelming military successes. Similarly, the Roman Empire met with different results in different areas. Despite the similarity of military superiority *Pax Romana* had a different cultural impact in Egypt, Greece, and Palestine. Rome never achieved a truly social amalgamation, however omnipotent the Roman legions may have been. While calling attention to the role of force in social development, Gumplowicz' unitary principle tended to proceed in isolation from any *internal* tensions besetting even the most powerful military society. We shall have occasion to refer to Gumplowicz' purely external view of conflict in the next section. For now, our focus is his contribution to the "natural history of society" technique; a method of social research which has claimed very important adherents in American thought. (*Cf.* Edwards, 1927; Brinton, 1938; Blumer, 1939; Hopper, 1950; Gross and Hopper, 1959; Lang and Lang, 1961).

Although the rudiments of the natural history of society technique had been known to Quetelet, and was also an element in the work of Gustave LeBon, it remained for Gumplowicz to work out the first rigorous methodology combining historical researches with sociological principles.

Gumplowicz saw in the natural history of society approach an advance upon, and an alternative to, Spencerian functionalism. Functionalism did not solve the problem of the relationship of facts to values any more than the organicist social philosophies then current in Germany. In addition, Gumplowicz was in search of a theory of social change rather than a theory of social structure. The natural history method held out promise for proving the existence of sociological uniformities, and not simply a description of "ideal types" and "functional aggregates." The natural history technique furthermore draws attention to cyclical patterns in social events, that is, continuous and recurring aspects of supposedly discrete events. "Whatever strikes us as new and original is only a new combination of very old thoughts and opinions—a combination springing of course from a new individual conception, for in nature only individuality is endlessly varied" (Gumplowicz, 1905c:355-56).

The natural history method held a particular fascination for of events, and an avoidance of a one-sided particularistic explanation. The starting point for Gumplowicz was that every society obeys "natural laws" of society; for were any society to be "unnaturally" constituted you could not seriously entertain the idea of a science of society. This view has much in common with the later philosophical formulation offered by Wittgenstein: "We cannot think anything unlogical, for otherwise we should have to think unlogically" (1918:43). For Gumplowicz, we cannot think anything unhistorical, otherwise we should have to think unhistorically.

The natural history method held a particular fascination for Gumplowicz since it appeared to be the closest link with the method of natural science in general. Observation, description, classification, and the forecasting of events in terms of a larger system of explanation and prediction, these properties of the empirical sciences satisfied Gumplowicz' desire for sociology to be distinguished by its precision as well as by its legality. "The alpha and omega of sociology, its highest perception and final word is: human history is a natural process; and even though, shortsighted and captivated by traditional views of human freedom and self-determination, one should believe that this knowledge derogates from morals and undermines them. Yet it is on the contrary the crown of all human morals because it preaches most impressively man's renunciatory subordination to the laws of nature which alone rule history" (Gumplowicz, 1905c: 360).

The natural history method held a particular fascination for sociological tabulations of whole systems, rather than an explanation of individual events taking place within the group or the society. Gumplowicz shared with LeBon and Sorel a concern with the forms of elementary collective behavior, rather than with the supposed purposes or goals of an action or a movement. This emphasis is shown in Gumplowicz' discussion of social justice. "That which comes to pass in the world and in life, or property, in life and history is in no sense human justice, rather it is historical justice which to man's mind must seem to be harsh injustice; though here again the fault is due to that false individual standard which man applies to human events." Events take place lawfully enough, but since our predictive propensities are based on abstract desires conditioned by individualist sentiments, events rarely happen the way the anticipated measurement would dictate (Gumplowicz, 1905c:356).

The natural history approach is aimed at being a correct estimate of the relationship between social change and social consensus; an effort to explain in particular why and how changes occur. Gumplowicz took his stand on the deterministic character of human life. Needs are economic and ecological, to earn a living and to reproduce the species. These needs are "blind natural forces" moving in "conformity to law." But these "blind forces" are in turn subject to developmental laws. Despite his profound philosophical animus for dialectical theories of history, Gumplowicz comes close to historicism when he notes that "the fall of many a powerful civilized state under the assault of rather small barbarian hordes could not be comprehended if it were not known that domestic social enemies of the existing order let the secretly glimmering hatred of the propertied and ruling classes burst into bright flame in the moment of danger" (Gumplowicz, 1905c:350). Thus, human action, far from upsetting the course of social history, is the main agency for the execution of its determinist will.

In the final instance the natural history of society method was found by Gumplowicz to be a useful variant of sociologism by placing a priority on social movements at the expense of the individual aims of participants in such movements. The natural history technique assumes that social changes are explainable by events in which human beings are agencies and actors in a drama of which they are not conscious. Gumplowicz is firm on this point: "we do not hesitate to recognize that the most cruel and barbarous conquerors are blind instruments of human progress" (1905c:57). Gumplowicz' philosophical monism spills over into sociological fatalism. "In life and in history every man suffers whatever fate is conditioned by his natural constitution." But even his "natural constitution" is a consequence of the "social milieu." Individual differences, of course do exist. But in terms of the long pull of social history such differences are unimportant. This is the point of sharpest cleavage between Gumplowicz and more recent advocates of the natural history of society technique. The latter tend to adopt a more open and pluralistic attitude towards historical evolution and the place of personality in the promotion of social change. Nonetheless, while these present day advocates have taken a more viable stance, they have done so at the expense of the *logical* consquences of the doctrine as such.

The reasons why the natural history of society has never quite caught hold of the sociological imagination either in Europe or in America, has squarely to do with the fact that more problems are raised than resolved by this methodology. Considering the importance of this method for Gumplowicz, it is not amiss to summarize the shortcomings most in evidence.

The "laws" found by the natural history of society method on inspection turn out to be little else than a refinement of the cyclical theory of history as worked out by Ibn Khaldun and later by Vico. Rather than function as explanations for social changes, the natural history technique reduces itself to fatalism. Conflict leads only to the re-establishment of equilibrium under the management of new "hordes," without producing anything genuinely novel in the social complex.

The attention Gumplowicz gave to developmental patterns was confined to the recurrent features of an event (*e.g.*, in wars of conquest there are stages of preparation, organization, attack, etc.), without sufficient regard for differences in these patterns as determined by an authentic historical picture, by attention to specific and unique elements and phases in particular conflict situations. The "law" of sequential patterns, once considered to be the main feature of every social change, simply becomes a new form for expressing the mysterious workings of the doctrine of *ricorso*.

What aims at a synthetic accounting, rather than a "one-sided" functionalist, phenomenalist, or historical method, in Gumplowicz' hands turns out to be an eclectic combination of each of these. The theory of stages represents an ideal-typification of a series of similar (but hardly identical) events occurring at different times in different places. But since events themselves are never examined within a specific matrix, what the synthesis amounts to is a rendering of the obvious in an interesting way rather than the interesting in an obvious way.

The use of scientific method in sociological explanation requires more than a faith in the general worth of observation, description and classification. In the case of Gumplowicz' natural history of society method, if we offer an account of civilizations, revealing formal similarities in the rise and fall of Egyptian, Greek, Roman, and Assyrian civilizations, we have not really arrived at an assessment of the specific social order being examined, only (and perhaps) the mechanism whereby a rising culture may become dominant or prominent. If it is said, for instance, that all "mobs" are characterized by temporary leadership, a focused object of aggression, anonymity, etc., and illustrate these by reference to certain events, one still has not made a forecast or an appraisal of particular mobs and their particular causation. And without causation, it is difficult to know what is meant by laws of society as distinct from statistical uniformities.

Gumplowicz' effort to unite history and sociology was conditioned by the genetic fallacy, by an explanation of events solely in terms of its origins—with the corollary assumption that no other variables could have developed to alter the situation. In effect, he denied even in theory the possibility of the relative independence of social forces in arriving at new policies and decisions. He assumed a determination in the realm of collective dynamics, omitting from his account the likelihood that the same sort of event can be "caused" in differing historical contexts by different agencies. Without the admissability of alternative possibilities, sociological investigation can have no authentic predictive value. The social world is thrown back on the shoals of a binding fatalism, not far removed from a Calvinistic sense of predestination.

Gumplowicz' concern was with the forms of social conflicts. The substitution of fatalism for causalism assumed a unilateral relation between society and personality that condemns even a collective population to a passive role in its confrontation with the historical event. And while Gumplowicz only partially drew conservative conclusions from his position, there is no doubt that his methodology tended to a cynicism in which striving for social progress became an absurd and useless task, since what can be achieved is only a hastening of a return to the same place, and not any genuine improvement in the social or moral fate of man. Not even Ward's faith in evolution could quite disabuse Gumplowicz of this fatalism (1905a: 649-51).

These shortcomings in Gumplowicz' methodological principles

noted, it remains to be said that his efforts were not in vain. The natural history method helped put an end to the organicist social metaphysics that threatened to engulf sociology in a specious sort of special pleading on behalf of mythic "rights" of the State. It also marked a real development over Spencer's functionalism, with its biological and physiological imagery that in truth explained and predicted little in the way of social behavior. In addition, his functionalism had a similar conservative consequence as organicism in that the functioning social system was in some sense held to be a good social system simply because it existed. Gumplowicz was one of the earliest sociologists to recognize that for sociology to transcend the non-scientific requirements of Statecraft it must forge a methodology that would distinguish between predicting and prescribing without sacrificing either. In this way he was able to escape the *optimistische Weltanschauung* that made German thought subject to every form of illusion and skullduggery fostered by "reasons of State."

4. Rassenkampf *and* Klassenkampf: *The Sociology of Conflict*

"Race is like the theory of numbers; it drives mad those who study it."
— *Kingsley Martin, 1953* —

"The effectual division of interest and sentiment is beginning visibly to run on class lines."
— *Thorstein Veblen, 1923* —

"The sociological gains as one moves from organismic positivism to conflict theory are immense."
— *Don Martindale, 1960* —

Conflict theory, which in an immediate sociological form represented a reaction to organismic social doctrines, in a deeper sense evolved out of the long history of political philosophy. Gumplowicz was, after all, a professor of political science as well as sociology. And despite his animus for the political theory of contemporaries, he had an abiding regard for the lessons of such conflict theorists as Machiavelli, Hobbes and Bodin (1926:127-50). The theoretical premises of conflict theory are fairly simple: (*a*) A society can only be established in the process of group conflict in which victory goes to the better organized force. (*b*) Leadership and authority are intrinsic properties of power and courage. (c) Society is an unstable equilibrium of forces, since contradictory interests are involved in both the origins and maintenance of set patterns of organized life. (d) The social system is cemented by sovereign power, which itself is simply the legalization of force. (e) The basic impulse of both collective dynamics and social structure is self-interest at the psychological level and group-interest at the sociological level.

However divergent conflict theorists were in stipulating these "main interests"—with views ranging from Rousseau's doctrine of the social contract to Marx' doctrine of class necessity—few doubted the function of material interests in the determination of any social structure. The whole of Gumplowicz' world of social struggle was determined by the supposedly ceaseless efforts to impose specific interests as the general and dominant interest of society as a whole. The instruments used to gain pre-eminence is determined by interest factors. "Thus the ruling classes through their parliaments exercise the legislative power and are able by legal institutions to further their own interest at the cost of others." This symbolization of interests is promoted by every group. "In the cities the middle class very early resorted to the use of guilds and representatives. The priesthood also organized into hierarchies and created synods and councils, consultative and representative bodies. The fact that the great mass of people by the very nature of things could not thus organize made the conduct of the struggle in their interest more difficult. It is in consequence of having entered upon this struggle that laborers now organize and wily agitators even established peasant unions" (Gumplowicz, 1905c:245-46).

The wide use to which Gumplowicz put conflict theory, particularly his effort to relate forms of social struggle to differential interest factors, requires that we clearly distinguish his theory from the conflict *ideology* of Marx and the conflict *policy* of Sorel. For Marx, conflict characterized all societies in which there was a division of classes based on antagonistic economic interests. But there is the further assumption that the harmonization of interests through the rational uses of productive forces would no longer require a process of development through conflict. In short, the terminal point of conflict inheres in the resolution offered by revolutionary practice in the victory of the exploited over the bourgeoisie, "the last antagonistic form of the social process of production" (Marx, 1859:329). The theory of conflict thus functioned in Marx primarily as a galvanizing force for social action, *i.e.*, as an ideology and not as a necessary deduction from historical laws. In Sorel, conflict is the mark of the dynamic society, or those forces within society capable of social, moral and intellectual regeneration. The employment of violence is constantly being fought by the forces of conservation and pacifism. Conflict theory, what Sorel calls "the ethics of violence," is thus a tactic of the strong and the rising, and not an explanation of social change as such (Cf. Sorel, 1908:202-40).

There are indeed powerful points of contact between conflict theory and conflict as an ideology and as a policy. Gumplowicz shared with Marx the idea that change proceeds primarily through a conflict of basic interests, and that such interests can be historically defined. Similarly, he shared with Sorel the belief that in some deep sense the ability to pursue one's interests, even if they come into sharp struggle with competing attitudes and institutions, is the mark of a vigorous and growing society. But the big divide between Gumplowicz' *sociologism* and the *socialism* of Marx and Sorel is that the doctrine of conflict and divided interests is used by the former as an *explanation of social change*, while for the latter two it represents *a justification of social revolution*.

This is not to say that Gumplowicz' view was free of ideological moorings. As the previous section tried to show, the natural history of society method is essentially a device which substitutes a theory of change for a theory of progress, and hence does not threaten the impulse to equilibrium and stability that characterizes conservatism, and no less characterized the pioneer stages of sociology. Martindale's distinction between conflict ideology and conflict theory is well taken. "The sociological conflict theorists are, as a whole, even more positivistic than their organicist colleagues. They can afford to be: they have not had to close their eyes to whole blocks of empirical facts . . . The normal task of on-going society can be seen as a constant movement toward what is variously called adjustment, stability, equilibrium, or the termination of conflict. Hence, bad as things sometimes seem, it is conservative wisdom not to make matters worse, nor to make the world over, nor to interfere with 'the normal processes of society,' but rather to leave well enough alone and keep whatever peace is possible" (Martindale, 1960:176-77).

What in particular eliminates any possible radical uses for Gumplowicz' theory of social struggle is the notion of conflict cycles. Social groups can only alter the particular formal relationships of authority to freedom, elites to masses, and superordination to subordination, they cannot genuinely alter the structure of this bipolarization of social life. Thus the theory of *Rassenkampf* and *Klassenkampf* provided Gumplowicz with a realistic formula for explaining group conflict, without at the same time entailing any radical demands for the reformation of the Austro-Hungarian Empire, or any other existing social establishment. This is well underscored in his discussion of might and right, which attempts to "adjudicate" conservative and liberal opinion in Germany by seeing the Bismarckian State as both the instrument of might and no less as the creator of rights. Thus, despite Gumplowicz' fulminations against organicist social doctrines from Hegel to Lilienfeld, he only proved that sociological positivism is no less capable of reaching conservative political conclusions through a less circuitous route.

The content of Gumplowicz' thought nonetheless provides a valuable guide in the analysis of the interlocking processes of social stratification and differentiation. It can only be viewed as a tragedy of sociological history that the rich mine of Gumplowicz' theory of *Klassenkampf* and *Rassenkampf* has been disqualified from serious consideration in consequence of the racist fanaticism of German nazism. Social critics such as Lukacs (1953:ch. 7, sect. 3) who have taken at face value the statement that the conflict theory of Gumplowicz and Ratzenhofer shared responsibility for the material and ideological successes of fascism and nazism, at best are guilty of permitting good sentiments to interfere with sound scholarship and at worst are subject to the charge of deliberately distorting the substance of conflict theory.

Specific types of social change exhibit two layers of operations, which we may call primary and secondary in consequence of the distinctive qualities of homogenous and heterogenous groups. In the first place, social groups are essentially homogenous in their concrete interests and bound together by commonly felt needs. Alterations in these homogenous groups are socially produced by the contrary demands and interests of other social groups. Thus, Gumplowicz speaks of social change as coming into being "when two or more heterogenous groups come into contact." This is the essence of the "sozialer prozess" (1905c:128).

As a consequence of the socialization of groups (in which the conqueror and the conquered are welded together in common language, religion, and political and economic interests), and no less as a consequence of syngenism (natural solidarity which manifests itself in the spontaneous association of individuals into groups), nations, states, classes, races—as well as other forms of aggregate groups—come to be formed. In this fashion relatively simple groups become amalgamated with, aligned to, or associated with complex and large-scale units. At this juncture Gumplowicz makes one of his more profound contributions to the sociological theory of groups. For this extension of the size of the group does not disrupt or transform the operation of the "universal law" of social change. The process of heterogenous group conflict only continues at a higher and more exacting level, *i.e.*, between nations, classes and races. It is for this reason that such phenomena as nationalism, socialism, and racialism, while they appear as questions of politics, are for Gumplowicz, actually questions for sociology.

Gumplowicz sees this process of group formation and amalgamation in terms of the larger framework of social equilibrium and social revolution. The dynamics of equilibrium and revolution, consensus and conflict, is the basic law of sociology, or at the least of political sociology. This process is dynamical rather than dialectial since the results of change is but a shift in the structure of formal organization, and not essentially a new stage in human evolution.

It can be seen that Gumplowicz' sociology of complex groups rests upon an "external" rather than an "internal" theory of change. Social change is not viewed as a consequence of rumblings in the bowels of any single social group or social system, but rather a consequence of the inevitable clash between groups. In this way, he managed to firmly "de-radicalize" the theory of change—since change is a matter of subordination to another group, or in turn, subordinating another group, rather than struggles taking place within the homogenous group. The historical *Geist* is seen in terms more akin to Toynbee than to Marx since a social system is measured exclusively by its capacity to respond and repulse challenges received from other civilizations, with the role of internal agencies of change limited to their capacities for absorption in this ultimate clash of civilizations. The task of analysis is somewhat simpler for Gumplowicz than it was for Spengler because the unit of measurement was taken to be the homogenous group rather than the more diffuse and conceptually abstract homogenous State. Racial, class and ethnic elements were seen as more intimately representative of true group cohesiveness and exclusiveness.

We now turn to the most controversial, and perhaps least understood, aspect of Gumplowicz' sociology—the doctrine of racial conflict. The utopian dogma that because *conceptually* it might be pleasant if all men were recognized as *social* equals because we can establish without a doubt that they are *biologically* equal is only a blatant illustration of the wish-fulfillment character of psuedo-social theory. To mistake declarations of the rights of men, for the actual conditions of men is not to take seriously the existence of imperfection and irrationality in the social world. The type of sociological positivism expounded by Gumplowicz, precisely because it came at a period in European history in which oracular social theory had been emptied of radical consequences, had the sobering effect of separating sense from sentiment, deed from desire, and, above all, *racial theory* from *racialism*.

Initially, it has to be seen that Gumplowicz' theory of race and race conflict is sociological and not anthropological. In *Der Rassenkampf*, he rejects any view which holds that there is an intrinsic physiological, intellectual or moral superiority of one racial group over another. "In nature, there are no relationships based on superiority or inferiority. Racial designations are part of human society, made to satisfy its impulse to systematize all relations" (1883:23). As such, Gumplowicz anticipates the general skepticism about the concept of race as an anthropological category which now prevails.

There seems little evidence for a biological theory of race or racial types, and even less evidence for any theory of the historical superiority of one group of people over another in terms of genetic findings (*Cf.* Gumplowicz, 1905c: 362-65). Since races are sub-specific taxonomic units it follows that they can, given any kind of social interaction, inter-breed. The only factor preventing the total inter-breeding of the different races of mankind has to do with

issues of social isolation and social distance. There can be no sharply
defined morphological boundary between groups which constantly
exchange genes. The arbitrariness of every known anthropological
typology is too well established to require any further elaboration
here (*Cf.* Howells, 1959; and LeBarre, 1954). Racial taxonomies
which are founded on biologically distinct elements invariably
collapse in the face of close analysis since "some biological differences between human beings within a single race may be as great
as, or greater than, the same biological differences between races"
(*Cf.* Unesco, 1950:15).

Gumplowicz was one of the earliest social scientists to see the
ineluctable dilemmas attached to any racial theory grounded in
biology, anthropology, and certainly history. Yet he did not abandon
the idea of race. Indeed, he made wider use of the *Rassenkampf* than
most legitimate social investigators of his time or since. Why?

The answer is neither simple nor simplistic. In the first place,
distinctions of race functioned as one of the major pivotal forces of
the social group. Second, Gumplowicz took the statements relating
to race at face value, that is to say, in an age of "white man's
burden" (and perhaps no less in an age of "white man listen") it
was difficult to discard a large scale social frame of reference by
means of which people defined themselves and in turn, were defined
by others. If a designation serves not only as a criterion of measurement and meaning, but no less, as a framework for social action, it
is indeed difficult to liquidate such a criterion on the basis of its
"unscientific" or "undemocratic" character. The sociologist cannot
expect all human actions to be based on rationally proven statements
about man and his world. His task is first to explain, account and
classify action situations—whatever the source of their stimulation,
mythic or scientific (*Cf.* Gibson, 1960:39-46). Sociology can no more
demand that social motivation be completely "rational" than the
psychologist can expect private behavior to be "normal." This may
indeed be the ideal striven after; but it serves no purpose to make
believe that ideals sought are identical with gains registered. It is
primarily in this sense that Gumplowicz' examination of racial conflict must be considered.

Arguing the case for a sociological theory of race first involves
Gumplowicz in a critique of theories of alleged racial superiorities

based on craniological or other biological characteristics. He took heated issue with those investigators who spoke of "different racial stocks" for the thoroughly unscientific purpose of upholding the superiority of the "Germanic" stock. National prejudice illustrates nothing but its own ignorance. The search for unitary racial types so prevalent at the turn of the century finds no anthropological support. "Even in the remotest tribes, whom the current of migration does not touch, who have no intercourse with others, and who are apparently beyond the reach of every other agitating force of history, there was nothing which could be called a 'unitary type' " (1905c: 145). Gumplowicz then goes on to show that a system of racial measurements and typologies based on observation of physiognomical factors is no less a blind alley than craniology. Thus the division of races in terms of skin pigmentation is as superficial as it is crude. The deeper the anthropologist searched for a racial typology based on skin color the more pronounced did the crisis of such an approach become. From three races, later studies evolved a typology based on hundreds of skin types. Anatomically based studies of racial differences ran into similar paradoxes of multiplying the number of skeletal differences to a point where it no longer had any general scientific value in the study of man.

Gumplowicz was not interested in making a frontal assault on the possibility of a theory of races. Basically, he remained convinced that *in some sense* a racial typology could perform useful functions in scientific clarification and codification. But in what sense? Since "every means of investigation fails to disclose racial purity in prehistoric times" (much less in modern times), the basis of racial theory must be shifted from anthropology to sociology. "Anthropological changes have not affected the social relations of either ancient or modern human groups. Sociologically they are still distinct groups. Sociological dissimilarities are independent of the structure of the bones and skull. They consist in very different factors" (1905c:155). Among these factors are distinctions between native and alien, distinctive linguistic, hygienic, educative, religious, and like elements found in the social constellation. These are the bonds of complex group membership. It is precisely such large groups that by convention and self-designation we call races.

Gumplowicz employs the Lamarck-Darwin theory of adaptation

as a purely environmental variable (a not inappropriate reading of
evolutionary doctrine given the *Zeitgeist* which then existed). Thus
a racial type is for him in effect a social type. "Who does not recognize an Englishman, a Frenchman, an Italian, a north or south
German among a hundred different nationalities" asks Gumplowicz.
"It is difficult to say exactly how we recognize them. Only the artist's
crayon can express it. But we recognize John Bull, the 'Honest Swabian,' the Frenchman polite and tractable and even the Parisian, the
Italian somewhat uncanny and Mephistophelian, and so on." He concludes this point with another rhetorical question: "Who has not
observed how living for years among a people of a pronounced type
of culture transforms a foreigner's whole external appearance and
bearing to theirs?" (1905c.275-76).

Clearly, Gumplowicz mistakes stereotyping for scientific generalization. It is by no means necessary that *Der Nationaltypus* are
self-evident to the observer—skilled and unskilled alike. For while
it is correct that "John Bull" is a symbolic representation of a certain sort of Englishman, and that life in England may even give
substance to the production of such an aristocratic type, the actual
number of such "pure types" who walk the streets of London are
extremely few in number. Indeed, so few as to be singled out for
their distinctive qualities, *e.g.*, the "Colonel Blimp" type, the "Lant-
ern Jaw" type, etc. *ad infinitum*. The plain truth is that national
identification is no sounder a basis for racial determination than
religious affiliation. As an instrument for moving beyond craniological or genetic theories of race Gumplowicz' insights do not carry us
very far. Stereotypes are not necessarily better because they are
sociological rather than anthropological.

Gumplowicz' position suffers from a taxonomic confusion. He
deals with some racial groups as if they were national, *e.g.*, the
British "race;" at other times a racial group is identified with a
caste, *e.g.*, the Brahmins; and at other times still, Gumplowicz speaks
of a race in terms of religious groups, *e.g.*, the Hebrew people. This
diversionary and confusing linkage of race to "folk groups,"
"nations," and "religions" only serves to detract from Gumplowicz' general theory of the group and group conflict.

Nonetheless, a sociological approach to race and racial relations
does have importance, since men do in fact employ stereotyped,

artificial criteria to differentiate themselves from "the others." The national race theme has been used to justify both social pride and social oppression. It cannot be denied that a high measure of social solidarity was achieved by nineteenth century English colonialism by a self definition of roles in terms of Rudyard Kipling's "White Man's Burden." Conversely, social cohesion of underdeveloped African nations is no less underscored by the concept of race. In part at least, the new African nations tend to define their social roles and their "generalized other" in terms of Richard Wright's slogan: "White Man Listen." The justification of "white" and "colored" positions is not herein at stake. What does matter is that Gumplowicz viewed political and economic delineations on the basis of race; which is not necessarily pernicious nor socially dysfunctional.

The fact that gradations in skin pigmentation are nearly infinite, and that any other device for the physical differentiation of men into races has yielded only one result, that the only "pure race" is homosapiens, does not basically alter the terms of the social struggle. Racial antagonisms are real in so far as they have authentic social consequences. Stigmata of inferiority can be quickly transformed into marks of social superiority. For every segregationist who considers deep chestnut brown skin a lamentable representation of natural inferiority, there is the Negro who proudly sings of "my fine brown skin," and may even go so far as to insist that brown is superior to either white (underbaked) or black (overbaked) on the basis of Providential design. Again, it must be added that no judgment is entailed by such a strategic accounting of "social types." Simply the realization that preservation of social distance for one group may heighten a sense of social solidarity for another group.

As long as the "racial question" is considered strictly in anthropological terms, one can only come up with a single result: that racial theory is an anti-scientific myth, with largely destructive consequences in terms of the unity of human goals. But the task of sociology is precisely to see the operation of such racial myths in terms of overall social structures and social policy. From this point of view, Gumplowicz courageously contributed to a more profound understanding of the social forces confronting each other in the modern world. The lesson is simple and clear: to be done with the racial question anthropologically is not to be finished with it sociologically. It might be argued that when all men become scientific, there will be no need to locate mechanisms of defense on so shoddy a basis as race. Quite true. But the same claim can be made for other, equally "absurd" bases for action, such as magical rites, ideologies, political slogans, etc. In short, when inter-group relations can proceed on the basis of scientific knowledge alone, the race struggle will be at an end. But a similar statement might be proffered by others with equal force. For when inter-group relations can proceed on the basis of a perfect rationalization of the economic system, the class struggle will be at an end. Meanwhile, that sociological science which exists prior to the millenium must continue to take account of the role of racial struggles in defining the behavior of small groups, communities, nations, and even continents.

In the furor caused by Gumplowicz' forthright attitude to the sociological implications of race, it has been overlooked that he had an equally firm attitude towards classes and class struggle. Both are products of the social conflict between heterogenous groups. His attitude to social classes stands at a mid-way point between Marx and Mosca both in time and in theory. The former influenced Gumplowicz more than the references might indicate (Cf., Gumplowicz, 1926:381-87), while the latter was in turn powerfully influenced by Gumplowicz (Mosca, 1896:62-64). Both political and economic functions define the limits of a class for Gumplowicz. The antagonisms which build up between classes is in turn a consequence of the general universe of group conflict.

The political aspect of this definition of class entailed the belief that "universally there is a ruling minority and a subject majority. This is the essence of the State as it is the essence of sovereignty." But although the growth of class stratification has a political impulse and a political origin, the purposes of a class remains basically economic. The formation of the political State, maintains Gumplowicz, is to secure economic advantages. Superordination and subordination, what he terms the party which commands and the group which accomodates itself, becomes enshrined in all stages of social life. As in Rousseau, the power distribution is naturally unequal. Since power is in the hands of the ruling class, only habit, custom and law, and other elements of social equilibrium, come into existence. Equilibrium is thus not a consequence of Providence, Utopia, Social Contract, or Natural Law, or any other essentially social metaphysic; it is simply a function of the distribution of power. "Inequality is stamped on every right; the husband orders his wife, the parent in the strength of his years commands his children, the owner excludes all others from enjoying the fruits of his property. All these are rights expressing the orderly relations of unequals." From this statement of authority as a function of class divisions, Gumplowicz moves to a pessimistic reading of society in general. "It is an error and a delusion to think that rights have been or can be equally distributed. They arise only in the relations which exist in the State; they express them and measure their inequality" (1905c:198-99).

Social stratification and differentiation is not restricted along the lines of capital and labor, but assumes many variegated forms from generational strife to sexual competition. Nonetheless, the relationship between economic classes does possess a *prima facie* importance denied to other forms of conflict. Gumplowicz sees the whole weight of political organization, the State, mobilized to harness the services of the subject majority. The forms of economic rivalry alter in each historical epoch, and are differently represented as such physical variables as climate and natural resources differ, but the content of the political State, the maintenance of patterns of socio-economic inequality, of *Herrschaftsordnung*, are essentially undisturbed by such external considerations.

The organization and rationalization of the labor process entails a supreme act of coercion, training and discipline. This the State alone is equipped to accomplish through the process of *Rechtsordnung*. The State "demands of the laboring class in the beginning at least, untold sacrifice of life and health; but finally in a rising civilization they become participants in the material and moral possessions." But since this participation can never really change the *character* of State authority, but only possibly shift the balance of such authority from one oppressor group to another, "the life of the State is summed up in this common though unequal labor" (1905c:201-2).

In Gumplowicz' view then, the fundamental source of social *stratification* is political and economic exploitation; while the main source of social *differentiation* is need satisfaction. In this interactive process, racial, ethnic, religious and class distinctions promote the end of exploitation and satisfaction. Enshrined norms of superiority and inferiority assist in making possible that violence necessary to capture and maintain exploited labor. When the laborer can be treated as "less than human," maximum exploitation is possible. Hence, satisfaction of minority needs, that is, material abundance for an elite, can be achieved in a scarcity economy. This in turn is hypostatized into the "theory" that the exploited need much less to satisfy their needs. So great is the need to rationalize the basis of class distinction, that Gumplowicz insists that "where natural ethnic distinctions disappear artificial 'social' distinctions arise to perpetuate the antagonism of human groups" (1905c:202-3).

But when this struggle for subsistence is achieved, and is replaced by a condition of relative affluence, the contest between social forces becomes immeasurably more complex. At this point psychological and directly political considerations help in shaping the structure of social distinctions. New factors such as personal ambition, the search for glory and power, dynastic dreams, etc. emerge to further differentiate men in the social group. Here Gumplowicz terminates his examination of social stratification, since the advanced state of social development, with its multitude of social strata and occupational roles, makes a strictly sociological accounting of the situation impossible. The more or less direct confrontation of social groups is considered the upper limits of a sociological (*i.e.*, factual) study of the subject. The study of social stratification in modern society must proceed from the "case-study" method, that is, the selective approach to groups which are presumed to typify stratification arrangements in a complex society.

The replacement of the anthropological approach (which seeks to exhaust all cases of human association and differentiation within a group) with the sociological approach (which seeks to examine selectively human association and differentiation between groups), enabled Gumplowicz to make a solid contribution to political sociology. His observations on the development of rank in the political and economic life of the group presaged the rise of the concept of "status." His approach to social stratification as the classification and rank ordering of people on a scale of power and preference still satisfactorily defines the field. Furthermore, his efforts to evolve a theory of classes in terms of the specialization of functions and divisions of labor this brings about, anticipated Durkheim's work in the same field; while his examination of the changing historical functions of classes and the role of intermediate occupational groups helped in placing economic systems within a broader context of social organization. This last represented a true broadening of the question of class *membership* in contrast to class *allegiance* in a way which was to be made familiar to later generations through the efforts of Weber's *Class, Status and Party*, but which must nonetheless have sounded a discordant note in the anti-sociological climate of the turn of the century. While Gumplowicz was hardly alone in his efforts to promote a realistic theory of social stratification, his work was in advance of most others in that he did not allow his philosophic monism to dictate the kind of determinism of *Geld* and *Geist* that was so rampant among organicist sociologists and even among the "younger generation" typified by Ratzenhofer in Germany and Giddings in the United States.

The phenomenon of social class and "class-building," represents one of Gumplowicz's "universal laws." It is part of the utilitarian drive to satisfy one's group interests. Social classes survive only to the degree that they satisfy the social wants of class membership. As new wants emerge and old ones expand, further functional differentiation takes place and new castes and classes arise. But Gumplowicz stops short of extending his concept of utilitarian differentiation to those phenonomena which Veblen saw as "parasitic" and which obey laws of "conspicuous consumption." Such classes are doomed to disappearance since they have little relation to a social "other." That the State, which Gumplowicz agrees comes into existence as a consecration of superordination and subordination, can ever perform a role of preserving dysfunctional social classes is nowhere entertained. While an approach which considers class divisions as functional barriers preserves Gumplowicz' theory of the external nature of the conquest of political power (through war rather than revolution) it fails to really distinguish between warfare (the struggle between sovereign powers) and revolution (the struggle between classes within a single State for sovereign power). And it was precisely on this point that Mosca along with Michels, Pareto and Sorel, moved sociology out of its pristine nineteenth century condition.

To discuss war between nations as "higher forms of the simple social struggles" is to nullify the distinction between the relationship of men to each other and the actual process of material satisfaction. Gumplowicz' theory of groups likewise suffers from its inability to distinguish between *intensities* of group relations and between *levels* of group interaction. Thus, in his framework differences in group interests and group interaction tend to be held uniform for all aspects of social relations. Gumplowicz failed to pursue his earlier train of thought, of distinguishing political, economic and psychological variables as such variables affect group life. All problems of class life became problems in *inter*-group relations which meant that questions of *intra*-group relations tended to become submerged. Homogeneity became another word for uniformity, while heterogeneity was used as virtually synonomous with dis-equilibrium.

Gumplowicz' approach was a provocative response to the organismic school of sociology, which could only view conflict situations as dangerous to the life of the social organism. For his part, Gumplowicz managed to convey an urgency to issues in social stratification by treating problems of class, race and ethnicity as special conditions of the general law of social evolution through social conflict. The conflict situation became in his hands neither rigidly defined nor fearfully avoided, but simply an object of study. If Gumplowicz was unable to perceive the significance of his work for the study of homogenous groups no less than for heterogenous groups, it was a failure of perception that was corrected with the collapse of mechanistic biology and sociology, and its replacement with a broadened view of social dynamics in which norms of personal behavior could be seen as interacting with, rather than nullified by, the social group.

5. Belief and Behavior: The Sociology of Knowledge

"In the presence of the total reality upon which our conduct is founded, our knowledge is characterized by peculiar limitations and aberrations. In view of our accidental and defective adaptations to our life conditions, there is no doubt that we cherish not only so much truth, but also so much nescience, and attain to so much error as is useful for our practical purposes. We may call to mind in this connection that vast sums of human knowledge that modify human life, which, however, are overlooked or disregarded if the total cultural situation does not make these

modifications possible and useful. At the other extreme, we may refer
to the *Lebensluge* of the individual, so often, in need of illusion as to
his powers and even as to his feelings, of superstition with reference to
God as well as men, in order to sustain himself in his being and in his
potentialities. In this psycho-biological respect error is co-ordinated with
truth. The utilities of the external, as of the subjective, life provide that
we get from the one as well as from the other precisely that which
constitutes the basis of the conduct which is essential for us."

— *Georg Simmel, 1906* —

While it has been said, in error, that Gumplowicz' sociology
represented an attempt to reduce social laws to biology (Tiumeniev,
1935: 260), a certain reductionist residue is nonetheless present in
his work. A powerful strand of social physics, much like that exhibited by Quetelet in *Physique Sociale* (1869) and by Bagehot in
Physics and Politics (1872), is evident in his "universal laws" of
behavior of which sociology develops "special applications." The
classical physics of Newton relating to the laws of motion and matter
continues to inform Gumplowicz' methodology (1883:158; and
1905c:114-17). Due to this physicalism, Gumplowicz never felt the
need for a theory of internal change, *i.e.*, changes occuring within
a social system which are *causa sui*. In Gumplowicz' thinking there
is a "universal law of persistence" which upon inspection is little
else than an application to social groups of Newton's First Law of
Motion: "Every body perseveres in its state of rest." By extension,
conflict arises in a social group in conformity to the second portion
of this First Law: "as it is compelled to change that state by impressed forces" (*Cf.* Dampier, 1949:155).

Social groups are supposedly at rest, and like atomic clusters,
remain at rest until put in motion by an external and moving object
with which the group comes into contact. As Gumplowicz says,
"each alteration in the social condition of a group must always have
a sufficient social cause, which is always the influence of another
group" (1905c:128). Again, in *Der Rassenkampf*, we see how Gumplowicz escapes the problem of disorganization or deviance within
a group by assigning conflict making factors to external agencies
in line with his Newtonian convictions. "The extent to which science
is permeated by the hypothesis that heterogenous elements reacting
upon each other are necessary to a natural process is best indicated

by the atomic theory. Obviously, it is conceded that the origins of
all natural processes cannot better be explained than by the assumption of the existence in bodies of invisible particles, each of which
has some sort of separate existence and reacts upon the others. The
entire hypothesis is only the consequence of the concept of a natural
process which the observation of nature has produced in the human
mind" (1883:159-60).

Gumplowicz' sociological reflections on belief and behavior
must be understood against a general physicalist background in
which social relations are only complex representations of atomic
facts. His sharp condemnation of all forms of idealism has as its
basis the desire to see problems of behavior in group life as essentially unconditioned by personality differences or by the influence of any
single individual in the historical process. But if this kind of sociological physicalism limited Gumplowicz' understanding of the range of
group dynamics it at the same time made possible a brilliant examination of the social sources of mental production—an understanding
which broadly defines the scope and operations of the sociology of
knowledge as an empirical discipline.

The basis of sociological investigation is the behavior of men.
How men *believe*, the forms of perception, is a question for social
psychology. How men *behave*, how they translate perceptions and
conceptions into forms of action, this is an object for sociological
study. The basis of society is the act. The basis for the social study of
ideas is how the act is conditioned by mental needs, and in turn
how actions of the group affect the belief systems of men. The social
struggle of groups generates the intellectual struggle of ideas.
Thought is itself a social product, the composite result of group
existence. "The great error of individualistic psychology is the supposition that man thinks. It leads to the continual search for the source
of thought in the individual and for the reason why the individual
thinks so and not otherwise; and prompts naive theologians and
philosophers to consider and even to advise how man ought to
think" (1905c:268). The correct view, according to Gumplowicz,
is to recognize that what we think is a necessary reflection of our
views and attitudes; and such views and attitudes are a direct outgrowth of social intercourse.

Social classes arise in response to human needs, and the proof that such needs are social rather than strictly economic, is that the rise of a "priestly class," bearers of religious ideas, perform a *useful* task even if such tasks are economically unproductive. Thus a distinction has to be drawn between social utility and economic use. Classes satisfy needs by providing "services" no less than by producing "goods." To the objection that such forms of social production of ideas are less meritorious than economic production of artifacts, Gumplowicz retorts that "the same might be also said of the services of the ruling class. But what are these objections against the fact that men's religious wants are as peremptory as their material wants, and that the ruling class also fulfills its function in social economy and has no substitute" (1905c:222). In this way, Gumplowicz sees the mental needs of men no less a subject of sociology than his material needs. Both are produced in the process of social interaction.

Social classes each have specific interests which they attempt to advance at the expense of others. But the advancement of such interests is an indirect process taking place in abstract spheres of law and morality no less than in the open conflict of groups. In *Rechtsstaat und Sozialismus,* he explains how the conflict between classes creates the basis for superordination in public law. A legal scaffold "begins only where the dominating classes come into conflict among themselves regarding the sphere of authority belonging to each of them. Thus, the first big political struggle which we encounter in the second half of the European middle ages, the struggle between the secular and the ecclesiastic authority, the struggle between the Emperor and the Pope, gave the first impetus to the development of the German science of public law" (Gumplowicz, 1881: 124-25). However, Gumplowicz does not pursue the point completely. For though he recognizes a special set of ideas as linked to class interests, he does not make an effort to distinguish these interest bound ideas from the germination of scientific ideas. That is to say, those ideas which are intrinsically restricted to justification and rationalization of political systems were not seen by Gumplowicz as part of the task of sociological investigation.

Moving over to the social psychology of mental production, Gumplowicz holds that for the large majority of men, thought is developed only to the point of its social utility, *i.e.,* only for its use in the promotion of the group needs. Education as an end, scientific knowledge, is not "thought" in any sense useful to the majority of men. Gumplowicz, lacking any general theory of ideology, limited his distinction to thought in general as contrasted with specialized branches of knowledge. Expertise such as that possessed by physicians and engineers is the basis of science but not of social solidarity. "Hard conflicts of interest" take priority in the majority of instances. And the settlement of such conflicts is not so much a matter of scientific precision as it is of power and authority. For this reason, the "science" of public law cannot be ranked alongside the science of astronomy, in that the mode of primary "verification" in the former is *interests*, while in the latter it is objective *evidence*.

In this situation Gumplowicz' man of knowledge is akin to Mannheim's "freischwebende Intelligenz," holding himself apart from the social conflicts of the age as best he can. But unlike Mannheim's notion of the intelligentsia *as a class* transcending the cycle of ideologically conditioned actions, for Gumplowicz the condition whereby exact knowledge transcends interest elements is a "personal fate," what perhaps we would now consider the exclusive property of the social isolate. As a general phase rule, Gumplowicz tells us that "a man's behavior is determined immediately by his economic status, which constrains him to follow a certain mode of life and awakens the corresponding mental conditions within him" (1905c: 277).

Mental states which reflect economic class interests are at first relatively simple, divided as they are into aristocratic, bourgeois and peasant sectors. But as society becomes a complex network of intertwined economic relations and occupational roles, these mental sets likewise become subdivided and specialized. In this way interests come to be construed in terms of specific occupational tasks, and not just limited to large scale social group needs. Thus, each "social circle," such as that which exists among professional groups like teachers, lawyers and physicians, "creates its own peculiar spirit, so to say a moral atmosphere of principles, ideas, views and conceptions" (1905c:281).

The production of moral ideals and moral types is a consequence of the social circle. Adhering strictly to the positivist distinction between matters of fact and matters of value, Gumplowicz allows that "morals are nothing but the conviction implanted by the social group in the minds of its members, of the propriety of the manner of life imposed by it on them" (1905:285). The development of a science of ethics is not dependent on any given moral code of any given social circle, but is tied to the stage of development reached by the exact sciences. You can have a science of ethics only at that point in history when science pre-empts the field of religious ideas, thus making possible a naturalistic explanation of moral beliefs. For Gumplowicz, an ethic is itself fashioned to meet the rigors of nature and society. Because of this the natural and social sciences are alone in the unique position to explain the characteristic features of moral behavior.

Gumplowicz pursues his naturalistic mode of explaining moral statements with a boldness that is often absent in latter-day positivism, and in a manner that diverges sharply from contemporary functional-structural explanations. His discussion of rights and justice displays rare philosophic versatility. Human rights are the enshrined beliefs and customs of the group. As such they act as justifications for group practices. Rights exist only in relation to obligations. Every right is a concrete entity. Thus the right of the father in a patrilineal society implies the obligation of the mother and children to perform certain tasks. Similarly, the "rights" of the propertied entail certain well defined obligations for the propertyless. The concept of natural rights or rights of man is dismissed by Gumplowicz since "the maintenance of inequality is the sole and real principle of every right." To maintain this system of rights, the concept of justice is introduced by the State to act as the symbolic representation of power, of force. At the root of our ideas about property, marriage, and family is the need for the social group to maintain itself. Such notions of social justice are not arrived at capriciously, but take root only at the moment they receive the sanction of the organized force of the social circle. From the coercive power of the social circle ideas of natural rights and social justice emanate and even come to be viewed as divinely ordained.

The easy dismissal of natural rights doctrine is based on Gumplowicz' failure to acknowledge the possibility that justice involves equality in some respects only. Thus, natural rights theory does not automatically lose its legitimacy upon demonstration of factual inequality. Justice may be said to possess an "ideal" dimension as well as a power dimension.

In his discussion of scientific ideas, Gumplowicz adopts a strict determinist mode of explanation. True ideas are likened to finding and fitting correct size corks to the bottles we have on hand. The method of trial and error is thus useful to the degree it helps turn up the proper size cork. Other methods are likewise useful in so far as they can uncover the right cork more rapidly. Gumplowicz' scientist is the man who understands the "universal law" of necessity. His social role is to bend every effort to further distinguish the necessary from the accidental in whatever area of investigation the scientific mind is engaged in. The production of scientific truth is thus a direct response to "natural necessities" in contrast to the social production of mistaken ideas. The scientist in this way becomes the only social force that can transcend the provincialism and regionalism of an interest bound social group.

In part, Gumplowicz' view of the social role of the scientist was itself conditioned by an image of the heroic isolate; an image which was at the same time a self-image. Despite this autobiographical note, there can be no question that he was one of the first sociologists to see the problem of the "man of knowledge" as a very special one, stimulated by the growth of occupational specialization and role differentiation in western society.

In this distinction between the scientist, the man who uncovers natural necessities, and the citizen, the man who lives within the protection of his social circle, lies the further distinction between genuine progress and simple cycles of change. While Gumplowicz was far more disabused of the much heralded idea of progress than his co-workers in sociology, he was spared the swamp of pessimism by an abiding faith in the actual advances of science and technology. This distinction between material *corso* and social and political *ricorso* was not based on any notion of "culture lag," but rather on the differences between *clarification by men* and *manipulation of men* which the truth discovering process entails. Political and economic systems in Gumplowicz' view are not true representations of natural necessities. Aberrations in ideas about social systems are therefore not only possible but inevitable. The history of morals, for example, is in no way translated into a steady improvement in the behavior of men. This must be contrasted with the history of science, which is precisely defined by a steady improvement in the knowledge and control over the physical universe.

Gumplowicz came close to adopting the engineering principle as a possible way out of the paradox of machines and men. At that point when moral behavior comes under the aegis and sponsorship of the sociologist of morals, it is possible to speak of genuine ethical "progress." But until that point is reached, until that time when all ideas are scientifically grounded, the possibility of actual progress for the human race seemed slender to him. And indeed, Gumplowicz' attitude on this subject has much to recommend itself, particularly in an age of mass extermination and massive warfare (Gumplowicz, 1883:6-9). The deference for past ages shown to Providence and Progress has often turned out to be a defense of the caprice of unscrupulous men. Thus the scientific analysis of political rhetoric has much to offer the political sociologist.

The lengthy discussion in Gumplowicz' work of the social role of knowledge and its relation to interests and institutions provided a basis for further considerations of the sociology of knowledge and science. Gumplowicz' thoughts while by no means exhaustive or necessarily correct in its details, were far from the shallow homiletics offered up in the name of progress by the pious *literatteurs* of the 19th century. Gumplowicz shared with Sorel a deep-seated suspicion that not everything which changes must necessarily be for the better. To attach a moral judgment to simple changes of function or place is already to adopt a pejorative or horatory view of history— a posture as unbecoming to the sociologist as say, chauvinism would be for the physicist. Precisely this effort to take a non-moralistic attitude to social order raises Gumplowicz' efforts above the mundane.

That Gumplowicz never arrived at a general theory of ideology (something which was theoretically possible given the antecedent work in this direction by Feuerbach and Marx), was in part a consequence of his glorified conception of State authority. The one time in which his sense of objectivity utterly failed him was in his Bismarckian vision of State authority as the *deus ex machina* of contending social forces. For Gumplowicz well realized that such coercive authority can never reach its goals given the natural propensity of

social circles for exclusivity. The coercive features of federal authority are not connected up with the parallel task of mass persuasion,
i.e., the transformation of beliefs held by the dominant social elements into the ideas of society in general. Gumplowicz can only see
the State's attempt at "self-justification" as an aspect of its elevated
role in promoting higher moral standards. The very physicalism
which enabled him to posit a struggle of ideas as a consequence of
contending social forces, never permitted him to move beyond a
conservative frame of reference, *i.e.*, the "need" for the State to
regulate and control such conflicts in the realm of ideas no less than
in political affairs. The analysis of how the State, the Nation, and
the bureaucratic apparatus in general creates nothing so grandiose
as a "higher morality" but simply a rationalization and justification
of its specific interests; and how in turn, oppositional organizations
bring contrary systems of ideas into being (counter-ideologies and
counter-utopias), became the next step in the development of an
accounting system for belief and behavior, for the sociology of
knowledge. Martindale's pungent statement on this point sums up
matters succinctly. "Conflict sociology emerged as the second form
of sociological theory precisely because while correcting positivistic
organicism in a realistic manner it was conformable to the same
ideological requirements" (Martindale, 1960:177).

Gumplowicz' dismissal of the possibility of explaining the *origin*
of things no less than their operations, and his parallel contempt
for the possibilities of ordinary men learning more than they need
for survival, severly cramped his understanding of the social production of ideas which ran contrary to the supposed needs of the
social group. New ideas, like new modes of economic production,
become a force only at the point of conflict *between* different groups.
This injection theory of idea systems assumed the homeostatic completeness of the social group, and as a result could not explain the rise
of conflicting ideas *within* the social group. In addition, such a view
as Gumplowicz offered could not account for the rise of competing
classes or races *within* the same social system. The view that a homogenous group was somehow also a hermetic group dominated Gumplowicz' thinking to the end, so that his theory of conflict rarely
managed to come to terms with the group as such, with the nation
as such, or with the system of State as such.

6. The Reception of Gumplowicz in American Sociology

"Those who would think about the nature of society and history in our time have been living off the big men of the nineteenth century. There has not yet appeared any twentieth century political theorist, sociologist, historian or economist whose work is truly up to their level . . . The trouble is that many of us do not know it."

— C. Wright Mills, 1955 —

"There are few really fundamental and important concepts in the sociology of 1935 that were not definitely formulated or at least adumbrated by Gumplowicz."

— Frank N. House, 1936 —

The attitude taken towards Gumplowicz' empirical sociology in Germany was by and large critical if not completely hostile. Not an insignificant portion of Gumplowicz' last years were taken up with a dissemination of his views, a defense of them against ungenerous critics, and a reaffirmation of the broad contours of *Der Rassen-kampf* and *Grundriss der Soziologie*. The failure of Gumplowicz to enlist the support of any sizeable portion of German speaking social scientists led him to search out contacts elsewhere in the world who would be in a position to translate and disseminate his ideas in more receptive intellectual climates. The success of this approach can be gathered by the number of languages in which his work appeared (French, Spanish, Russian, Polish, Japanese, Italian, and English), and also by the intense loyalty his work commanded from men like Pedro Dorado Montero in Spain, Franco Savorgnan in Italy, and Charles Baye in France. These men not only translated, but were instrumental in getting Gumplowicz' work reviewed, commented upon and employed in further sociological studies.

For all of this fame and notoriety later conflict theorists such as Simmel hardly acknowledged Gumplowicz' existence much less his influence. The main line of European sociology from Durkheim to Weber shows no apparent impact directly traceable to Gumplowicz (although the parallels at certain points between Gumplowicz and Durkheim are nothing short of remarkable). Later generations of European sociologists likewise proved not particularly responsive to Gumplowicz' sociological investigations. From the outset Gumplowicz was plagued by labels: reductionism, racism, too revolutionary, too reactionary, etc. We might single out two recent examples of this consignment of Gumplowicz to sociology purgatory.

Sorokin accuses Gumplowicz of a crude biological reductionism, and is highly critical of the Austrian sociologist's "one sidedness and exaggerations" concerning the origins of social stratification in warfare. Sorokin likewise disliked Gumplowicz' sociological theory of personality. He does modify his attitude toward Gumplowicz to the extent of rating his work in "the history of social theories much higher" (Sorokin, 1928:484-87). Unfortunately, Sorokin did not see fit to examine the relationship between Gumplowicz' work in the history of social theory and sociological theory as such. Georg Lukacs is even sharper in his condemnation of Gumplowicz' sociologism. He is accused of having eliminated the study of "social character" from sociology, thereby reducing the study of man to a vulgar biological determinism. The ultimate irony is that Gumplowicz, the transplanted Polish Jewish sociologist, is accused of preparing the way for Hitlerism and nazism, the most virulent form of anti-semitism ever to emerge. Gumplowicz' writings are said "to constitute an important stage in the historical conception of fascism" (Lukacs, 1953: ch. vii, sect. iii). But since Lukacs places just about all post-Marxian sociology in the same position with respect to nazism, the allegations against Gumplowicz are not quite as damaging as they might seem.

The case of Mosca's treatment of Gumplowicz deserves special attention. Mosca himself makes clear that the basic canon of his political sociology: the division of men into ruling and ruled classes, is in large measure a derivation from *Der Rassenkampf*. He rejects, however, Gumplowicz' alleged position that occupational and class divisions are ethnologically heterogenous. Mosca goes on to argue with Gumplowicz and "other neo-Darwinians" by noting that there is nothing racially bound about class superiority; that in fact biological inheritance has nothing to do with either intellectual prowess or moral behavior (Mosca, 1896: 62-64). However, Mosca is clearly arguing with a straw man and not with Gumplowicz. For as we have already noted, Gumplowicz takes essentially the same position, namely, that the intellectual and moral qualities of a class are in no sense the consequence of biological or anthropological superiority or inferiority. As a matter of fact, for Gumplowicz, the talk about natural superiority is an ethnocentric device assiduously practiced

by devotees of *Kulturwissenschaft* and *Geisteswissenschaft* that has
no place in empirical sociology.

In his excellent study of Mosca, James H. Meisel helps shed
light on Mosca's strange distortion of the work of his predecessor.
Mosca "made it too easy for himself when he represented Gumplowicz as a crude racialist. He knew that this characterization was un-
fair, and his short reference to the work of his predecessor fails to
do him justice. Gumplowicz did not claim more than that the racial
factor was a starting point, the first cementing influence which later
on gives way to others, cultural and economic. The two races of the
conquerors and the conquered merge, become one nation with a common consciousness in which the memories of racial cleavage are
transformed into, and absorbed by, the new rationale of class. To
Mosca this must have appeared as some sort of biological Marxism,
the acceptance of which would have placed him ominously close to
the very system he wanted to disprove. And so we end up with finding the erratic block of 'syngenism' in Mosca's workshop; what had
been a capstone in another structure has become mere ornament"
(Meisel, 1958:133).

This fear of Mosca's that Gumplowicz was perhaps too close to
Marx for comfort, was later expressed by Max Scheler. In his pioneer
work on the sociology of knowledge Scheler expresses the opinion
that Gumplowicz shared with Marx and Ranke a "one-sidedness"
stemming from a common regard for "naturalism" (Scheler, 1924:
30). Paradoxically enough, while for Mosca and Scheler the sociology of Gumplowicz was too radical, for such orthodox Marxians as
Bukharin, the work of our sociologist "castrates Marx, corrodes the
revolutionary content from him, distorts him unrecognizably"
(Bukharin, 1935:9-10).

Caught in the cross-currents of European social ideologies
Gumplowicz' stock, never to high to begin with, suffered a steady
decline. This sad neglect of a major pioneer in modern sociology is
perhaps best reflected in the retrospective symposium on *La Sociologie au XXe Siècle*, the second volume of which concerning *Les
Etudes Sociologiques dans les Différents Pays*, makes no mention of
him either in connection with German, Austrian or Polish trends in
sociology. (Gurvitch and Moore, 1947). Surely, if pages can be
given over to an examination of Jacob Burckhardt and Wilhelm

Dilthey, neither of whom were either twentieth century figures nor sociologists (*Cf.* Salomon, 1947:593-620), some recognition of Gumplowicz' work would seem to have been in order.

If Gumplowicz' reception among his fellow sociologists proved less than enthusiastic, it must be remembered that his inflence extended beyond the discipline into other fields of social science. A good case in point is the Austrian economist Joseph Schumpeter. While Schumpeter's relation to Gumplowicz can hardly be said to be of paramount importance, it was nonetheless substantial enough for Schumpeter to design his famous study of social classes in terms of Gumplowicz' work in the same area. He writes in the preface to this essay that "the qualifying phrase, 'in an ethnically homogenous environment,' is not meant to deny the significance of racial differences in explaining concrete class formations. On the contrary, my early thinking on the subject followed the paths of the racial theory of classes, as it is found in the works of Gumplowicz, upon which I came while I was still at school" (Schumpeter, 1955:102).

Nor were Schumpeter's remarks intended as a formal gratuity. He was convinced that class formations were essentially a dynamic and internal process, rather than an imposition from external sources such as conquest and warfare. That is why the *homogenous* group rather than the *heterogenous* group served as a model for Schumpeter's exposition of the issues. Social classes are in a process of continual change, no less than individual membership in such classes. Even Gumplowicz' belief in the military basis of social stratification was "homogenized" by Schumpeter. "The army of knighthood had really grown obsolete and inferior. There was a stronger power in existence now, and this meant a fundamental change in the total social-class structure." This power was individually owned landed property. Schumpeter internalized the whole problem of social change. Where Gumplowicz might have said that "the army of knighthood failed because the mercenary army came into being," Schumpeter declared the reverse: "Rather that the system of mercenaries arose because the knightly host failed from inner causes" (*Ibid*, 150-51).

There can be no question that Schumpeter's internalization of class change had the effect of considerably weakening Gumplowicz' theory of class change as a consequence of invasion, immigration and group solidarity. While ethnic heterogeneity may account for the formation of the social or racial group as such, the structure or mobility of that group is itself a subject for separate inspection. With reformulation of the sociology of stratification and different-iation, Gumplowicz' *Rassenkampf* became an "accidental property" rather than the "essential nature" of social classes.

Schumpeter, who came to the University of Graz shortly after Gumplowicz committed suicide in 1909, thus honored his predecessor in the best and most meaningful of ways—by utilizing the work of Gumplowicz to move decisively beyond him.

In the United States, where the weight of old metaphysical dispositions and entrenched academic separations were not especially potent factors in the spread of social science, the reception accorded to empirical sociological theory was highly favorable. A further stimulus to close ties between Central European and American soc-iology was the relatively unencumbered social position of the Amer-ican sociologist. However restrictive the horizons of American colleges were at the turn of the century, such hoary phenomena as religious or racial tests of allegiance (like those endured by Simmel and Gumplowicz), or national tests of loyalty (as that which Roberto Michels was subject to), or the more common system of promotion through classroom popularity, were either openly combatted or just barely and uncomfortably tolerated. Evolutionary doctrine, belief in social reform, faith in technological progress, each in its own way created a receptive intellectual climate for sociology. If there were university administrations and faculties which made capital out of the linguistic similarities between the words sociology and socialism, there existed an even larger block of academic personnel who per-ceived that sociology (either as social theory or social reform) was filled with a content no less hostile to socialism than the most ardent industrialist ideology. An examination of the reviews tendered social-ist and muckracking literature in *The American Journal of Sociology* of the early decades of the twentieth century would probably show that sociologists were less receptive and more jaundiced to radical ideas than editorial writers of the captive press. From the outset American sociology sensed that its "life-chances" were related to how well it could distinguish sociology and social reform from the spectre of socialism.

Among the pioneers in American sociology, Gumplowicz was held in very high esteem. Indeed the recognition extended his sociology stands in contrast to the general neglect and critical reaction to the work of Durkheim (*Cf.* Hinkle, 1960:273). The efforts of Lester Ward to popularize and disseminate the work of Gumplowicz was perhaps decisive to his gaining a hearing from other American sociologists. The mutual respect each had for the other was deep enough so that they have been designated as collaborators (*Cf.* Stern, 1933:3). Gumplowicz' greatest impact on Ward was in compelling him to refocus his efforts away from an evolutionist and philosophic approach, in which "civilization" and "society" become obscurely fused, and towards the acceptance of the human group as the main center of sociological enquiry (*Cf.* Ward, 1898: chs. 5-7). Gumplowicz, for his part, altered two very precious cornerstones of his sociological edifice as a result of Ward's criticisms. First, he changed his attitude towards the heterogenous nature and origin of the human race, and accepted the idea of the single origin and common heredity of the races of mankind. However, this was less a shattering blow to Gumplowicz' sociology than might be imagined since he still maintained that such phenomena as the formation of the political State and the differentiation of races, were features of the present geological epoch (*Cf.* Gumplowicz, 1905: ch. 2).

The second point on which Ward had a profound influence was to disrupt if not shatter Gumplowicz' long-standing belief that progress in the political or moral domains does not exist. Ward indicated that Gumplowicz' general allegiance to *Darwinismus* made the confinement of a theory of progress to only science and technology an inconsistency within the system. Evolutionary theory disallowed a dualism between "science" and "man" in which the former "progressed" while the latter only "moved." Faced with the choice of surrendering his dualistic attitude toward change or his monistic sociology, he yielded on the former. Thus while he still reaffirmed that "the naturalistic monist regards the 'historical process' as remaining eternally the same" (Gumplowicz, 1905b:643), he did so with much less force than in the *Soziologie*. "I was already acquainted with Ward's works. I had already been led by his letters to personal appreciation of him; that he would succeed, however, in fiery debate, if not in converting, still in silencing me, I never should have believed, and yet that is what happened . . . I am free to confess that in place of the former feeling of confidence in my own views, perhaps of my own superiority to a 'utopian,' there had come a feeling of hesitation, still more a feeling of admiration for a *Menschheits-Idealismus*" (1905b:645).

Despite the close friendship between Ward and Gumplowicz, there was an overriding difference in sociological interests. Ward was searching for a principle of democratic consensus, while Gumplowicz saw such a consensual apparatus as being at best a temporary abatement of the *Rassenkampf* and *Klassenkampf*. A quote from one of Ward's last articles reveals that in the texture of language, no less than in conception does he distinguish himself from the Austrian sociologist. "All social structures taken together constitute the social order. The problem is to inaugurate a condition of social progress. This cannot be done by disturbing the social order. Order is the condition to progress, and progress consists in setting up dynamic activities in the social structures themselves" (Ward, 1905:605). As Ward earlier indicated, he was concerned with problems of social *integration* and *equilibrium* much more than with the European sociological models of conflict and differentiation (*Cf.* Ward, 1903: 199).

Albion W. Small, who received his basic sociological training in Germany, took less notice of Gumplowicz than did Ward. In Small's view, the major figures and stages in sociology revolved about Spencer, Schäffle and Ratzenhofer. Gumplowicz was considered a participant in these stages rather than a formulator (*Cf.* Small, 1905: 176). Although Gumplowicz' work is well regarded, Small's concern was to place conflict theory in a larger context of group interaction. In order to do this, Small once again placed social psychology, the theory of personality, in the forefront of sociology as an independent variable, rather than as something dependent for its structure on either the group, the race or the class (Small, 1910, 1913). Small also differed markedly from Gumplowicz in philosophic assumptions. He had a general aversion for the sort of militant naturalism found in the *Soziologie*, and clearly preferred the Jamesian "wide open universe" to Gumplowicz' universe of law (*Cf.* Small, 1924).

Interestingly enough, if Gumplowicz had considerable effect on the politically liberal wing of early American sociology, he seemed to exercise only a little less effect on the conservative wing. Thus William Graham Sumner's *Folkways* clearly showed its indebtedness to Gumplowicz' use of the *Volk* doctrine. Social habits or customs imply a standardization of norms which arises out of the bio-social struggle for existence. This standardization through social stereotypy determines particular folkways. But as with Small's work, Sumner was concerned with social statics more than with dynamics. Thus, in place of Gumplowicz' dominant minority and dominated majority, Sumner evolved a theory of in-group and out-group patterns to account for social evolution (*Cf.* Sumner and Keller, 1927:I: 400). By so doing, Sumner was able to account for the exploitation of labor as an "out-group" phenomena and was not called upon to explain the differentiation of a single *Volk* into classes and races (*Cf.* Sumner, 1906:262-63).

Sumner's attitude toward Gumplowicz involved a decided shift in emphasis. For Gumplowicz, linguistic differentiation signified that groups symbolically represented their separation by a unique and standardized language, which in turn provided cohesion to the social group in contrast to others (Gumplowicz, 1892:93). For his part, Sumner saw this same phenomena of language as a "product of the need for cooperative understanding" (Sumner, 1906:134). In sum, although Sumner was deeply interested in the sort of problems raised by Gumplowicz and Ratzenhofer, his real aim was to achieve a sociology which could explain social stability, maintenance of institutions, and peace-making groups. From the point of view of the history of sociology Sumner represents the first decisive break with the European focus on social conflict and social change. Despite Sumner's obvious erudition and pan-Germanism in matters intellectual, he set American sociology on the high road of consensus theory from which it has hardly strayed since.

A rekindling of interest in Gumplowicz took place after World War One. In some measure this was a consequence of the kinds of social issues the War unleashed. Once again attention focused on the social sources of conflict, on the rules of war no less than on the rules of peace, on reason and unreason regarding nationalism, socialism, and revolution, etc. Out of this came the first serious effort to fashion a political sociology on American soil. The work of Harry Elmer Barnes in this respect is singularly noteworthy—and noteworthy from our perspective for his effort to re-acquaint American sociologists with Gumplowicz' writings. The title of Barnes' early effort at a political sociology reveals the extent of Gumplowicz' influence: "The Struggle of Races and Social Groups as a Factor in the Development of Political and Social Institutions" (Barnes, 1918-19:394-419).

During the next decade Barnes elaborated upon this theme in his famous work on *The New History and the Social Studies.* Barnes here notes that "it remained for Ludwig Gumplowicz in his *Rassenkampf* and other writings to develop the thesis [that the first form of State was the military type specialized for war] in its modern completeness and in convincing character" (Barnes, 1925:485-86). Barnes' own view, that the national State arises in the Middle Ages as a result of military conquest, and that nationalism and militarism have thus been intimately linked from that point onward, constituted for him "an excellent exemplification of the theory of Gumplowicz concerning the military nature of political origins and an equally admirable illustration of the class-building process within the State, which accompanies the process of conquest and ethnic and political superimposition" (1925:366). That Barnes never lost interest in Gumplowicz is evident by the full due he receives in his monumental history of sociology (*Cf.* Becker and Barnes, 1938:II:1050-53, 1059-60). In this way, a bridge was provided by means of which the work of Gumplowicz was transmitted from the early to the modern period in American sociology.

The decade of the "twenties" in American sociology belonged in large measure to the famed "Chicago School." The group, led by Robert E. Park, Ernest Burgess, Walter Reckless, and Louis Wirth, were all thoroughly versed in European sociological developments. And while Gumplowicz never loomed as large as either Tönnies or Simmel in their orientation, they did not fail to take his work into account. The sociological study of nationalities as conflict groups made by Gumplowicz proved particularly valuable in the formation of concepts of how human groups operate at smaller scales, *e.g.*, gangs, unions, parties and sects (*Cf.* Park and Burgess, 1921: 212). Recognition of Gumplowicz' pioneer work in the general theory of social interaction, the logic of the social sciences, and the function of social conflict in unstructured situations (1921:340-41, 420) all played an important, albeit a peripheral role in the evolution of the Chicago School toward a sophisticated conception of the relation of conflict to consensus in the life of the social group.

Independent lines of inquiry were undertaken in this decade which placed Gumplowicz in the very forefront of the "development of social theory." In his work by the same name, Lichtenberger (1923:432-64) reserves the closing chapter for an examination of the main points in the work of Gumplowicz and Ratzenhofer. Influenced a great deal by Ward and Giddings, this analysis is sympathetic (and unfortunately uncritical) in every detail. While in general revealing a keener regard for Ratzenhofer's softening of the lines in conflict theory, that is, a sociology in which *intra*-group rivalry is seen as more basic to social change than *inter*-group conflict, Lichtenberger's text is remarkably free of bias or of factual error. He perhaps tends to make too much of the common note struck by Spencer and Gumplowicz concerning the need for "universal laws." Nonetheless matters are righted by showing that "unlike Spencer, Gumplowicz does not build upon these laws a complete descriptive sociology. He seldom refers to them. They constitute a basis for his thoroughgoing determinism rather than for his sociological system" (1923:445). While Lichtenberger's work is easily the most generous in space to Gumplowicz, the book itself has severe limitations. In its nostalgia for the past, the book somehow fails to deal with Durkheim's contributions, even though Tarde merits an entire chapter. Furthermore, the monumental contributions of Simmel and Weber are not so much as mentioned. One would gather from Lichtenberger's work that American sociology had neither a beginning nor a present status—only the lonely figure of Ward emerging from Spencer on one side and feeding Tarde on the other. In a real sense then, this is a peculiarly European text, although its author did his studies and teaching in the United States.

Floyd Nelson House in his work, *The Development of Sociology*, offers a warm and sympathetic appraisal of the *Grundriss der Soziologie*. He sees Gumplowicz as basically within the framework of "Social Darwinism" (although he takes note of the difficulties in such a classification when applied to him). House sees the "Austrian" as "one of the great pioneers of modern sociology, second in importance among them only to Spencer, and in some respects unquestionably greater than Spencer" (1936:163). One of the reasons for his greatness, according to House, was Gumplowicz' unfailing and unflagging attention to the work of his predecessors. And since House himself took an avowedly historical approach to sociological theory, he is more than grateful for Gumplowicz' "painstaking thoroughness, not only as regards the review of what has already been done in the field but also as regards the logical analysis of the matters dealt with" (1936:165).

Perhaps the one debatable interpretation made by House concerns Gumplowicz' view of the relative position of society and polity. House maintains that Gumplowicz is so concerned with the functions of State authority that it dominates his sociology completely. It is, however, doubtful that the State is "the most important social phenomenon" (1936:164) for Gumplowicz. The likelihood is that House basis this remark exclusively on the *Soziologie,* in which the State does emerge as the most general expression of the group-making potential of men in modern societies. But basically, Gumplowicz considered the State an expression of the group, and for that reason, political theory was viewed by him to be a special case of sociological inquiry. Nonetheless, House's closing remark on Gumplowicz stands as a significant testimonial, and requires neither criticism nor commentary. "The sociology of Ludwig Gumplowicz was on the whole the first to conceive the nature and scope of sociology, and its general point of view in the manner that has since characterized its central trend of development. It is particularly notable that he was the first to break with the conception of sociology as the philosophy of history or as the theory of social evolution and to substitute the concept of 'social process' for that of 'progress.' It is useless to attempt to divide credit between him and Spencer for the rapid development that subsequently took place in sociological thought, but at any rate, the opinion seems justified that Gumplowicz made fundamental additions to the work that Spencer had begun" (House, 1936:173).

Howard Becker, having imbibed Gumplowicz' lessons from Barnes in turn passed this enthusiasm along to his younger colleague Alvin Boskoff. In their recent joint volume on *Modern Sociological Theory in Continunity and Change,* Boskoff points out that despite Gumplowicz' discredited polygenetic theory of races, he was none-

theless "one of the first to achieve full emancipation for sociology
from the non-social sciences by insisting that social phenomena are
distinctive and can be understood only by reference to social causes"
(Boskoff, 1957:12). However, at the time of this statement a whole
new generation of sociologists have emerged who are either indiffer-
ent to or ignorant of Gumplowicz' work. Comments on his work grow
scarce, and praise of his work becomes guarded and cautious. This
stands in marked contrast to the earlier statements of Barnes, Lichtenberger and House.

A case in point is Nicholas Timasheff, who in his work on
Sociological Theory deals seriously with Gumplowicz' sociology.
Although in Timasheff's case the reason for the interest is probably
not so much due to prior estimates of American sociologists as it is
a reflection of Gumplowicz' enormous impact on the Russian sociology of pre-revolutionary Russia. Perhaps this is also why, contrary to the evidence, Timasheff maintains that "the teaching of
Gumplowicz shows a strong Marxian flavor." Although just what
constitutes this flavor is not revealed. Nonetheless, Timasheff's
pages on Gumplowicz contain a careful synopsis of the main con-
tentions of *Der Rassenkampf*. And his further observation that
Gumplowicz' theory of group conflict represents "an interesting
anticipation of Toynbee's views" is surely on target. Timasheff also
shows a cautious sympathy for Gumplowicz' views on the limited
nature of social progress (Timasheff, 1957: 62-63).

The most recent inventory of sociological theory in historical
perspective is Don Martindale's thoroughly informed *The Nature
and Types of Sociological Theory*. Strongly influenced by Germanic
currents in sociology, Martindale offers a workmanlike summary
of Gumplowicz' *Soziologie*. And he is unique among American
sociologists in locating its place in the general development of conflict theory both in Europe and America. Unfortunately aside from
calling Gumplowicz "perhaps the most influential of the conflict
theorists of his time" (1960:180), Martindale does not attempt a
critical evaluation of Gumplowicz' work specifically. Nevertheless,
his overall estimate of the conflict theorists shows none of the easy
slogans and stereotyping that are to be found in present-day European texts of a similar variety (*Cf.* Eisermann, 1958).

The most recent acknowledgment of Gumplowicz' role as a formulator of sociological principles is contained in the work of an American sociologist and jurist of Austrian descent, Egon Bergel. In his volume on *Social Stratification*, he points out that Gumplowicz demonstrated classes to constitute a "natural strata." He further notes that the substitution of the phrase ethnic heterogeneity for racial differences comes closer to the truth of Gumplowicz' position. Bergel also emphasizes Gumplowicz' rejection of the racialist theory of biological, intellectual or moral superiority of victors or rulers (*Cf.* Bergel, 1962:163-64). In this same volume, reference is made to Gumplowicz' pioneering work on classes as a political strata. In all, it must be said that Bergel's work on stratification makes greater use of earlier conflict theorists than is usually the case at this point in American political sociology. However, it is no less true that he draws manifestly conservative conclusions.

Before concluding our survey we might note one glaring deficiency in the treatment of Gumplowicz in American sociological literature—his complete absence from any of the readers or anthologies in sociological theory. Thus no mention of him is found in the group of readings prepared by Coser and Rosenberg on *Sociological Theory* (1957), despite their preference for questions of social conflict, power, authority, and class. The same situation obtains in the reader prepared by Borgatta and Meyer (1956). Here again the omission is unfortunate since the chief interest of the editors is on problems of social structure and group life. Finally the absence of any selection from Gumplowicz' *corpus* in the monumental collection, *Theories of Society*, edited by Parsons, Shils, Naegele, and Pitts (1961) can only be termed unfortunate, since in all likelihood an entire generation is going to be guided by the figures represented in *Theories of Society*.

In good part there can be no doubt that the general inaccessibility of Gumplowicz' *Soziologie* and the absence of his other writings in the English language, has contributed to his absence from the anthologies. It might also be the case that his "fate" has been tied to the general neglect in American sociology of informal, unstructured, and spontaneous modes of social behavior, and the consequent disregard of conflict problems. Other elements which may have worked to the detriment of Gumplowicz' thought in modern American sociology are: first, the general decline of *theoretical* inter-

est in the sociology of race relations and problems of ethnic and
minority groups; and second, the relatively underdeveloped condition
of studies in the history of sociology. However, with the rapidly
changing climate in American sociology towards "fundamental
questions," and towards keener attention to such long neglected areas
as collective dynamics, the sociology of international relations, and
the scientific study of conflict resolution, the likelihood is that attention will once again be focused on Gumplowicz' unique contributions
in these areas.

7. A Note on Gumplowicz' Grundriss der Soziologie

In his polemic with Rümelin, Gumplowicz clarifies the *ideology*
motivating the creation of the *Soziologie*. It is an ideology which
sees philosophy as positive science, and sociology as the only authentic movement beyond traditional social metaphysics. The *Soziologie*
is a justification of monism and naturalism no less than a discourse
on group interaction. The book was forged in the heat of the on-going
battle between positivism and idealism in all areas of intellectual
creation. Nor was this battle a one-sided affair, there were titans to
be found on both sides: Dilthey, Rickert and Meinecke pushed the
Kantian-Hegelian complex to its upper reaches and not without
lasting benefits to sociology. Likewise, Le Bon, Ratzenhofer, Tarde,
Ward, Mosca, and of course Gumplowicz, could all be counted on
the side of "anti-metaphysics" in social theory.

Positivism was able to galvanize social theory precisely because
of its oft-stated pledge to eliminate all metaphysics. Positivism became a euphemism for the popularization and generalization of the
results of the sciences—especially of physics and biology. Increasingly, the better philosophic minds of the age were drawn from those
with some training in the sciences. Mach in physics, Huxley in
biology, James in psychology, Sorel and Pareto in engineering.
Positivism, which socially may indeed have represented a mediating
role between radical and conservative political thought, and likewise
a "curse on both your houses" attitude to such long standing philosophic questions as materialism versus idealism, empiricism versus
realism, and monism versus dualism, nonetheless performed a scientific role of emancipating the social sciences from teleologically pre-
conceived goals and aims. Positivism enabled sociology to emerge

from its prior function as apologist for (or critic of) social events to analyst of these events. That such an emancipation was often more proclaimed than authentic, and that it involved sociology in a series of naive postures, is not a critique of its success, but only a catalogue of the necessary agonies which attended the breakdown of the nineteenth century romantic *Zeitgeist*. Seen in this light the frequent polemics against the idea of progress, justice, etc., and the excessive self-praise which arises in the pages of the *Soziologie* are understandable if not completely forgiveable.

Gumplowicz himself placed greater stock by his *Rassenkampf* than his *Soziologie*. Nonetheless, by present-day standards the latter is undoubtedly the more important of the two. We are less concerned with the novelty of ethnic, class and racial conflict in social history than with the general theory of conflict as such. And here the latter work excels. For the *Soziologie* is at once an historical accounting of early efforts to forge an empirical sociology, a settlement of accounts with the older disciplines that went under the name "human sciences," a definition of the method and content of sociology, and a symbol of the emancipation of sociology from the grips of organicism and historicism.

Which element in the *Soziologie* is the most interesting or novel seen from present day perspectives is of little account. Certainly we have had more incisive definitions of the group and the person, more impressive analyses of the history of social thought; and so great has the shift in the "power position" of sociology (at least in the United States) become that the problem is no longer whether sociologists have emancipated themselves from philosophic predilections, but whether or not such an emancipation has not gone so far as to cause the present generation to worry over the reverse problem; the need for sociologists to become more philosophically aware and sophisticated.

What may well strike the contemporary reader first upon coming to the *Soziologie* is how *philosophical* the work is—the very reverse of Gumplowicz' claim. The book was an entry in the great nineteenth century debate over the place of determinism in human affairs; or phrased differently, the function of science in the social studies. This was a controversy that enlisted the passions as well as the reasoning power of all involved. And it was a necessary tactic for Gumplowicz to claim more for his science than it could possibly deliver. But this very exaggeration had the effect of setting sociology as a science on an empirical path from which it has reaped so many benefits both as a discipline and as a socially viable instrument.

Perhaps Lipset and Smelser (1961:41-51) are correct in pointing out that the purpose and need for "great debates" is now vitiated by the "secularization" of sociology. However, such a thesis is predicated on the notion that ideology must necessarily have a destructive effect on a science, when in fact Merton (1938), Zilsel (1942) and Schumpeter (1949) long ago noted that an ideology may also have a stimulating and positive effect. Theoretical physics has continued to carry on the most intense sort of philosophical and ideological discussion concerning the ultimate constituency of matter, the actual status of complementarity, the possibilities of a unified field theory, etc. without being the worse for these debates. Indeed, the idea that sociology does not require an analysis of fundamentals because it is now "secular" is simply a rationalization for its failure to keep abreast of theoretical issues in *all* of the sciences by an appeal to its obvious successes in research activities. By its concentration on fundamentals, Gumplowicz' *Soziologie* may yet continue to focus attention on theoretical moorings that have been covered with moss and so taken to be non-existent, when in fact these moorings are still with us and still in need of scientific explication.

Negotiations for the English language rights to the *Soziologie* were entered into long before its actual appearance. While permission was granted to the *American Academy of Political and Social Science* sometime around 1890, the translation did not appear for another decade. In the meantime, an English publisher made enquiries of the translation rights and was notified by Gumplowicz that such rights had already been granted to the *Academy*. Perhaps this accounts for Gumplowicz' heavy sarcasm over his ill-fortune at the slowness with which the translation proceeded. Writing to Ward in 1897, his impatience over the matter was made manifest. "Since that time (1890) the gentlemen in Philadelphia have left me waiting, still not having distributed anything or given me any report on what they planned to do in the future" (1933:5). We can gather from the remainder of the correspondence that Ward was urged to use his good offices to elicit action on the English translation—which finally appeared two years later, in the autumn of 1899.

We have no correspondence as to what Gumplowicz thought of the edition as it was finally brought out. However, to someone as obviously concerned with the details of publication and translation as was Gumplowicz, the edition could not possibly have been a completely happy event. Indeed, his stony silence on the matter (in contrast to his general pleasure at seeing works of his appear in translation) speaks eloquently enough. While the translator, Frederick W. Moore, prepared the translation with diligence and with the assistance of other colleagues at Vanderbilt University where he was at that time Assistant Professor of History and Political Economy, there is no evidence that he took the trouble to consult with the author on some knotty translation problems. Thus, both *Volk* and *Rasse* are rendered by the English word race, when in fact they are not interchangeable; and *Heterogen* is sometimes translated as "unlike," other times as "distinct," and still again as "foreign," when in fact the root term "heterogeneous" is quite appropriate to cover all instances in which the word appears in Gumplowicz' text.

The additional fact that the translator had little apparent training in or understanding of sociology, and what is even more damaging, little sympathy with his task, is made plain in his perfunctory two page introduction. But this absence of sympathy reveals itself most directly in the *Abstract* which Professor Moore prepared for the book. The bracketed elaborations not infrequently spill over into arguing with the positions taken by Gumplowicz. The intellectual level of these editorial inserts can perhaps best be gathered by a direct quote. "Were the author (Gumplowicz) as fully impregnated with democratic ideals as Americans are, his language at this point, though not his idea, would be somewhat different" (Moore, 1899:12). Thus poor Gumplowicz had to wait fourteen years for a translation to appear in America, and then to have the misfortune of drawing an editor who was less than enthusiastic about the task.

The edition itself was not produced with an idea of its complex subject matter in mind. Thus the care and detail that went into the production of scholarly books at the turn of the century was conspicuous by its absence. A newspaper print was used, a very poor quality of paper stock was used, and the binding was of the "penny novel" variety. This is not meant so much as criticism as commentary on the relative incapacity of social scientists of the time to distinguish between types of "social questions." Thus, Gumplowicz' *Soziologie* appeared in the same series with a study of *Relief Work at the Wells Memorial Institute*. Nonetheless, in spite of the interest of *Annals* in the popularization of German sociological classics, its relative lack of technical concern for the *Soziologie* could not but have a deleterious effect on the circulation of Gumplowicz' work among interested persons. At this point, the original printing is more of a curiosity than a rarity in the *corpus* of translated social science treatises.

The main changes which I have made in this edition of Gumplowicz' *Grundriss der Soziologie* are as follows:

I have incorporated the major additions which Gumplowicz saw fit to introduce to the 1905 German edition. This includes the lengthy new "Foreword," a section on "Sociological Method," a third section on "Positive Ethics," and a fourth section concerning "Designs of Philosophical History." The other addition, on the history of sociology, is so perfunctory and uninspired in character, that it would only serve to detract from the original. The uncritical spirit of this nation by nation survey of sociology stands in marked contrast to the other new materials Gumplowicz introduced to the second edition.

The two "Supplements" to the original German edition have been inserted in their proper places. The first supplement on "LeBon" presented no problem, since it was already incorporated in the chapter on "The History of Sociology" by Baye in the French edition of the work. Gumplowicz himself did likewise in the second German edition of the text. The second supplement, called "Might and Right," was retained by Gumplowicz as an Addendum, although in the first edition he indicated that this additional material relates to the fourth chapter on "Social Psychological Phenomena and the Individual." Thus in order to present the book as a continuum, I have taken the liberty of placing this second supplement at the end of the fourth chapter, with an indication that this analysis of "Might and Right" is supplementary to, rather than an organic portion of, the text.

All materials added to the text by Professor Moore have been deleted. What might have been a useful guide at the turn of the century has by this time become quite well known to the community of social scientists. And since as an interpretation of Gumplowicz' thought Moore's introduction and abstract are seriously deficient, there seemed no purpose to their inclusion in this edition. Yet it should be said that Moore's translation has basically been retained. The translator shared in the *Zeitgeist* of social science at the turn of the century. Both Gumplowicz and Moore used a common scholarly vocabulary inherited from *die Jurisprudenz* that would be difficult to recapture, and pointless to restructure. The temptation to substitute more recent conceptual terminology has best resisted by retaining the Moore translation wherever this was feasible, and it was so in a large majority of cases and pages.

I have employed a completely different notation system from the one originally provided by Gumplowicz. He tended to list references in the cavalier fashion that was customary at the time. Complete names appear rarely, titles often are listed incompletely (or even inaccurately), and places and dates of publication are, by and large, altogether absent. One large scale advantage of the present system of notation, beyond the obvious introduction of uniformity, is that it provides the reader with a useful and rare bibliography of texts which were never in wide currency even at the time Gumplowicz wrote. It is thus particularly interesting to the student of European sociological history.

Throughout, I have attempted to be faithful to the meaning as well as the content of Gumplowicz' work and thus to show that contrary to his own pessimistic inclinations, there is perhaps some "progress" even in the field of "historical justice." We might conclude by saying of Gumplowicz' *Soziologie* what he had written of Bastian's work. "Insight here discovers a hard intellectual struggle from the darkness of intimation to the light of cognition—the severe birth-pangs of a new science."

BIBLIOGRAPHY

Bagehot, Walter
  1872   *Physics and Politics: Thoughts on the Application of the
          Principles of "Natural Selection" and "Inheritance" to Polit-
          ical Society.* New York: The Colonial Press, 1900.

Barnes, Harry Elmer
  1918   The Struggle of Races and Social Groups as a Factor in the
          Development of Political and Social Institutions, *Journal of
          Race Development.* vol. IX, 1918-19.
  1925   *The New History and the Social Studies.* New York: The
          Century Co.
  1940   Sociological Contributions to Political Thought, *Contemp-
          orary Social Theory,* edited by H. E. Barnes and Howard
          Becker. New York: Appleton-Century Co.

Barth, Paul
  1897   *Die Philosophie der Geschichte als Soziologie.* Leipzig: O.
          R. Reisland, 1922.

Becker, Howard and Harry Elmer Barnes
  1938   *Social Thought From Lore to Science, Sociological Trends
          Throughout the World,* vol. II. Washington, D. C.: Harren
          Press, 1952.

Bergel, Egon Ernest
  1962   *Social Stratification.* New York: McGraw Hill Book Co.

Blalock, H. M., Jr. and Ann B. Blalock
  1959   Toward a Classification of System Analysis in the Social
          Sciences, *Philosophy of Science.* vol. 26, no. 2.

Blumer, Herbert
  1939   Collective Behavior, *New Outline of the Principles of Soci-
          ology,* edited by Alfred McClung Lee, New York: Barnes
          and Noble, Inc., 1946.
  1957   Collective Behavior, *Review of Sociology,* edited by Joseph
          B. Gittler. New York: John Wiley and Sons, Inc.

Borgatta, Edgar F. and Henry J. Meyer
  1959   *Sociological Theory: Present Day Sociology From the Past.*
          New York: Alfred A. Knopf.

Boskoff, Alvin
1957 From Social Thought to Sociological Theory, *Modern Sociological Theory in Continuity and Change*, edited by H. Becker and A. Boskoff. New York: Holt, Rinehart and Winston, Inc.
Bramson, Leon
1961 *The Political Context of Sociology*. Princeton: Princeton University Press.
Brinton, Crane
1938 *The Anatomy of Revolution*. New York: W. W. Norton and Co.
Bukharin, Nikolai I.
1935 Marx's Teaching and Its Historical Importance, *Marxism and Modern Thought*, edited by Ralph Fox. London: George Routledge & Sons.
Chamberlain, Houston S.
1912 *Foundations of the Nineteenth Century*, translated by John Lees. New York: Lane Publishers.
Comte, Auguste
1853 *Positive Philosophy (Cours de philosophie positive)*, translated by Harriet Martineau. London: Kegan Paul Ltd., 1893.
Coser, Lewis H. and Bernard Rosenberg
1957 *Sociological Theory: A Book of Readings*. New York: The Macmillan Co.
Dampier, William Cecil
1949 *A History of Science and its Relations with Philosophy and Religion*. Cambridge: Cambridge University Press; and New York: The Macmillan Co. (fourth edition).
Dewey, John
1930 *Individualism Old and New*. New York: Minton, Balch & Co.
Dilthey, Wilhelm
1883 *Einleitung in die Geisteswissenschaften (Gesämmelte Schriften*, vol. I.). Leipzig and Berlin: B. G. Teubner, 1922.
Durkheim, Emile
1897 *Le Suicide, Etude de Sociologie*. Paris: Felix Alcan.
Edwards, Lyford P.
1927 *The Natural History of Revolutions*. Chicago: University of Chicago Press.

Eisermann, Gottfried
1958   *Die Lehre von der Gesellschaft: Ein Lehrbuch der Soziologie.*
       Stuttgart: Ferdinand Enke Verlag.

Gerth, Hans and C. Wright Mills
1946   *From Max Weber: Essays in Sociology.* New York: Oxford
       University Press.

Gibson, Quentin
1960   *The Logic of Social Enquiry.* London: Routledge & Kegan
       Paul Ltd.

Gross, Felix and Rex Hopper
1959   *Un Siglo de Revolucion.* Mexico, D. F.: Biblioteca de En-
       sayos Sociologicos, Instituto de Investigaciones Sociales.

Gumplowicz, Ludwig
1877   *Philosophisches Staatsrecht.* Vienna: Manz.
1879   *Das Recht der Nationalitäten und Sprachen in Oesterreich-
       Ungarn.* Innsbruck: Wagner.
1881   *Rechstaat und Socialismus.* Innsbruck: Wagner.
1883   *Der Rassenkampf: Sociologische Untersuchungen.* Inns-
       bruck: Wagner'sche Universitäts Buchhandlung.
1885   *Grundriss der Sociologie.* Vienna: Manz.
1892a *Die sociologische Staatsidee.* Graz: Leuschner & Lubensky.
       [Second edition, 1902, Innsbruck: Wagner].
1892b *Soziologie und Politik.* Innsbruck: Wagner'sche Univ. buch-
       handlung.
1897   *Allgemeines Staatsrecht.* Innsbruck: Wagner, 1897 and 1902.
1899a *Sociologische Essays.* Innsbruck: Wagner.
1899b *The Outlines of Sociology.* Philadelphia: American Academy
       of Political and Social Science.
1902   *Das Oesterreichische Staatsrecht.* Vienna: Manz.
1905a *Geschichte der Staatstheorien.* Innsbruck: Wagner'sche Uni-
       versitäts-Buchhandlung.
1905b An Austrian Appreciation of Lester F. Ward, in *The Amer-
       ican Journal of Sociology.* vol. X, no. 5.
1905c *Grundriss der Soziologie.* Vienna: Manz'sche Verlag und
       Universitäts-Buchhandlung.
1910   *Sozialphilosophie im Umriss.* Innsbruck: Wagner.

1926 *Geschichte der Staatstheorien* (*Ludwig Gumplowicz Ausgewählte Werke*, edited by F. Oppenheimer, M. Adler, and F. Savorgnan). Innsbruck: Univ.-Verlag Wagner.

1933 *The Letters of Ludwig Gumplowicz to Lester F. Ward*. Edited by Bernhard J. Stern. Leipzig: C. L. Hirschfeld Verlag. (In German and French).

Gurvitch, Georges and Wilbert E. Moore

1947 *La Sociologie au XXe Siècle* (vol. 2, *Les Etudes Sociologiques dans les différents Pays.*) Paris: Presses Universitaires de France.

Heller, Erich

1952 *The Disinherited Mind*: *Essays in Modern German Literature and Thought*. Cambridge: Bowes and Bowes.

Hempel, Carl G.

1958 The Logic of Functional Analysis, *Symposium on Sociological Theory*, edited by Llewellyn Gross. Evanston: Row, Peterson and Co.

Hinkle, Roscoe C., Jr.

1960 Durkheim in American Sociology, *Emile Durkheim, 1857-1917*, edited by Kurt H. Wolff. Columbus: The Ohio State University Press.

Hopper, Rex D.

1950 The Revolutionary Process: A Frame of Reference for the Study of Revolutionary Movements, *Social Forces*, vol. 28, no. 3.

Horowitz, Irving L.

1957 *The Idea of War and Peace in Contemporary Philosophy*. New York: Paine-Whitman Publishers.

1960 *Philosophy, Science and the Sociology of Knowledge*. Springfield: Charles C. Thomas - Publisher; and Oxford: Blackwell Scientific Publications, 1961.

1961a Arms, Policies and Games, *The American Scholar*, vol. 31, no. 1.

1961b *Radicalism and the Revolt Against Reason*: *The Social Theories of Georges Sorel*. London: Routledge & Kegan Paul Ltd.; and New York: Humanities Press.

1962   *Conference on Conflict, Consensus and Cooperation.* Sponsored by the New York State Sociological Association. Geneva, New York: Hobart & William Smith Colleges.

House, Floyd Nelson
1936   *The Development of Sociology.* New York: McGraw Hill Book Co., Inc.

Howells, William
1959   *Mankind in the Making: The Story of Human Evolution.* New York: Doubleday & Co.

Kluckhohn, Clyde
1951   Values and Value-Orientations in the Theory of Action: An Exploration in Definition and Classification, *Toward A General Theory of Action,* edited by Talcott Parsons and Edward A. Shils. Cambridge: Harvard University Press.
1959   Common Humanity and Diverse Cultures, *The Human Meaning of the Social Sciences,* edited by Daniel Lerner. New York: Meridian Books, Inc.

LaBarre, Weston
1954   *The Human Animal.* Chicago: The University of Chicago Press.

Lang, Kurt and Gladys Lang
1961   *Collective Dynamics.* New York: Thomas Y. Crowell Co.

Lazarsfeld, Paul F.
1961   Notes on the History of Quantification in Sociology—Trends, Sources and Problems, *Quantification: A History of the Meaning of Measurement in the Natural and Social Sciences,* edited by Harry Woolf. Indianapolis-New York: The Bobbs-Merrill Co.

Lichtenberger, James P.
1923   *Development of Social Theory.* New York and London: D. Appleton-Century Co., 1938 (second impression).

Lilienfeld, Paul von
1873   *Gedanken über die Sozialwissenschaft der Zukunft,* vol. I. Berlin; G. Reimer.

Lipset, Seymour M. and Neil Smelser
1961   Change and Controversy in Recent American Sociology, *The British Journal of Sociology,* vol. XII, no. 1.

Lukacs, Georg
1953   *Die Zerstörung der Vernunft.* Berlin: Aufbau-Verlag.
Mannheim, Karl
1952   *Essays on the Sociology of Knowledge,* edited by Paul Kecskemeti. London: Routledge & Kegan Paul Ltd.
1953   *Essays on Sociology and Social Psychology,* edited by Paul Kecskemeti. New York: Oxford University Press.
1956   *Essays on the Sociology of Culture,* edited by Ernest Mannheim and Paul Kecskemeti. London: Routledge & Kegan Paul Ltd.

Martin, Kingsley
1953   *Harold Laski (1893-1950), A Biographical Memoir.* New York: The Viking Press.

Martindale, Don
1960   *The Nature and Types of Sociological Theory.* Cambridge-Boston: Houghton Mifflin Co.

Marx, Karl
1859   Preface to the *Critique of Political Economy, Selected Works of Karl Marx and Frederick Engels.* Moscow: Foreign Languages Publishing House, 1950.

Meisel, James H.
1958   *The Myth of the Ruling Class: Gaetano Mosca and the Elite.* Ann Arbor: University of Michigan Press.

Merton, Robert K.
1938   Science and the Social Order, *Philosophy of Science.* vol. 5.
1957   Manifest and Latent Functions: Toward the Codification of Functional Analysis in Sociology, *Social Theory and Social Structure* (revised and enlarged edition). Glencoe: The Free Press.
1960   The Ambivalences of LeBon's *The Crowd.* Introduction to *The Crowd: A Study of the Popular Mind.* New York: The Viking Press (Compass edition).

Mills, C. Wright
1955   Introduction to W. E. H. Lecky, *History of European Morals From Augustus to Charlemagne.* New York: George Braziller.

Mirek, Francois
  1929 *System socjologiczny Ludwika Gumplowicza.* Posen.
Montero, Pedro Dorado
  1915 Proemio to Gumplowicz' *Derecho Politico Filosofico.* Madrid: La Espana Moderna.
Moore, Frederick W.
  1899 Introduction to Gumplowicz' *The Outlines of Sociology.* Philadelphia: American Academy of Political and Social Science.
Mosca, Gaetano
  1896 *The Ruling Class (Elementi di Scienza Politica),* translated by Hannah D. Kahn. New York: McGraw Hill Book Co., Inc., 1939.
Nagel, Ernest
  1957 A Formalization of Functionalism, *Logic Without Metaphysics, and Other Essays in the Philosophy of Science.* Glencoe: The Free Press.
Park, Robert E. and Ernest W. Burgess
  1921 *Introduction to the Science of Sociology.* (second edition). Chicago: The University of Chicago Press, 1924.
Parsons, Talcott
  1937 *The Structure of Social Action: A Study in Social Theory With Special Reference to a Group of Recent European Writers.* New York: McGraw Hill Book Co.
  1951 *The Social System.* Glencoe: The Free Press.
Parsons, Talcott and Edward A. Shils, Kaspar Nægele, Jesse Pitts (editors)
  1961 *Theories of Society* (two volumes). New York: The Free Press of Glencoe.
Posner, Stanislaw
  1911 *Ludwik Gumplowicz.* Warsaw.
Quetelet, Lambert Adolphe Jacques
  1839 *Popular Instructions on the Calculation of Probabilities.* London: J. Weale.
  1842 *A Treatise on Man and the Development of His Faculties.* Edinburgh: W. and R. Chambers.
  1869 *Physique Sociale.* Bruxelles: C. Muquardt.
Ratzenhofer, Gustav
  1898 *Die Sociologische Erkenntnis.* Leipzig: F. A. Brockhaus.

Sabine, George H.
1937 *A History of Political Theory*. New York: Henry Holt & Co.

Salomon, Gottfried
1926 Vorwort des Herausgebers, *Ludwig Gumplowicz Ausgewählte Werke*, (Vol. I, *Geschichte der Staatstheorien*.) Innsbruck; Universitäts-Verlag Wagner.

Salomon, Albert
1947 La sociologie allemande, *La sociologie au XXe Siecle*. (Vol. 2, *Les Etudes Sociologiques dans les différents Pays*.) Paris: Presses Universitaires de France.

Schäffle, Albert E. F.
1891 *The Quintessence of Socialism*. Translated by Bernard Bosanquet. London: S. Sonnenschein & Co. Ltd., 1902
1893 *The Theory and Policy of Labour Protection*. Edited by A. C. Marant. London: S. Sonnenschein & Co. Ltd.

Schumpeter, Joseph
1949 Science and Ideology, *Essays of Joseph Schumpeter*. Edited by R. V. Clemence. Cambridge: Addison-Wesley Press, 1951.
1955 Social Classes in an Ethnically Homogenous Environment, *Imperialism and Social Classes*. Translated by Heinz Norden. New York: Meridian Books.

Simmel, Georg
1906 The Sociology of Secrecy and of Secret Societies, translated by A. Small, *The American Journal of Sociology*, Vol. II.
1950 *The Sociology of Georg Simmel*. Edited by Kurt Wolff. Glencoe: The Free Press.

Small, Albion
1905 *General Sociology: An Exposition of the Main Development in Sociological Theory From Spencer to Ratzenhofer*. Chicago: University of Chicago Press.
1910 *The Meaning of Social Science*. Chicago: University of Chicago Press.
1924 *Origins of Sociology*. Chicago: University of Chicago Press.

Sorel, Georges
1908 *Reflections on Violence*. translated by T. E. Hulme and J. Roth. Glencoe: The Free Press, 1950.

Sorokin, Pitirim
  1928 *Contemporary Sociological Theories.* New York and London:
        Harper & Bros.
Spencer, Herbert
  1874 *The Study of Sociology.* New York: D. Appleton Co.
Stern, Bernhard J.
  1933 *The Letters of Ludwig Gumplowicz. Sociologus,* Vol. 1,
        Supplement 1. Leipzig: C. L. Hirschfeld Verlag.
Sumner, William Graham
  1906 *Folkways.* New York: Dover Publications, 1959.

Sumner, William Graham and A. G. Keller
  1927 *The Science of Society.* New Haven: Yale University Press.
Timasheff, Nicholas S.
  1957 *Sociological Theory: Its Nature and Growth* (revised
        edition). New York: Random House.
Tiumeniev, A. I.
  1935 Marxism and Bourgeois Historical Science, *Marxism and
        Modern Thought,* edited by Ralph Fox. London: George
        Routledge & Sons Ltd.
Tönnies, Ferdinand
  1887 *Gemeinschaft und Gesellschaft. (Fundamental Concepts of
        Sociology),* translated and supplemented by Charles P.
        Loomis. New York: American Book Company, 1940.
United Nations Educational and Scientific Commission
  1950 *The Race Concept: Results of an Inquiry.* Paris: Unesco.
Veblen, Thorstein
  1923 *Absentee Ownership and Business Enterprise in Recent
        Times: The Case of America.* New York: The Viking Press,
        1938.
Ward, Lester
  1898 *Outlines of Sociology.* New York: The Macmillan Co.
  1903 *Pure Sociology.* New York: The Macmillan Co.
  1905 Evolution of Social Structures, *The American Journal of
        Sociology,* vol. X, no. 5.
Weber, Max
  1922 Wissenschaft als beruf, *Gesammelte Aufsätze zur Wissen-
        schaftslehre.* Tübingen: J. C. B. Mohr (Paul Siebeck).

1951   *The Religion of China: Confucianism and Taoism,* edited and translated by Hans H. Gerth. Glencoe: The Free Press.
1952   *Ancient Judaism,* edited and translated by Hans H. Gerth and Don Martindale. Glencoe: The Free Press.
1958   *The Religion of India: The Sociology of Hinduism and Buddhism,* edited and translated by Hans H. Gerth and Don Martindale. Glencoe: The Free Press.
Wittgenstein, Ludwig
1918   *Tractatus Logico-Philosophicus.* London: Routledge & Kegan Paul Ltd., 1922.
Wolff, Kurt H.
1959   *Georg Simmel* 1858-1918: *A Collection of Essays, With Translations and a Bibliography.* Columbus: The Ohio State University Press.
Zebrowski, Bernhard
1926   *Ludwig Gumplowicz: Eine Bio-Bibliographie.* Berlin: R. L. Präger Verlag.
Zilsel, Edgar
1942   The Sociological Roots of Science, *The American Journal of Sociology.* vol. XLVII, No. 4.
Znaniecki, F. and E. Znaniecki
1932   Ludwig Gumplowicz, *Encyclopaedia of the Social Sciences,* Vol. III. Edited by E. R. A. Seligman and Alvin Johnson. New York: The Macmillan Co.

Outlines of Sociology

Preface to the First Edition of 1885

Two years ago I published some of my sociological investigations under the title of *Der Rassenkampf*; diffidently offering them as the "first lispings of a great science of the future, sociology." The favorable reception accorded this work by competent authorities at home and abroad has encouraged me to present the following *Outlines of Sociology*. From the widespread attention accorded sociological problems it is evident that sociology is not an ephemeral idea, but is in fact becoming a science. I succeeded, I believe, in laying down a few of its principles in *Der Rassenkampf*. In the present *Grundriss der Soziologie* I have earnestly striven to project a complete and unified plan of the science; to show the distinction between sociology and other sciences, and to call attention to the most important questions which must hereafter be subjected to sociological analysis. May this book meet with the same tolerant criticism as its predecessor.

Graz, April, 1885.

Preface to the Second Edition of 1905

Twenty years ago, when I published my *Grundriss der Soziologie* with the above introduction, the critics especially Merkel in *Schmoller's Jahrbuch* of 1886, considered it an "audacious undertaking to write the outlines of a science which is still a science of the future." At that time, this opinion was quite justified. For until then, in the German language at least, there neither existed a sociology under the title "sociology" staking a claim for scientific independence, nor were the works occasionally called "science of society" or "sociological" and "social philosophical" identical with or related to what I consider to be sociology. Likewise at present, there are "social philosophies" and "sociological" publications which in the true sense of the word, do not have anything to do with sociology.

For at that time, and probably now as well, one considered to be sociological mainly researches in political economy and writings on social philosophy containing psychological and ethical views on "society" which are everything but sociology. (*Cf.* Stein, 1897).

Since the eighteen-seventies there have existed writings in the German language that deal with the "body of society," with the "social organism." Those were the works of Schäffle and Lilienfeld. But they were only further realizations and the final outpourings of "organic political science" as it was occasionally presented by Bluntschli (1885) and Ahrens (1889). And even if at a later period they were described by their authors as "sociological," they still did not have anything to do with the nature and fundamental basis of positivist sociology. Today they are mentioned when the development of sociology is examined only to serve as an example of how one should not treat sociological problems.

Thus the critics were entirely correct twenty years ago, at least for the domain of the German language, when they denied the existence of a science of sociology. Since my *Outlines* was the first draft of a new science which did not again traverse the biological paths of Comte and Spencer, but took its own course, one can easily understand the disapproving attitude of the specialists toward this intruder.

At first, the popular, already oft resorted to instrument of "total silence" was employed. (For example, the Zarncke periodical *Literarische Zentralblatt* did not offer any review of my sociology.)[1] But when that failed to suffice, when in the larger world the sociology that everyone treated here with absolute silence was already being considered a pathfinder, when Frenchmen, Italians, Spaniards, Americans, Russians, and Japanese translated into their languages the sociological works that had been treated with complete indifference, then the suppressed resentment gave vent to a diverse, anonymously directed attack upon sociology.[2]

[1] At a later time though, my sociological writings were appreciatively reviewed by the *Literarische Zentralblatt*.

[2] In 1894, Richard Hildebrand (1894) mentioned in a rectorial address that

But when sociology increasingly advanced to the fore, when in the areas employing the German language, Gustav Ratzenhofer arose to become its powerful defender, who in a series of ingenious works confirmed and elaborated the new science in a deeper way than ever before, then the specialists humbled themselves. The same authorities (as for instance the Berlin-Jenenser coterie grouping themselves around the *Staatswörterbuch*) who previously wished to stifle sociology through utter silence, thought the better of it. And after they finally realized that sociology is a true application of scientific method to the social world, they offered a prize for the best solution to the question: "What do we learn from the principles of the theory of descent in relation to the inner political development and legislation of the State?" This intricate formulation was meant to cover their embarrassment and to take the wind out of the sails of the odious "totally silenced" sociology. It was meant to bring sociological works into existence which were then to sail out into the world (if it was really inevitable) under the flag of the Jenenser specialists, so that the new science with the falsified label *Nature and State* would then appear as their achievement.

This attempt failed (*Cf.* Gumplowicz, 1905: 556). In the first place the inexperience of the selection committee in the area of sociology, and also personal vanities and trivial considerations, have induced the gentlemen to "crown" quite a number of inferior writings. Secondly, they could not escape the evil fate of awarding a prize (even though a third one) to a genuine work in sociology (by Eleutheropulos). In this manner the admission was forced that the purpose of this deceitful prize competition, which intentionally avoided the term "sociology," was to present sociology (that discipline about which they had hitherto been dumb) as a discovery of the selection committee. Beyond this, Eleuthropoulos' work on sociology, disregarding every single intricate stipulation put forth in the prize competition, treats the sociological problem frankly and honestly. It is the only one of the award publications which can claim

---

"the right of existence of a proper science of sociology seems to the orator more than dubious." However, to me it immediately seemed entirely indubitable that the poor contents of this address had been borrowed from a sociological work, namely Lewis H. Morgan's *Ancient Society* (German edition 1891: 15) — without mentioning the source.

to have scientific value. And so this undertaking which had evidently been planned against sociology, ended quite differently from the intentions of its initiators; with the recognition that sociology, even in the terrain of the German language, is on the threshold of success.

Gustav Ratzenhofer, in his last speech, made to the *World Congress* in St. Louis, referred to these unpleasant conditions when he said: "One must, as I do, live in the world of German scholars, to get an idea of the embittered struggle which the entrenched sciences wage against sociology. However, this struggle is already decided in favor of the sociologists in spite of outbursts of hatred against the founders of sociology, as toward Gumplowicz. The book market is already deluged by bungling pieces of work which gratuitously give themselves an imagined sociological perception." The label "sociology" is quite inappropriately being bestowed upon various spheres of thinking.

In view of this victorious struggle of sociology against shop talk and diverse eccentricities, the book, *Outlines of Sociology*, published twenty years ago, and the first of its kind to appear in German, constitutes at least a literary-historical document. Thus I do not consider changes in order. It therefore appears in its original form with the exception of insignificant word corrections.

I was allowed to do this since in, my later publications (Gumplowicz, 1892a; 1892b; 1897) I further developed several ideas that were contained in the *Outlines of Sociology* only in abbreviated form. Therefore, I did not have to be afraid of being reproached today for the relative incompleteness of their first formulation.

All the more so will this be apparent to the sympathetic reader's mind, given the primitive stage in the development of sociology when these *Outlines* were written. Indeed, the entire highly developed sociological literature of the present time was created during the past twenty years, when sociology had to fight every step of the way to gain acceptance and recognition. As has already been indicated, this struggle was triumphant. My book on the foundations of sociology thus makes its reappearance in a thoroughly changed climate.

What animated activity now prevails in what only a short time ago was the uncultivated ground of sociological literature! The antagonistic voices have for the most part become silent and the opponents of sociology who were in the past angry, would today like to be considered sociologists themselves. Wherever one looks, in the special fields mined by historians, lawyers, economists and philosophers, one encounters the attempt at gaining a sociological gloss. What a change! From every quarter the vision of the best special researchers is directed toward sociology with great expectations. "All symptoms speak in favor of the fact" writes the well informed ethnologist Friedrich S. Krauss, "that in the near future, sociology will move into the forefront as the leading social science" (Krauss, 1903: 13). It is already being considered as such in France, Italy, and the United States. The excellent historian of religion, Giovanni Pascot, calls it the "true science of man" (Pascot, 1896), while the anthropologist Allievo talks about "scienza sovrana di sociologia" (Allievo, 1899).

In Italy, Spain, France, Holland and Belgium, there already exist numerous academic chairs of sociology. While in America there are hardly any universities at which they are missing.[3] In London, the recently founded Sociological Society has developed a promising program of activity.[4] After these important twenty years for sociology, with such an exhuberant growth in its literature, my *Grundriss der Soziologie* may sound somewhat inadequate and sketchy today. However, I hope that it will be given credit for having been the first to enter the fray, where the battle was fought against a multitude of opponents that led to a victorious conclusion.[5]

Graz, March 1905.

---

[3] Ratzenhofer alludes to the fact that American sociologists extend open-hearted sympathy with, and awareness of, Austrian sociology when he says: "Although the screw-propeller was invented in Austria, it was used first in England." (Ratzenhofer, 1902). I call special attention to this point because the philosophical historian, Ludwig Stein, wrote in the *Neue Freien Presse* (October 1904) that it is not quite clear to him what the aims of these allusions are.

[4] See their *Sociological Papers*, 1904.

[5] Where the advanced development of sociological literature made it necessary, I have added supplements to the original text. [These supplements are integrated into the text of this edition.—*ILH*]

Part I

The History Of Sociology

IT IS USUAL BEFORE PROCEEDING to the systematic presentation of a science to give a sketch of its literature. A bibliographical introduction informs the reader how much effort has been expended on the science, how it has progressed and what stage of development it has reached. If the sketch is also critical, and it can hardly fail to be so, the reader is also informed of the new writer's attitude toward the work of his predecessors. Such an introduction gives a comprehensive view. But it involves disadvantages of a technical nature. If every system should be described in detail, the introductory sketch would become a history of the science. The reader would have to wander through system after system, each one represented as more or less false before learning how the writer would correct them; which is not practicable. Or should the writer make and substantiate his criticisms in the introduction itself, he would anticipate his own system; whatever followed would be merely tiresome repetition. This too would be impracticable; especially since the refuting arguments can be used much more effectively as the author proceeds to unfold his own views. In this way he is not bound by historical sequence nor need he present the older systems in their entirety.

Accordingly, we shall mention only the most important pioneers in the domain of sociology, noting with all possible brevity the most prominent and most general points of view in their systems and deferring criticism and refutation until we present our own system.

Young and imperfect as the science of sociology still is, a history of its literature has already been written (Bärenbach, 1882). But its author makes the "socialistic" doctrines his starting point, and his failure to distinguish clearly between socialism and sociology greatly diminishes the value of the work. Further bibliographical material may be found in the literature on the development of constitutional

91

law, politics, political economy, and the philosophy of history
(Rochol, 1881; Raumer, 1883; Bluntschli, 1885).

1. Comte

Probably the first author to cherish presentiments of a "science
of the common nature of nations" was Giambattista Vico (1725).
But he adhered to Biblical tradition and did not emancipate himself
from contemporary theories of natural rights. Neither should we
expect to find in St. Simon, the world reformer, an objective science
of society. Full justice has been done when it is recognized that
it was from him that Comte received his inspiration.

To Auguste Comte unquestionably belongs the honor of having
been the first to recognize the real character of sociology. In his
Positive Philosophy he declared repeatedly, plainly and correctly
what this science should be. "All that can be rationally proposed in
our day," he says in one place, "is to recognize the positive character
in social as in all other science, and to ascertain the chief bases on
which it is founded." The scientific character of the future sociology
is thus indicated. Further, "it is the exclusive property of the positive
principle to recognize the fundamental law of continuous human
development, representing existing evolution as the necessary result
of the gradual series of former transformations." Thus Comte conceived mankind to be subject to the law of evolution and the present
to be the necessary consequence of the past. Though his conception
of mankind was erroneous, as will be shown later, both ideas are
nonetheless true and important; and the general principle has been
maintained firmly in sociology ever since. Moreover, an admonition
of broad scientific application was added: "True resignation, that
is, a permanent disposition to endure steadily and without hope of
compensation all inevitable evils, can proceed only from a deep
sense of the connection of all kinds of natural phenomena with
invariable laws" (Comte, 1839:II, lect. 46). Without such resignation, there can be no sociology.

> "If there are (as I do not doubt) political evils which, like
> some personal sufferings, cannot be remedied by science,"
> he went on, "science at least proves to us that they are in-
> curable, so as to calm our restlessness under pain by the
> conviction that it is by natural causes that they are rendered
> insurmountable" (Comte, 1839: II, lect. 47).

Would that he had acted upon this wise principle himself. But he violated it by suggesting plans for the "practical amelioration" of "conditions of the lower classes." The error is one for which his master, St. Simon, is to blame. It finally forced him from the path of objective science and into the false ways of subjective politics.

How clear and precise is his statement of the task of sociology in contrast with the older doctrines of the philosophy of history. "Social science could not exist so long as men were ignorant concerning what constitutes development; for this science studies the laws of development" (Comte, 1839:II, lect. 48).

Yet he himself failed to apprehend its true nature, for he accepted Pascal's "admirable aphorism" that "the entire succession of men, through the whole course of ages, must be regarded as one man always living." And he misconceived the results of sociology most egregiously, saying "that this science fulfills the famous suggestion of Pascal by representing the whole human race, past, present and future, as constituting a vast and eternal social unit whose different organs concur in their various modes and degrees in the evolution of humanity" (Pascal, 1660). But it is false to conceive mankind to be a unit; as we shall later show. It led Comte into a thousand and one errors.

In his time, it is true, historical and ethnographical material was very meagre. His personal knowledge of mankind was limited; and his investigations into the laws of human development were restricted to the Teutonic and the Latin races of Europe. Indeed, France was often his sole example. The "great revolution" was to his mind the overturning of all humanity, whereas the greater part of mankind was by far not influenced at all by this local European event.

Not only were his "laws of human development" based on this narrow experience; they were also so distorted by personal predilections that they possess little value. The historical and ethnographical horizon of his time was far too confined. His sociology failed from absolute lack of information. The epoch-making character of his work is solely due to the brilliant generalizations upon which he founded it. They are the basis, as we shall see, of all sociological efforts from his day to ours.

2. Quetelet

The prospect of verifying his laws of human development by means of numerical calculations must have been all the more enticing, to a mathematician like Quetelet, given the fact that Comte himself seemed directly to suggest it.[1] Quetelet's interest centered in the *Natural History of Society, i.e.,* in sociology. Even his earlier work on *Man* has the sub-title *Social Physics,* and he states that "it is the body social that we propose to study" (Quetelet, 1835: Sect. 3).

His task is obviously allied to that of Comte's sociology. But the "law of the great number" which he relied on to discover the laws of social development was ineffectual. His statistical works afford material for the theory of "man" and the thralldom of human will only. For sociology they could do nothing. He made no distinction between "mankind" and the unclear concept "society;" and many of his investigations begin with errors current in the social science of his day. He assumes, for instance, that "the simplest and most natural social union among men is the family[2] which is found in all ages and among all peoples" (Quetelet, 1835: Sect. 2-3). He did not know that the family, in the modern meaning of the word and the sense in which he uses it, is a very late social institution and an adaptation to political ends. Equally ingenuous is his idea that a nation "is a body composed of homogeneous elements performing their functions in unison and inspired with the same life principle." Whereas, in truth, every nation consists of unlike elements performing complementary functions under compulsion. His theory was that social unions originate in the "preponderance of the force of attraction impelling individuals to associate." He frankly conceded,

---

[1] "It is clear that this education [the preliminary sociological training] must rest on a basis of mathematical philosophy even apart from the necessity of mathematics to the study of inorganic philosophy. It is only in the region of mathematics that sociologists, or any body else, can obtain a true sense of scientific evidence and form the habit of rapid and decisive argumentation; can in short learn to fulfill the logical conditions of all positive speculation by studying universal positivism at its source" (Comte, 1839: II, lect. 49). However Comte warns against applying mathematical laws to the "complicated speculations of sociology."

[2] Comte makes the same statement: "The family presents the true germ of the various characteristics of the social organism. Such a conception is intermediate between the idea of the individual and that of the species or society" (Comte, 1839: II, lect. 50).

however, that "a nation is not always composed of elements of one sort. Indeed it is quite often the result of invasion and the fusion of conqueror and conquered." But this is the "exception." His theory is not based upon it. No wonder that he failed to get a clear conception of the laws of social development. Phenomena as common as the struggles of nation with nation seem a denial of nature; and he concludes his *History of Mankind* with the enthusiasm of an Elihu Burritt, saying:

> "To the credit of mankind be it told the nineteenth century is on the point of striking into a new path. It is recognized that there must be laws and tribunals for nations also; and that crimes practiced on a large scale by one people against another are just as much to be hated as crimes of man against man" (Quetelet, 1835).

These are beautiful effusions; but they attest to the scantiness of Quetelet's sociological information. Since he wrote them, the nineteenth century has witnessed, even in Europe alone, a half dozen wars: the Crimean and the Austro-Italian; the war of Prussia and Austria against Denmark; the Austro-Prussian; the Franco-Prussian and the Russo-Turkish. According to him they were all downright "crimes." Yet the victorious nations inscribed them in their annals in letters of gold, and succeeding generations exult at the thought of them. His "new path" is still a good way off. Is it not sociology that should take a new course?

3. Spencer

Herbert Spencer's words on this point are of inestimable importance:

> "Thought and feeling cannot be completely dissociated. Each emotion has a more or less distinct framework of ideas; and each group of ideas is more or less suffused with emotion. There are, however, great differences between their degrees of combination under both of these aspects. We have some feelings which are vague from lack of intellectual definition; and others to which clear shapes are given by the associated conceptions. At one time our thoughts are distorted by the passion running through them; and at another time it is difficult to detect in them a trace of liking or disliking. Manifestly, too, in each particular case these components of the mental state may be varied in their proportions. The ideas being the same, the

emotion joined with them may be greater or less; and it
is a familiar truth that the correctness of the judgment
formed, depends, if not on the absence of emotion, still, on
the balance of emotions which negates the excess of any one.
Especially is this so in matters concerning human life.
There are two ways in which men's actions, individual or
social, may be regarded. We may consider them as groups
of phenomena to be analyzed, and the laws of their dependence ascertained; or considering them as causing pleasures
or pains, we may associate with them approbation or
reprobation. Dealing with its problems intellectually, we
may regard conduct as always the result of certain forces;
or, dealing with its problems morally, and recognizing its
outcome as in this case good and in that case bad, we may
allow now admiration and now indignation to fill our consciousness. Obviously, it must make a great difference in
our conclusions whether, as in the one case, we study men's
doings as those of alien creatures, which it merely concerns
us to understand; or whether, as in the other case, we contemplate them as the doings of creatures like ourselves, with
whose lives our own lives are bound up, and whose behavior arouses in us, directly and sympathetically, feelings of
love or hate."

Here let me emphasize the conclusion that in pursuing our
sociological inquiries, and especially those on which we are
now entering [political institutions], we must as much as
possible, exclude whatever emotions the facts are calculated
to excite, and attend solely to the interpretation of the facts.
There are several groups of phenomena, which when
thought about, breed either contempt, disgust, or indignation. Our reactions must be restrained" (Spencer, 1880:II,
Sect. 434).

As the English statesmen cries "hands off" to the onlookers in
political quarrels, so Spencer cries "away with sentiment," whenever a sociological investigation is undertaken. On the portal of this
science he writes: "All sentiment, abandon ye who enter here." This
is not merely a practical admonition, it is a *conditio sine qua non,*
a stipulation indispensable in sociology, and which moreover fore-
stalls objections raised on moral grounds.

Fortunately, Spencer is in full agreement with Comte in recognizing "the positive character in social as in all other science." It
is to him the first principle of methodology, or rather it precedes

methodology. But in accepting the fundamental similarity of sociology and biology he made a well-nigh fatal blunder.

Comte affirmed emphatically that this similarity was an essential sociological principle.

> "The necessity of founding sociology upon the whole of
> biology is obvious. The subordination of social science to
> biology is so evident," he continues, "that nobody denies it
> in statement however it may be neglected in fact. Biology
> will be seen to afford the starting point of all social specu-
> lations, in accordance with the analysis of the social fac-
> ulties of man, and of the organic conditions which deter-
> mine its character. But, moreover, as we can scarcely in-
> vestigate the most elementary terms of the social sciences,
> we must construct them by applying the positive theory of
> human nature to the aggregate of corresponding circum-
> stances. . . . When the social condition has advanced so far
> as to exclude this kind of deduction, the second aspect
> presents itself; and the biological theory of man is impli-
> cated with the sociological in a less direct and special man-
> ner. The whole social evolution of the race must proceed
> in entire accordance with biological laws" (Comte, 1839:
> II, lect. 49).

The whole "theory of the organic state" which flourished so
luxuriantly in Germany from Rohmer and Bluntschli, to Schäffle
and his *Structure and Life of the Social Body*, should probably be
traced back to Comte directly or indirectly; and Spencer seemed
about to follow him too. "Setting out then with this general principle,
that the properties of the units [which it is the province of biology
to treat] determines the properties of the aggregate," he also concludes

> "that there must be a social science expressing the relations
> between the two, with as much definiteness as the nature of
> the phenomena permits. In every case [social science] has
> for its subject matter the growth, development, structure
> and functions of the social aggregate, as brought about by
> the mutual actions of individuals" (Spencer, 1874:52-53).

He is an individualist and endeavors to derive knowledge of social
events from the individual and his nature. If this were possible
sociology must be a higher order of biology, since we get our knowledge of the individual through the latter. But we may state here
that the social communities are the sociological units or elements,

and that it is not possible to ascertain their mutual relations from the properties of their constituent parts, *i.e.*, from the properties of individuals. No one starting from the latter can reach the nature of the group. Hence biological analogies are worthless in sociology except as illustrations.

Without saying so in words or even becoming clearly conscious of it, the English philosopher seems to have felt this. At least his scientific instincts have preserved him from such obvious exaggerations as others have made in consequence of false analogies between biology and sociology. Although he even affirmed such analogies in principle, he never based anything essential upon them, he never went so far but that the core of his sociology remained sound. Whenever he used biological terms, he treated them as similarities rather than as analogies. Notice, for example, how he describes the peaceful differentiation of authority in a primitive horde:

> "Setting out with an unorganized horde, including both sexes and all ages, let us ask, what must happen when some public question, as that of migration, or of defence against enemies, has to be decided. The assembled individuals will fall, more or less clearly, into two divisions. The elder, the stronger, and those whose sagacity and courage have been proved by experience. will form the smaller part, who carry on the discussion; while the larger part, formed of the young, the weak, and the undistinguished, will be listeners, who usually do no more than express from time to time assent or dissent. A further inference may safely be drawn. In the cluster of leading men there is sure to be one whose weight is greater than that of any other—some aged hunter, some distinguished warrior, some cunning medicine-man, who will have more than his individual share in forming the resolution finally acted upon. That is to say, the entire assemblage will resolve itself into three parts. To use a biological metaphor, there will, out of the general mass, be differentiated a nucleus and a nucleolus" (Spencer, 1880:II, sect. 464).

The passage quoted is typical. Spencer uses biological principles only to a very limited extent in investigating sociological laws. Social facts and phenomena keep reminding him of similar biological facts as is proper; but he always connects the two distinct species by a plain "similarly it happens," without identifying them at all. It is this quiet objectivity which makes him so superior to other

sociologists. Schäffle and Lilienfeld, for example, took these analogies seriously. They followed these will-o'-the-wisps over treacherous
ground. But Spencer does not confuse the nature of social and
organic phenomena for an instant, notwithstanding anything which
the title "Society as an Organism might imply (Spencer, 1880:I.
Pt. II, ch. 11). Every fact presented as common to both classes of
phenomena is so general that we may concede it without detracting
from the lucidity of the thought. He finds that societies grow as
truly as living organisms do; though this comparison holds only
because we have but one expression (growth, *Wachstrum*) for two
ideas, organic growth and social enlargement. If there were a special
expression for each there would be no temptation to falsely compare
or identify them. Likewise, nothing but want of verbal precision
makes it possible to say that both an organism and a society increase
in "structure" at the same time that they increase in scope. The
word "structure" is biological and should be only metaphorically
applied to the development of social classes, departments of government, and the like. In that case, there would not appear to be any
common quality. The same criticism is true of Spencer's third comparison, that both in an organism and in society "progressive differentiation of structures is accompanied by progressive differentiation of functions" (Spencer, 1880: sect. 216). The thought is perfectly clear, if we interpret the words according to the nature of the
respective phenomena. His comparisons with biological processes,
therefore, do not make our ideas of social processes less precise.

Although such comparisons are frequent, the positive inductive
methods of natural science is not a mere phrase with Spencer. He
really applies it to the domain of sociology; whereas Schäffle and
Lilienfeld, as we shall see, are misled by biological analogies, deduce
sociological laws from *a priori* biological laws, regardless of consequences. For the real subject matter of sociology their method
substituted a spurious organism from another domain of knowledge.[3]

But Spencer attacks social phenomena directly, examines them

---

[5] In the chapters of Spencer's *Sociology*, on "Social Structures," "Social
Functions," "Systems of Organs," etc. (Part II), the phenomena of organic
life are always presented first, then those from social life are described. But
the two sorts are kept distinct. There is no confusion. If the reader should omit
biological similes, the presentation of sociological phenomena would be clear.

calmly, with no predilections whatever, and formulates his results in sound doctrines and general laws. His method is correct, but still his results were only partial. He could not cut loose from the unitary conception of mankind, the *fable convenue*, the old conventional assumption of all former sociologists and philosophers, although often after a calm examination he is fairly compelled by the logic of facts to attribute the beginning of social development to the mutual effects of heterogenous ethnic elements. The "first internal cohesion" of "small hordes of primitive men" is due, he notes, to their "combined resistance to external foes."

> "While there exists only small wandering, unorganized hordes, the conflicts of these with one another work no permanent changes of arrangement in them. But when there have arisen the definite chieftainships which frequent conflicts tend to initiate, and especially when the conflicts have ended in subjugations, there arise the rudiments of political organizations" (Spencer, *Ibid*, sect. 250, *et seq.*).

And he adduces ethnological facts to illustrate every social phenomenon arising from the contact of social groups. But when he wishes to attribute phenomena to the mutual effects of the individuals of a group, he is forced to fall back on loose logical reasoning and biological similes. Had he appreciated this himself, perhaps he would have given up attempting individualistic explanations and would have, from the beginning, accepted the plurality of human hordes as not susceptible of further sociological analysis.[4] But as it is, there is a perpetual contradiction throughout his sociological investigations. On the one hand he tacitly assumes a unitary mankind descended from a common origin; on the other, where he really explains social phenomena, he goes back to a "plurality of primitive hordes." As we have demonstrated in *Der Rassenkampf*, the assumption of primitive plurality of human hordes is the only possible rational basis; the only one upon which all social phenomena can be satisfactorily explained. We have elsewhere made it sufficiently clear that this assumption does not contradict Darwin's theories.[5]

[4] Though Spencer does not affirm plurality of primitive hordes to be the first natural fact in sociology, he does note incidentally that "social evolution begins with small simple aggregates" (*Ibid.*, sect. 257).

[5] "Darwinism is so fully occupied with the questions of evolution and natural selection that no opportunity is found to consider the question of single or plural descent carefully. Yet, not only must Darwin's theory assume one line,

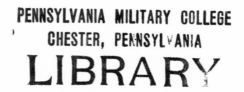

Primitive plurality is often the only possible explanation and we shall adopt it exclusively, thus sparing ourselves the vacillation between the unitary and plural conceptions of mankind from which Spencer suffers. Had he followed it consistently, he could have still more easily applied his formula of evolution, of which we shall speak later, to the development of social phenomena. His universal law is so ill-suited to the development of mankind as a unit that the insufficiency of this assumption is manifest at every step. Fortunately the importance of his work does not rest on the formulas which he superimposes upon the facts; but to his acute observations and his method of treating them. He has command of more material than anyone save Bastian, and he is enough of a positivist to test its complicated mass objectively, calmly, without prejudice, drawing conclusions regardless of metaphysical presuppositions. This has made Spencer the real founder of sociology and he will long remain its most powerful champion. Next to him stands Bastian; his superior, perhaps, in knowledge and in calmness of observation, but less skilled in presenting scientific conclusions. But before turning to this phenomenal scholar and investigator, we wish to mention several other attempts at sociology.

4. Holbach

Monism is the thought underlying all early attempts at sociology. They culminate in the endeavor to find a universal law for events in the whole domain of nature. They all fail to distinguish between universal and social laws, seeking to explain social events by universal laws, which is impossible. They revive the dispute between idealists and materialists. The former attribute everything to the mind's efficiency; the latter, to the effective force of matter. The first grand attempt to explain all events, natural, human and social, by a single universal law of matter, was Holbach's *System of Nature*. The author

---

but, naturally and logically, it must admit a number of parallel lines of evolution. Otherwise it must be assumed that at the moment when organic cell life began there was only one cell from which the whole animal world has developed by successive changes. Such a silly assumption is foreign to Darwinism; indeed, it has been expressly emphasized that reference is made only to the 'original forms' under which existence began, and that the question whether there were one or more individual forms was considered unessential" (Gumplowicz, 1883: sect. 14).

is a skillful reasoner; so we find the demonstration complete in every
detail, showing how those two primordial forces, attraction and repulsion, not only sustain the heavenly bodies in their paths and
regulate all life and motion on our planet, but also help to establish
the relations between man and man and build up every social community. Indeed there would seem to be nothing that attraction and
repulsion do not accomplish (Holbach, 1781:Bk. I, ch. IV). Mole-
cules attract one another and bodies are formed; they repel one
another and bodies are dissolved; by the process of accumulation
plants and metals, animals and man are made:

> "in short never to separate physical from moral laws—it
> is thus that men, mutually attracted to each other by their
> reciprocal wants, form those unions which we designate by
> the terms marriage, families, societies, friendships, connect-
> ions. In all phenomena man presents, from the moment he
> quits the womb of his mother, to that wherein he becomes
> the inhabitant of the silent tomb, he perceives nothing but
> a succession of necessary causes and effects, which are
> strictly conformable to those laws common to all the beings
> in nature. All his modes of action—all his sensations—all
> his ideas—every act of his will—every impulse he either
> gives or receives, are the necessary consequences of his own
> peculiar properties, and those which he finds in the various
> beings by whom he is moved. Everything he does, every-
> thing that passes within himself, are the common property
> of everything he beholds. Nature, in the effects of inert
> force—of self-gravitation—of the attractive or repulsive
> powers contained in his machine— of the tendency he has,
> in common with other beings, to his own individual preser-
> vation; in short, of that energy which is the common
> property of everything he beholds. Nature, in man, does
> nothing more than show, in a decided manner, what be-
> longs to the peculiar nature by which he is distinguished
> from the beings of a different system or order" (Holbach,
> 1781: Bk I, ch. IV).

The idea of explaining all human and natural phenomena by
the law of attraction and repulsion has repeatedly reappeared since
Holbach's day; and we shall meet it again in Schäffle.

5. Schäffle

Comte and Spencer, as we have seen, derived sociological laws
from the less remote domain of biology. The "theory of the organic

state," so-called, which was current in Germany for decades, was based on Comte's ideas until, finally, Schäffle combined it with Holbach's thought. Everybody will acknowledge Schäffle's great intellectual power and scholarly ability. But the fundamental thought of his system, the alleged analogy between the State and an animal organism, is baleful, and all must regret that talent and experience were spent in elaborating an idea so extravagant. It is impossible to go into the details of his comprehensive work here, and it must suffice to quote the leading thought in the author's own words:

> "We have repeatedly observed that not only nature as a whole, but also the several organic and inorganic bodies in it seem to be great societies or systems whose parts, in turn, are either simple or more or less composite. Then, according to what has preceded, attraction and repulsion between the elements and the outside world would impart motion to these atomic kingdoms. Under such circumstances, can it be a misinterpretation to assume that the social body, which is the realm of persons and the most universal and spiritual realm of experience, cannot accomplish the ends of its existence without the manifestation of the same double force in each of its personal elements? Some parts would appear to be centripetal in virtue of one force, while others, obeying the other, would seem to assert their independence of the whole. But, as the units of the body-social are neither simple nor irrational, we ought not to consider the two fundamental impulses either simple or irrational; but we can and we must explain the total life of the body-social as the product of the multiform, reciprocal effects of all the active social elements, of all the subjects endowed with volition, of all persons and institutional groups of persons in a state of attraction and repulsion. For ethical movement is not imparted to the body-social by anything outside; but we see it arise within from the discharge of ethical forces between the constituent parts, both individual and collective" (Schäffle, 1875:I, pt. 5, ch. 2).

This language, though not quite clear, is not yet the mystical language of Kantian metaphysics, beneath which lie clear thoughts, for the illustrations are inept. Schäffle analyzes the "body-social," but he leaves us in doubt whether this mystical expression denotes mankind as a whole, or only a state or folk. It is as unclear and intangible as Quetelet's "society." The latter uses the "great number" to explain his meaning; the former demonstrates that there are social cells, tissues, bones, nerves, etc., which makes the matter worse. It needs a very lively imagination to correct Schäffle's lengthy excerpts from anatomy, physiology and psychology with social phenomena and social development. Sober reason turns in despair from the endless limp comparisons. If they contain a kernel of truth derived from experience and acute observation, as often happens, it is tedious to find it in the confusion of analogies.

6. Lilienfeld

Of Lilienfeld, we can, on the whole, say no more than has been said of Schäffle. He has the same erudition and equally great intellectual power and inventiveness and he displays the same degree of industry in executing a plan which is fundamentally wrong and in defending a cause which is lost from the start.

The fundamental concept of his ponderous work is expressed in these words:

> "There is only one way to make human society the subject-matter of a positive science. It must necessarily be classed among organic beings and regarded as an organism as much above man as man is above all other organisms in nature. On no other condition is it possible to treat human society inductively and to conceive of it as an inseparable part of nature. On no other condition can dogmatic social science beome positive. But on this condition it obtains a basis as real as that of natural sience" (Lilienfeld, 1873: I, 25).

The reverse of all this is true. Social science can never "obtain a basis as real as that of natural science" until the fantastic view that "society" is an "organism" has been thrown overboard and all biological analogies have been cleared away.

Lilienfeld's query whether "social organisms do not obey the same laws as all other beings" must be emphatically answered in the negative. The distinction between social organisms and organic beings is something more than a simple "preponderance of the principle of adaptation in the former and of the principle of causality in the latter." They are distinct species of phenomena and different laws control them. Laws of *organic* development and laws of *social* development are *toto genere* unlike and ought not to be confounded. When Lilienfeld further inquires whether "in relation

to us, the whole of mankind does not constitute an organic being
uniting in itself all social groups and related to them as the whole
is to its parts," we may be sure that we are confronted with a wretched scientific blunder. After mankind has been declared to be an
"organic being," what can be expected from any further investigation? Yet in the next chapter, on "Human Society as Real Being,"
he solemnly protests that he:

> "conceives the analogy to be something more than an alle-
> gorical parallel. If we had considered all the current
> scientific and popular expressions which point to a relation-
> ship between natural and social phenomena to be mere
> rhetorical figures, we should have trodden in the footsteps
> of all the doctrinaires and metaphysicians; we should have
> been working over the same barren soil on which in the
> course of centuries so many capable natural scientists have
> sacrificed their powers with no sociological results save
> doubts and contradictions."

Lofty statement. But it must be laid to his charge that in spite of
everything he was no more fortunate than they.

He seems to believe that a metaphor can be made real by
"conceiving" it to be real. "We must gain the conviction that this
or that social group, this or that state, is a real living organism like
every other in nature." He expects a great deal of the reflecting
reader. We have not been able to gain this conviction even after a
most earnest study of his five volumes. There are many honest and
deep thoughts, but nothing to enforce this conviction. In one place he
trenchantly criticises "metapolitics, which is busied with generalizing
from allegories, *i.e.*, from data that are themselves once removed
from reality." "Double nonsense" he calls it. We frankly confess
that between it and his methods we see no difference. As with
Schäffle, so we must say of Lilienfeld, that his work contains incidentally admirable observations; but his elaborate system is built on
a false foundation and can be of small profit to science."[6]

All in all, de Roberty is right when he laments that, notwith-

---

[6] Lilienfeld's first volume appeared in 1873 and Schäffle's in 1875. Although
the latter knew of Lilienfeld's work before his own was published, it is our
opinion that the two systems were independently conceived. Without doubt,
however, both writers were influenced by the theory of the "organic" state then
prevalent in Germany and very forcibly stated in the popular works of Bluntschli and Ahrens.

standing Schäffle and Lilienfeld, "social science still has its proper
course to seek" (de Roberty, 1881). The period of progress, since
Comte clearly outlined the social problem, was only one of incipiency, important though it be. Among other errors of this period,
de Roberty specifically mentions "setting the phantom light of
general analogies to guide the science." He recommends above all
that the "natural history of society" be made the basis of sociology,
saying that on it alone could an abstract social science be built.
But his work is occupied with preparatory questions of methodology.
As propaedeutics of sociology it has fulfilled its mission; he does
not claim more for it. The task which he urges upon sociology, the
construction of a science of "society," based on its natural history,
has since been undertaken with great success by a German ethnographer, Bastian.

7. Bastian

We have already called Bastian an amazing person. He has
done more for the "natural history of society," as de Roberty
called it, than all his predecessors together. The scope of his labors
is great and his plethora of deep and excellent thoughts is beyond
any man's power to reckon to-day. We can only make a few frag-
mentary observations upon them, being wholly unable to suitably
exploit the sociological treasures he has stored up.

Bastian could never succeed in systematizing his knowledge;
it was too great. Whenever he made the attempt, even in his early
work on *Man in History,* his system broke down at its very inception
and was swept away by the flood tide of his information. Significant,
however, is the thought contained in the sub-title to this work: *Contribution to a Psychological Conception of the World.* It recurs
in all his works, and is the great philosopher's pole-star on the
immeasurable ocean of knowledge, his inspiration in all his labors.

Probably this thought dates from the time when "race-psychol-
ogy" first flourished in Berlin. For in his preface he says:

> "Psychology ought not to be limited as heretofore to in-
> dividual self-observation and the pathological evidence
> afforded by schools and insane asylums. Man, as political
> animal, attains full development only in society. Mankind,
> than which there is no higher concept, must be made the
> starting point; mankind is the unitary whole in which the
> individual figures as an integral part" (Bastian, 1860:I,x).

He searches "mankind" far and wide for manifestations of "thought." He considers his task to be psychological. His object is to disclose the soul of races, which are the parts, and so finally to disclose the soul of mankind, the whole. In the later works, he calls these psychical manifestations "folk-thought" [*Völkergedanke*].

So he is really not a sociologist; he lays little or no stress on the process of social development. Still the material which he gathers from every nook and cranny to demonstrate "folk-thoughts," also illustrates social development. Bastian wanted to be a psychologist of race; but the problem he set himself was falsely proposed and impossible, and the force of facts drove him into another course. He became an ethnographer and built up a system of ethnology.

Some passages may be cited to show his views. He is a realist from the first and occupies the only correct realistic ground, materialism and idealism combined.

> "If so-called materialists have hitherto vainly attempted to construct new systems," says Bastian, "if they have been unable to satisfy public expectations and have found no surcease for that longing of the human heart which has always hovered over the earthly horizon of all races like the promise of dawn, it was because they neglected psychology, not knowing how to rescue it from the hands of dialectic speculation and to claim it as their own province. They opposed the idealist on party lines, instead of drawing his objects also within the sphere of scientific investigation. True science recognizes neither materialism nor idealism, for it includes both. Psychology, 'race-psychology,' based on ethnographical studies, had to wait until the other natural sciences developed, because it must build on them. But now that the preliminary work is done, it joins them, proposing to swing a bridge from the narrow circle of sense to the endless realm of ideas" (Bastian, *Ibid,* X).

What, then, is his attitude toward the facts of the social world? "No judicious investigator," he says," will give further heed to enthusiastic utopists and reformers. As soon as we learn that recognition of the caues proves development to be according to law, we accept whatever is as right, because it has become what it is (Bastian, *Ibid,* XVII-XVIII). He is equipped with all the requirements of true objective science. He wishes to "gather up evidence" and

"collect psychological statistics" in order "to acquaint the reader
with the course of thought peculiar to the various races of mankind." Unfortunately (or perhaps fortunately for the future science),
Bastian plans a task immeasurably greater than he can manage. His
plan is nothing more nor less than "to show by statistics that exactly
the same number of original psychological elements have coursed
regularly through the heads of all races in all ages of history." A
quarter of a century has passed since this was written and the tireless
statistician of folk-thought has never suspended his labors. That his
mind is still fresh and clear is proof of its extraordinary strength;
for his "statistics" have become impenetrable forests wherein ordinary mortals lose their way and become bewildered.

Future science will be able some day to utilize his labors and
will find them invaluable. But it seems to us that the laws of the
"regular" course of thought might have been made intelligible at
once if he had been a sociologist rather than a psychologist of race.
The fundamental characteristic of Bastian's investigations is the
endeavor to attribute all social phenomena to human thought. He
accumulates inexhaustible stores of social facts in order to unravel
man's thoughts from them and then to discover in the thoughts the
soul of races. With him thoughts are always primary and deeds are
an emanation from them; thoughts arises only under the influence
of external natural phenomena, and the social world emanates from
thought. The scheme of his system is: (a) nature, (b) man and
thought, (c) society and social thought. His scientific structure
culminates in the latter; his ultimate object is the psychology of race.
In sociology the point of view and the object must be totally different. The social process must precede; the social fact is primary. Man
disappears from the foreground of consideration since he receives
his thought, his soul, from the social fact. Social thought, the concept of social facts, appears in the individual human mind only by
reflection.

Hence, as distinct from Bastian's system, sociology includes:
(a) social elements: swarms, hordes, groups, etc., (b) man: their
product, both in body and mind, (c) the social process and its products, (d) the socio-ethical products of the reciprocal action of
society and the individual. Social phenomenon is always primary.
The thought of the individual, and socio-ethical products such as

religion, rights, morals, etc., are derivative. An undigested remnant of idealism still troubles Bastian and he continues to be a pronounced individualist (atomist), *i.e.*, he uses the individual and his nature to explain the nature and development of the whole.

The first volume of his *Man in History* treats psychology (*i.e.*, the psychology of the individual) as natural science; the second is on psychology and mythology, and examines the relation of the individual to nature; and the third is occupied with "political psychology," concluding with a description of society. But this does not seem to us the correct method for sociology. It has had little success in politial science and has fallen into disrepute as idealism and atomism. Yet he even attributes "property," in the traditional way, to the primitive possessive act of the savage seizing the "fruit from the tree" to still his hunger. He adheres to the old idealistic phrase that property is "the necessary extension of the sphere of personality in society" (Bastian, 1860:III, 217).

Likewise the state, to cite only one more example, is derived from the family, which has gradually "become a race." But in the later works every suggestion of idealism and the whole rationalistic theory of the state is omitted. He studies the "natural history of society" more and more objectively and finally gives the most striking expression to this tendency in a "system" of ethnology.

In the ethnographical works (Bastian, 1867; and 1872b), also here and there in masses of descriptive matter which is invaluable for its own sake, reflections crop out that are not only the result of acute observation and clear reasoning, but are besides really epoch-making in social science. As an example we will cite the discussion of the "ethnological conception of descent and relationship" in the introduction to his *Ethnological Investigations*, for we shall often have occasion to refer to it in dealing with social change.

The current use of the terms "native race" and "relationship" is criticised very sharply. It is shown that in the nature of the case they are only relative. If we know any of the circumstances at all our knowledge reaches back such a little way that we can never use these words in their proper framework.

> "When historical analysis is not able to go further the last race may provisionally be called native. Although classical authors described some races as earth-born autochthons

which were not known to have had an earlier dwelling-
place in general they applied the term regardless of historical considerations. Indeed some races called aboriginal
were notoriously immigrants, and were on that account
connected with the mountains in etymology" (Bastian,
1872a).

No criticism could be more destructive of the Biblical theory
of descent underlying every system of political and social science
other than that of Bastian. He shows that:

"every race tries to find the 'first man,' as the redskins call
him; the ancestor of man, or father of the race. For, as
examples from Asia, Australia, America and elsewhere
show, the name of the race always coincides with the general
name for man. No difference of origin is allowed for," he
continues, "except that the former race is said to have
sprung from the ground, into which it withdrew again before conquerors born of birds and wild animals; or, being
the offspring of trees and vines, was not adopted into the
family of the proud heaven-descended heroes . . . In Grecian
tradition Laos sprang from the stones, and in German the
Saxons from a rock. Assyrian traditions are revolutionary;
the Lybian repeat the myth of the Moxos,[7] and in Scandinavian story the first-begotten were divided into classes. But
since Christianity and Islamism made the Semitic legend
preponderant over large portions of Europe and Asia all
racial diversity is referred to the three patriarchs who survived the flood with their father."

The passage is typical of Bastian's ability to upset false ideas.
By citing notions that recur the world over, so as to show that they
are only a form of human thought, he thoroughly destroys the
delusion that they ever contained any truth.

Next to the Biblical explanation of man's origin nothing is
so fatal to sociology as the false views of tribal descent and kinship.
By correcting them Bastian rendered sociology another very great
service.

"Kinship and descent, like so many other words, have a
figurative as well as a real signification, whereas they ought
to be employed in the inductive sciences as technical terms
with one well-defined meaning. Descent from a common

[7] [The Moxos were a tribe of Bolivian Indians who believed that they originated on the spot, and who were restrained from migration by a superstitious
fear of the mountains, rivers, etc.]

ancestor implies kinship, but kinship may also arise from a union of races and is therefore the broader term. Strictly, descent should be traced through a limited number of generations, beyond which it is preferable to speak of kinship. The limit might be somewhat extended where endogamic marriages are the rule, as among the Incas, Achimenides and Wanes, and in the aristocratic circles of certain mountain peoples. But this practice is extraordinarily rare, whereas the marriage regulations among the Australians, Chinese, Abipones and many others must lead to the incessant crossing of families; for the degrees of relationship within which they prohibit marriage are even remoter than those the Pope once had much difficulty in enforcing in Bavaria. The term 'descent' should be avoided as much as possible in ethnology, unless one wants to grapple with the fruitless problem of ultimate origin. And yet many an historical clue is afforded by mythical traditions of descent, whether confined to the Teutons, as those given by Tacitus, or made to embrace a wider field, whether Celts, Scythians and Illyrians are grouped under one common ancestor, or the equally incongruous Galla, Waknafi and Wakamba, whose languages even are unlike, grouped under another; or whether Grecian eponyms are represented to be brothers, or genealogical tables are projected for the known and presumptively the whole world at once" (Bastian, 1872a: I, viii).

"In general, the more definitely a particular locality is circumscribed the broader is the sense in which kinship may be used. The recurrence of the same *kabong,* or brotherhoods, throughout the whole Australian continent gives a clue to the general similarity of type which continual crossing produces among savages at the same time that it prevents individualities from becoming constant."

It is important to bear in mind how relative the ideas "kindred" and "autochthonous" are, but it is equally vital to have an objective conception of race and stem.

"Nationality," says Bastian, "grows out of similarity of interests and views; it is furthered by religious and political union, and especially by the assimilation of language, and attains its greatest perfection within an area enclosed by natural boundaries."

According to Bastian, the earliest precursor of the nation is the race or stem, which is "earlier than the folk," since the "incorporation" of races "into folk is determined by political boundaries."

Important also is Bastian's confirmation of the fact that "the most favored regions of civilization are those in which several streams of foreign immigration meet." This amounts to saying that civilization is promoted by their union. Admirable also is his explanation of how the resulting civilization or, what is nearly the same thing, how the "national type" is related to the local conditions, *i.e.*, to "the local ethnological type," to the "anthropological province," to use his own words.

> "A great variety of inhabitants, may exist in every geographical province. The range of conditions within which like is possible is wide, and circumstances may cause very great differences to arise even between adjacent varieties. Hence the dispute over stability and mutability of races is, for the most part, fictitious, for both views are supported by examples, but the conditions which produce them respectively are not accurately distinguished. How far the national type produced by one cause or another shall approximate the ethnological or territorial type will depend on circumstances. A native stock, though capable of improvement in various ways, will never change much. Even if there should be an influx of strangers indigenous to another climate and permanent political changes should result, the influence of environment would still tend to mould the type into harmony with itself. But for centuries there might be a multiple series of transitional phases; and when growth finally ceased, the resultant type, while bearing the impress of historical and geographical environment, might differ widely from the autochthonous type, which was wholly or principally the product of the geographical province, as the modern Frenchman differs from the Gaul and the pre-Gallic Celt, or the Spaniard from the Hispanian, etc."

But, by the "original autochthons" we must understand that he means the type which is the earliest that historical investigation can discover, not an absolutely "original" type. For, as Bastian emphatically declares of the original representatives of the anthropological province of the Celebes, the Alfores, "our ignorance of any predecessors is not sufficient proof that there were none." This is the only worthy conception of anthropological history, and Bastian is consistent in contending that "questions of tribal descent have no ethnological meaning, since in the course of a few generations consanguineous relationships become so extended and involved as to obliterate tribal lines." So the "voluminous question whether the Slavs descended from the Illyrians, the Sarmates or the Veneti," seems to him "senseless;" but the point is to learn "the elements composing the tribe" and the process going on within it. In summing up the task of this ethnological science, he says: "In the ethnological treatment of nationality," by which, as we know, he understands an ethnic composite:

> "we must not divert attention into wrong channels by raising unjustifiable questions about descent and preventing insight into the springs of life; neither may we begin the investigation with an arbitrary hypothesis." (Biblical tradition, for example - LG)
> "But we must proceed from the given circumstances back ward, separating out the elements so long as we have a spark of historical light left, or so long as collateral proof still serves to guide us through the darkness of myth."

The outlines of the science thus incidentally sketched are not the product of *a priori* deductions and philosophical speculations. They developed part by part as he pondered over enormous piles of ethnological material collected in his research and on exploring expeditions. He was forced to proceed systematically. First of all, he had to make a critical estimate of similar previous attempts; thus he compiled his *History of Ethnology*. It's logical successor, *Folk Thought and the Science of Man* was probably intended to be a systematic outline; but the flood of facts makes the forecast of a system impossible. Finally, in the *General Principles of Technology*, he is more successful, as much as is possible with his overflowing information. These three late works best show his epoch-making importance in sociology (Bastian, 1880; 1881; and 1884).

Just as Comte assigns sociology a place after biology in the hierarchy of the sciences since it is the youngest, (the future science), so Bastian begins his *History of Ethnology* by pointing out that this science occupies the last place in order of development. This external coincidence of itself suggests that perhaps both have the same thing in mind.

Indeed, Bastian calls ethnology the "science of man;" which would also describe sociology. But by ethnology he means a science, or better, that science of man which takes races and not individuals

for the subject matter of its investigations. The problem cannot be
to find a "God in history" until man has been found there. The first
problem concerns man in his character as political animal, in the
social state; where it appears that thought is primary and that the
thought of the individual is secondary, first becoming clear as an
integral part of the whole in the exchange of thought through language" (Bastian, 1880:25). A good portion of his scientific program
is thus comprised in the name. This "science of man" is to consider
the individual only as a member of an ethnic group. Its identification with sociology which considers man as a member of a social
group is almost complete. Besides, hear what Bastian says of the
present position of ethnology:

> "Some inductive natural sciences like botany and chemistry
> have had a plain and definite field of observation before
> them; and though they could not have arisen before the new
> epochal age of discoveries dawned they have since devel-
> oped systematically, rapidly and fully; whereas ethnology,
> which as science of man should strive for ultimate conclus-
> ions, was incapable of such rapid progress. It had to wait
> upon the others. First induction must become fully estab-
> lished in chemistry and physics. Progressing from inorganic
> matter to organic, it must reach the limits of the corporeal
> in physiology. After that, continually supplementing its
> gigantic powers by the comparative method, it might ven-
> ture to invade the mental realm, transforming psychology
> into a natural science and analyzing race-thoughts in the
> name of ethnology" (Bastian, 1880: I, and *Passim*).

Thus the object of ethnology in Bastian's sense is the discovery
of folk-thought, and the means is ethnology. Hence Bastian sees the
germs of ethnology in the first of modern geographical discoveries,
and its continuation in the ethnographical and anthropological data
of the nineteenth century. "Firm footing was first gained" with
Adeling's *Mithridates* and Blumenbach's works. "After that the
the development of the science was only a question of time." It was
strongly promoted by a treatise on *Ethnology and the History of
Primitive Ages* and by the founding of ethnological museums. Then
Prichard, writing in a "religious sense," "to prove the unity of
mankind and descent from one pair" gave the science its first hand-
book (*Cf.* Prichard, 1855).

Herder, Rousseau and others contributed by discussing the

philosophy of history. Men like Auguste and Amadée Thierry hastened to adopt the new points of view. Interest grew and ethnological societies were founded in Paris and London and correspondence was opened with societies, journals and museums abroad. Bastian dwells on the significance of these steps, holding the energetic development of ethnological museums to be indispensable, a *conditio sine qua non* for his future science.

> "With suitable museums not only will many practical ends be realized but more important the basis of induction will be strengthened, which will be a great advantage in psychology where theoretical studies first come in contact with the domain of philosophy" (Bastian, 1880:79).

But he does not mean the psychology of Fries, Herbart, Beneke, Fichte, Schopenhauer, Ulrici, and Fischer; nor any "witch's concoction before which the philosophers stand dismayed," but the natural science of psychology. "In it lies our hope; so far as can be seen, the last hope of mankind" (Bastian, 1880:83).

The essential characteristic of the future psychology, which he desires should go hand in hand with ethnology, is that it does not start from the individual man. For he "is nothing, at best an idiot; only through spoken intercourse in society does he become conscious of thought, is his nature realized. The thought of society, social thought, is the primary result and the thought of the individual is won by later analysis from it" (Bastian, 1880:79). These words are golden and we shall accept them as the motto of sociology. Bastian aptly criticizes the current psychology by saying that "systems of philosophy generally begin with the individual and have to patch social thought together out of the tatters that have come into their hands they know not how; whereas, if social thought were looked upon as an unmutilated garment, each individual thought would be found woven into its right place." Then he unfolds his ethnological plan "to win from social thought sufficient material for psychological investigation." Not satisfied with considering "thought-structures, or thought-trees of civilized races only," he demands the assistance of the "ethnology of savage races," of those:

> "cryptogramic structures, so to speak, in which the processes of cell-life and growth may be more easily observed, in order that the laws discovered in them may be applied to phanerogamic complexes.

The laws governing every organism are firmly fixed within it; even ethical laws are unchangeable. Everywhere in the five continents, we see thoughts springing forth, similar where the conditions are similar or varying with local differences. As the same principles regulate the processes of cell-life in the tropic palm and the arctic fir; as the same plant may have its leaves broad, curled, or dwarfed to needles according to its habitat; as there are Asiatic, African and American varieties of the lion, so the pantheon of the Indian national mind differs from that of the Grecian and the Scandinavian.

In all the psychological creations of society, whether religious, social or aesthetic, there are primitive elementary thoughts indisputably recurring and passing through the same course of development, often with truly startling identity, like ghostly doubles of distant acquaintances. The organic bond is so close that one with such sharp eyes as Cuvier had for fossils might reconstruct the whole circle of ideas from the torn fragments and accidental traces" (Bastian, 1880:89).

Accordingly, Bastian proposes three specific ethnological problems. The first is:

"to determine the elementary laws of growth in race and national thoughts; to get something which will do for these what the cell-theory does for plant-physiology. The second would be to study the local influences of environment, to which Buckle in his philosophy yields a preponderating importance. The last is the investigation of what might be compared to grafting or to cultivating ornamental plants by artificial means. It is chiefly concerned with races just beginning to develop a civilization before they cross the threshold of history. All changes due to intercourse whether with friends or foes fall under this head; all such phenomena as were formerly supposed to be borrowed. For whenever similarity of ideas was discovered, historical hypotheses were immediately recast according to that principle; whereas, according to the psychological axioms of ethnology and the methods of comparative etymology, the explanation should be first sought in the most general and elementary laws. When there is no longer a possibility of finding it in them. resort may be had to historical intercourse so far as it seems reasonably certain. When work is begun in earnest, ethnology will have to arrange its investigations according to these three points of view" (Bastian, 1889: 90-91).

Such is Bastian's ethnological method. In his *Völkergedanke* he worked zealously to prepare suitable material and to arrange it properly according to this plan. The methodological and propae-deutic hints of the *History* come out more clearly. Carping criticism might complain of repetitions; but deeper insight here discovers a hard intellectual struggle from the darkness of intimation to the light of cognition—the severe birth-pangs of a new science.

Properly rejecting theories ascribing "the preponderating in-fluence to environment," he again lays it down as the problem of inductive ethnology:

"disregarding the somewhat superficial local phenomena for which an historical or geographical explanation must be sought later, to determine first of all and permanently the uniform laws of the growth of human racial thought. It can be done most simply by the genetic method, starting with uncivilized peoples as the lowest and most transparent organisms. How development proceeds from such germs to the most exalted mental products, must be discovered by comparing parallel series of phenomena according to uni-versal natural principles."

This is not mere repetition. Each thought is more fully devel-oped and more clearly expressed. As he progresses he more closely approaches sociology. He very properly hopes "by observing uncivil-ized races and gaining an insight into the human mind's processes of growth" to obtain a perfect key to its "higher stages," "even to its full development in civilized peoples." It will not always be possible, however, for:

"many primary ideas are so completely eliminated as civil-ization progresses that their relation to current ideas is lost and they have only an archaic value. But others with their offshoots, still permeate modern conceptions."

He has really projected a complete science of sociology. Indeed in spite of his peculiar views, he penetrates right to its heart as we shall see.

"Of the many series of conceptions touching the most im-portant interests of life, not a few," he says, "concern the condition of society when it is coincident with the state or when it is promiscuously stratified into ranks, castes, guilds, parishes, confederacies, etc. But before ethnology can expect to investigate, methodically and thoroughly, the ideas prev-

alent under such circumstances, it must first have comprehended the social organism within which they find expression." This organism is the state; and all depends on investigating its structure and biology. In considering man's
immanent social nature, the question of its origin must be
postponed temporarily before the fact of its existence . . .
Society, which morphologically leads up to family, tribe
and state, and, biologically, to kin, race and nation, exists
in greater or smaller proportion wherever man does. For
the conception of man as a social being is real; but the
conception of him as an individual is abstract" (Bastian,
1881:17).

Thus Bastian stands fully on sociological ground. The involuntary course of his thought proves, better than any logical argument
could, the intimate connection between his ethnology and our
sociology. The former is nothing but the necessary basis, the latter
is the crown of the ethnological structure.

So great is the power of thought over man, that often a mere
accident is sufficient to awaken a whole system of ideas in the
mind. Bastian scarcely graces the portals of sociology, whereupon
they open as of themselves; and the whole complex mass of problems, overruns him. Once under the influence of the sociological
idea he cannot escape a storm of perplexities and doubts. Suddenly he notices that "indefinite terminology leads to various misconceptions, as when "race" (clan, lineage, band, etc.), is used for tribe
and phyle, curia and phratry, and gens, etc." (*Cf.* Gumplowicz,
1883: 186, 200 *et seq.;* and 1875; sect. 8). Suddenly he sees
clearly what he did not see when he wrote *Man in History,* that
the "family, which is the substructure of the whole development
under prevailing conditions, must be abandoned in ethnology,"
i.e., in sociology.

"Since our idea of the family is abstracted from actual
conditions, it is a particularly definite concept. . . . We have
the schematic forms, family and race, and think of the
latter as arising out of the former because a race can be
analyzed into families; but an actual unit first appears in
the kindred" (Bastian, 1881:21).

The adverb "first," seems objectionable here. Sociology does
not "first" begin with the kindred or horde, but begins with it as
an originating natural fact; for it is not and cannot be known what

might have been earlier (Gumplowicz, 1875: sect. 8; and 1881: sect. 29). He does not clearly understand how the state arises from the first "actual" or, as we should say, "ultimate" unit, nor what the process of transition is, for he says that "even in the kindred or phratry there are traces of a half-conscious interference, which suggest to some the social contract as the origin of the state; but the state should be attributed to nature." He discards the social contract, as might be expected, and sets the kindred first, conceding the origin of the state from it problematically. But while emphasizing the natural origin of the state, he gives no clear account of the transitions from kinship to state, which we shall treat later in the appropriate place. However, when once the state has arisen, he understands its changes perfectly, both as ethnic conglomerates and as social clusters. By contrasting it with the kindred as the "actual unit," he points out that the "ideal state is never realized; for the boisterously waking life of the race-mind [better race minds] grows more boisterous still in the effort to unify and nationalize the currents of ethnic feeling by force of political authority."

In view of this deeper conception of the state, the ordinary theory of political organizations and of political rights had to be abandoned.[8] When the Semitic sphere of knowledge was added to the classical, theocracy was added to the chief Aristotelian forms of government: kingdom or monarchy, aristocracy, and city state (besides tyranny, oligarchy, and democracy or ochlocracy). But now that the whole globe is subjected to observation there are so many modifications to be noticed that the previous systems would be radically transformed were the types arranged comparatively.

Such reflections do not belong in ethnology. Without noticing it, Bastian has reached social and political science. Later, in his *Principles of Ethnology* (1884), he comes to realize this and sets forth the relation between ethnology and sociology, saying plainly that "ethnology, as ethnic sociology or sociology under many ethnic forms, has to demonstrate the physiological laws of the life of social organisms." In comparing savage races and civilized states he develops his most interesting ideas and proves the solidarity of folk-thought. But the comparison ought to be conducted sociologically

---

[8] *Cf.* Gumplowicz (1875: sect. 13, 14.) where we discussed the unsatisfactory nature of this theory, which rests on a one-sided conception of the state.

and not ethnologically. To obtain positive results it is necessary to
treat natural communities as such. As he says: "Within the ethnical
horizon it is the social organism and not its components that counts"
(Bastian, 1881:71). And it might be added whether that social organism is the most or least civilized race (Gumplowicz, 1875: sect. 7).

> "The problems which agitate the life of the most highly
> developed races should be apparent in embryonic form
> even among the lowest savages; and since it is so much
> easier to note all characteristic points quickly and correctly
> in such small and transparent organisms, they should help
> us to understand the more complicated wonders of creation
> and to reduce legitimate data to law."

It would be impossible to comprehend the intellectual genesis
of the "more complicated wonders of creation" without resorting
to the smallest organisms.

> "While modern races, like crystals clear and polished and
> radiant with beauty, stand out in history in such definite
> proportions that scientific measurement is quite possible;
> in the ethnology of savage races, we deal with a chaotic
> seething mass [*Eine wüst und verworren gährende Mut-
> terlauge.*] which, however, applying a chemical metaphor to
> folk thought, holds primary mental elements in solution."

These are what Bastian wants. To seek through the great variety
of living forms the earliest germinal stages of the "primary mental
elements" and to watch them growing into folk-thought is the task
of his ethnology. He has a noble object before him and, with true
and justifiable enthusiasm, he proclaims the way and the grand
vision that will meet the astonished eye when it is reached.

> "After we know the law of development, it is possible to
> take a perfected product and trace the stages backwards to
> the starting point, the relative beginning. Many historical
> principles have thus been established. Microscopic analy-
> sis may proceed even to the cellular basis of ethnology,
> wherein reliable facts may be obtained concerning the con-
> ditions precedent to existence, concerning the enigma of
> being and becoming. Hitherto the investigation has been
> purely philosophical; hereafter psychological inductions
> will be used . . . Diving into the stream of thought, we shall
> only raise the secrets of mysticism from the dark depths;
> but having the skeletal race-thoughts objectively before
> us, we can handle, measure and study them and, by suffic-

ient analysis, reason back to the law of development in thought itself" (Bastian, 1881: 76).

This law should explain everything, but it can be learned only from the "primary elemental thoughts of savage races and the changes they undergo."

> "In contrast with narrow ideas of history and the early efforts to attribute religious and social similarities to presumed intercourse in the past, the idea must arise, as the geographical horizon was extended and material increased, that the task of ethnology is to go back to the elementary laws of development in race-psychology; and then to make as much allowance for the admitted causes and only so much as topographical reasons require" (Bastian, 1881: 119).

We have perhaps dwelt too long on Bastian's *History* and *Folk-Thought*. Yet the fundamental sociological principles and methodological suggestions contained in them cannot be overvalued. These two works are positively epoch-making in sociology. It might have been expected that he would have carried out his ideas in the *Principles of Ethnology*, which soon appeared. It might have been expected that, after collecting material for thirty years and after preparing himself by such deep reflections on the character, problem and object of ethnology and "ethnic sociology," he would have finally given us an elaborate presentation of the science. But unfortunately he has not fulfilled this reasonable expectation. Our previous remark is confirmed. The abundance of the material interferes, preventing a clear and complete treatment of the *principles* of the science.

The most that the later work furnishes seems scanty beside the plan he projected in the two former studies. Not that the chapters seem deficient in form and matter; but six (!) chapters treating six topics do not comprise all the points which should at least be enumerated among the *principles* of the science. Bastian treats in succession (1) geographical provinces, incidentally touching on the question of the unity of the human race; (2) implements, the first agencies of civilization; (3) property, the foundation of political order; (4) marriage; (5) rights, and (6) religion. But what of phenomena so essential to "ethnic sociology" as, slavery, sovereignty, state and society, political economy, commerce and the like? Where is there the least intimation of social development in local centers of civilization? The development of single institutions, like property, gives no idea of the development of human societies themselves, which in "ethnic sociology" is the most important thing. This is Bastian's weak point. He is so absorbed with minutae that he loses sight of the object as a whole. There is also another mistake, mathematical, it might be called. He states the sociological problem incorrectly, and consequently cannot obtain the correct solution. Starting "from one given point," which falsely held to be the soul, he wants to explain the social development of human societies as the result of *thought*. "In the beginning was the thought." *Thought* grows and develops; all phenomena are but variegated forms of thought, changing with time and circumstances.

Strange that Faust's misgivings did not warn him: " *In the Beginning was the thought/This first line let me weigh completely/ Lest my impatient pen proceed too fleetly/It is the thought which works, creates, indeed?*" Had he taken to heart the deep meaning of the poet's words: *"In the Beginning was the act,"* he would have come closer to the sociological problem.

Much as he afterwards tried, he never succeeded in eradicating idealist philosophy even from his latest works. At bottom he is always a "folk-psychologist," seeking the cause of all social phenomena in the "soul" of each race, but (we speak not of combatting idealism with narrow materialism) do we not regularly see that it is always the act which excites reflection? Does not the thought follow? The act is produced by natural forces that have no connection with the soul. Man acts according to natural law and thinks humanly afterwards, notwithstanding the approved maxim, "first think, then act," the worth of which for the individual we would never challenge. Social development and the behavior of communities is another thing. Blind natural forces prevail; there is no thought, no reflection, always an onward tendency following eternal laws and manifested in the form of acts. Then the act creates the thought which the idealist terms the "soul" of the actor as "motive" of the act. As the acts arising from unitary natural laws are harmonious and regular, so are the thoughts. Hence, the law of the regular growth of folk-thought, Bastian's psychology of race. But we would not in the least deprecate Bastian's services by these criticisms. For perhaps no one human being has done so much for social science as he.

8. Lippert

We had to say of Bastian that finding so many trees he fails to see the forest or, at least, does not let us see it. Now we come to a younger writer, who manages his material masterfully and works the great array of scattered ethnological data into great mosaics. Julius Lippert always presents the whole object in broad contours.

He began with a special department of sociology, comparative religion, and has advanced in fact, if not in name, to sociology in the best sense of the word. His first two books, on *Soul Worship* and *Systems of Religion,* were thoroughly reviewed in *Der Rassenkampf.* Let us recall briefly that in them he clearly and convincingly establishes a universal law of the origin and development of religion, thus laying a totally new and a sociological foundation for its scientific study (Lippert, 1881a; and 1881b).

Undisturbed by the ill-natured criticisms of the *Literarisches Centralblatt,* this very productive author has since enriched science, and especially sociology, by two valuable works: *The History of the Family,* and *General History of the Priesthood.* He possesses a great talent for tracing the development of social or psycho-social institutions through the history of all races and ages. His history of the family is a model of sociological composition.

> "Every man considers his family organization the normal human form and is prejudiced in favor of the writer who treats it thus. But that is not looking at history objectively."

Then after gratefully recognizing the services of Bachofen, the discoverer of "mother-right," and showing us the original mother-family, "organized upon the basis of mother-love," he goes on to show the rising "father-right" and the older father-family, "not resting on the principle of kinship or any consciousness of it, but on the principle of might, sovereignty and possession." (Lippert, 1884:5; also see Gumplowicz, 1881: sect. 30). Finally he shows the latest phase of development, the "younger father-family—in which

the terms father and son have come to imply consanguinous relationship" (*Cf.* Bachofen, 1861).

He raised Bachofen's theory of mother-right, which several
writers have since accepted, beyond all further doubt, adducing
"rudiments in use and custom," and "allusions in myth and saga."
In this way he threw much light upon primitive groups and the
organization of human societies in which "stranger and enemy are
synonymous terms" and "all are strangers who are not united by
ties of blood or marriage to the same small organization" (*Cf.* Gumplowicz, 1883:195; and 1881: sect. 19).

He discovers that there was a prehistoric variety of the family
in Germany "later than the one with maternal succession," one in
which the man is "lord of herds and slaves," "the woman belongs to
the man as a part of his possessions" and "her children are his not
simply if and because he begat them, but because the mother is
his" (Lippert, 1884:95). This "ancient family" goes hand in hand
with a "developed system of slavery," for the latter "proceeds undeniably from rising father-right" in the older sense (*Ibid*, 141).

He shows various intermediate stages between the older and
the younger father-family.

"Whether the old union shall be preserved or dissolved into
separate families, depends on occupation and property-relations
largely; but eventually the question arises everywhere" (*Ibid*, 221).
Later, we shall consider whether he has made it perfectly clear that
the motives he alleges are sufficient to produce the change. But
it must be recognized that he was the first, so far as we know, to
prove that this is the course of development and to attach importance to it. He was the first to call attention to the contrast between
the older family and the younger one in which we live. This is no
ordinary service, for the problem was a difficult one. "Have we
any idea," he asks justly, "we who are wont to think that family
relations are natural and have always existed, have we any idea by
what tortuous, weary paths mankind reached this form of existence?"
(*Ibid*, 216). He has pointed them out with great clarity. The task
of the future will be to investigate each stage of the long way in
detail.

Lippert's third sociological problem, the priesthood, surpasses,
if that were possible, both the others in scope and difficulty. For it

is intimately connected with almost everything that is sociologically important. The priesthood, as a body, has always and everywhere striven to control all spheres of social life; so that its history necessarily involves considerations of the most important of them: religion, custom, rights, sovereignty, state and society, etc. He did not shrink before the difficulties of the task but has produced a significant sociological work which is a pioneer in several directions.

He starts with the same theory that the root of all religions is in "soul-worship" and that religious ceremonies are derived from religious conceptions.

> "Especially is it a fact that the unseen is not thought of as a natural force, even when manifested in a natural effect; but it is conceived to be a personal spirit analogous to the human soul. The savage is utterly unable to comprehend a natural force; but as soon as he begins to think logically every death suggests the idea of a personal spirit. It is only by grasping this fact firmly that we can see how religious observances, however complex, originate in human logic and how the unity of the latter explains the essential similarity of the former even to the remotest corners of the earth" (Lippert, 1883-84:13).

This citation indicates the plan of the work and justifies the method of general treatment adopted. At bottom, Bastian's thought is the same; but his terms, racial-soul and folk-thought, are less clear than Lippert's plain "unity of human logic." Since human logic, when stimulated by one and the same fact, soul-worship, cannot conceal its character even in the complex texture of religious observances, it must be universally demonstrable that the principle underlying them is unitary; and this Lippert has succeeded in doing by separately describing the life of groups. For though soul-worship originated everywhere in the most primitive human logic, its development varied with the kind and degree of social life in each group. It would be impossible for us here to present the development of the priesthood in detail, the world over, as he does or discuss the purely sociological questions involved. But his view on the question fundamental to all sociology, the origin of political organizations, must be presented because it differs essentially from that which we have hitherto defended and upon which we base the present work. While we hold that every political organization, and hence every developing civilization, begins at the moment when one horde permanently subjugates another. And while we do not hesitate to recognize that the most cruel and barbarous conquerors are the blind instruments of human progress and powerfully promote civilization, nay, even found it; Lippert sees nothing but the victory of "barbarism" over "civilization" in the undeniable fact that states are founded by conquest. He holds that civilization begins and grows in "peaceful" companionship within the primitive horde, defending the view warmly and decrying the opposing view attributed to the "school-books." We are free to confess that his views enlist our sympathies; we would gladly accept them in preference to our own if we could be convinced of their truth. But we will reserve the discussion until later, simply citing some of his statements here.

> "Mexican history is full of tales of invasion, but in every case dominion fell to the rude sons of barbarism. Not one of the conquering races, Toltecs, Chichimecs, and Aztecs in turn, brought civilization to the charming land of Anahuac. Rather, the old tragedy was oft repeated. The races which had been hundreds and perhaps thousands of years in rearing a civilization in their upland valleys are the 'good housewives' of history, of whom nobody speaks. But the Bedouins, repeatedly breaking in from the wilderness of barbarism, often beaten off, but finally victorious, made civilized man with all his skill their slave, and they are praised as the creators of it all. In the school-books they are called the founders of civilization, as if they had brought it from the wilderness. The sympathizer with those quiet and ceaseless workers, the lineage of peace, must be satisfied if the object of his regard is not accused of the most profligate 'corruption' which a healthy breeze from the desert needs blow away. Fortunately the conquerors do not always want to destroy all of it. They are ready to adopt the most serviceable parts and even to increase and extend them by the power of organization" (Lippert, 1883-84: I, 288).

Lippert makes no secret of the fact that his judgment is influenced by sympathy with the conquered; which makes his opinion less objective. Moreover, he concedes to the "rude sons of barbarism," a "power of organization" sufficient to "increase and extend"

* *Ibid.*, Vol. i, p. 288.

the civilization of the "lineage of peace." We are thankful for both the confession and the concession. Later we shall have occasion to show that "power of organization" is an invaluable trait of the "rude sons of barbarism" and that the "lineage of peace," after being powerfully organized, will add not "sand upon sand" but block upon block, to rear a civilization. But reserving the discussion, let us hear further evidence in support of his views.

Historians have generally followed Garcilasso de la Vega in dating the beginning of Peruvian civilization from the time when the Incas conquered the ancient Peruvians and founded a kingdom. Lippert discards this conception and agrees with the views of the English traveler Hutchinson, who is "convinced from personal inspection that we are here dealing with a civilization that began long before the time of the Incas and progressed gradually." Lippert adds that "this opinion will doubtless gain ground." He believes himself justified in considering that the government of the Incas, as well as that of the Toltecs and Chichimecs, was "the dominion of an energetic conqueror over races that had already founded a settled civilization." This may be the case, however, without justifying Lippert's theory. Everywhere we see repeated instances of civilized states subjected by more or less "barbarous" conquerors; as China was by the Mongols and Roman Italy by the Goths and other German tribes. The Incas were not necessarily the first conquerors, the "Anglo-Saxons" of Peru; they may have been its Normans. This argument alone is not sufficient to confirm Lippert's theory of the *generatio aequivoca*, the problematic genesis, of civilization.

Again, ancient Egypt is cited. The historical events seem to Lippert not "essentially different from those which welded the Peruvian state together." But they may be explained in more than one way and, it seems to me, justify Lippert's views even less than the Peruvian and Mexican cases cited.

> "As there the low country on the holy lake, so here the rich delta lands of the holy river between desert and wilderness first invited permanent occupation. The races in the delta, pressed by the nomadic hordes to the border of the sea, had to sustain life in permanent settlements by provident labor; they subdued the waters and made the first stride toward civilization, learning to feel their higher human value in comparison with the barbarians."

Let us not forget that Lippert is here speaking of the object of his sympathy:

> "We may assume," he continues, "that there was in antiquity a like number of small tribes leading a pastoral life and cultivating a piece of land incidentally, as many modern Africans do, yet never leaving a certain definite territory. The fertility of the inundated lands permitted such an arrangement and the 'red-land' of the desert remained the home of the nomads."

After this rather apodictic description of the settlement of the "lineage of peace" on the lowlands of the Nile, he continues somewhat dubiously:

> "Naturally we do not know how the lowland races of antiquity became politically united. But the union might very well be due to the advance of the nomadic hordes which even to-day sweep over the plains and neighboring deserts. Certain it is that in historical times, as well as in prehistoric Mexico, tribes of higher civilizations have been united politically under the sovereignty of tribes of younger civilizations; among whom the tribes spreading over both plain and desert must doubtless be reckoned" (Lippert, 1883-84: I, 380).

However much we may sympathize with Lippert's theory, is this statement of the facts sufficient to convince us of its correctness? He is unable to explain "how the prehistoric lowland races became united politically." We should explain, though only by analogy from historical experience, that political union and organization were in all probability due to subjection by the "sons of barbarism." This is not a pleasant explanation either to Lippert or to us; but it seems to be the only correct one. We hold that sociological laws prevail unchanged whether we have historical evidence of the fact or not. Applying Lyell's geological method to sociology, we should say that the "sovereignty" of the "rude sons of barbarism" was necessary to organize the "lineage of peace" and to cause the succeeding development of civilization (*Cf.* Gumplowicz, 1883:172 *et. seq.*). As Lippert concedes that he knows no explanation, he should not take it amiss when we say that his theory is simply an interpretation of the facts dictated by sympathy with one party and consequent antipathy toward the other. But we leave the question unsettled. It is possible that in some lands civilization arose from the subjection of one tribe to another and that in other lands it was autogenetic in the "lineage of peace." However, autogenesis is contrary to the experience of historical times and needs to be established beyond a doubt.

This indication of the contents of Lippert's work must suffice. It is not possible even to trace the course of his investigations into the development of the priesthood, much less to do justice to the many historical and sociological questions which he treats from new standpoints. He is master of the art of giving life and artistic shape to the sociological material which others have collected. With that we must stop.

Comte, Spencer, Bastian and Lippert are the leading figures in sociology. What others have done is of secondary importance and will be mentioned incidentally as the discussion proceeds. But we must speak of several whole branches of science which concern sociology more or less intimately and cooperate to prepare the ground for it in various ways.

9. Mohl, Gneist and Stein

First in order are economics and politics, from which it was very difficult to get an adequate conception of society. What Mohl, Gneist and Stein did in this direction, we have duly pointed out elsewhere (Gumplowicz, 1877: sect. 12; and 1881; sect. 15-28). It is only necessary to recall that these scientists conceived society to be preponderantly economic. Especially Stein has only "economic" groups of men in mind though, to be sure, he is thinking of their relation to the state as political power "above society." This simple economic conception of society, partial as it is in view of social questions, pervades political economy so thoroughly as to make it in common speech *the* social science. Carey's *Principles of Social Science,* wherein he handles only political economy simply, had the same effect. Bärenbach, in his bibliographical sketch of the social sciences, chiefly treats political economists, noting their relation to "social questions" in particular. Likewise Menger, discussing the *Method of the Social Sciences,* only treats the method of political economy, which he looks upon as preeminently, *the* social science. In spite of this narrowness, the great sociological importance of political economy should not be overlooked. It was the first science that recognized that men's actions, when specifically considered, were controlled by economic laws. Seeing that the regular transitions from one economic phase to another were determined by external factors, political economists were forced to accept the idea of development in accordance with law. What is still more important, political economy had in the nature of the case to treat not individuals, who might evade every rule and law, but social groups: landlords, manufacturers, merchants, artisans, laborers, agriculturists, etc. So political economy became the best school for sociology; and economic thought led the way to sociological thought.

10. Carey and Post

The connection between political economy and sociology nowhere appears so prominently as in Carey's works. But this is due to his versatility. His field of view extends far beyond the simple economic events of social life. The man who defended the unity of science in Comte's sense and strove to demonstrate it in all the phenomena of life, could not be content to consider economic events exclusively. He made very instructive digressions on various sociological matters (Carey, 1857-67).

The socialists also were pioneers in sociology. They pointed out that the relations between laboring and propertied classes, between large and small industries, etc., develop in conformity to law (Gumplowicz, 1881: bk. ii).

Next to political economy, the science of comparative law has accumulated the most valuable sociological material and awakened the most fundamental ideas. Since every domain of social life fashions its own rights, this science embraces the whole social order and every domain may be considered from its point of view.

Sporadic attempts at scientific comparison long since demonstrated that, among the most various people of ancient and modern times, similar rights rise and develop analogously to a degree that is inadequately explained by assuming historical relationship and transfer of ideas. We have seen how Bastian protests and offers instead an explanation based on the psychology of race. In any event reflective comparison suggests that rights develop according to law; and from this idea it is only a step to a Natural Law and a *Natural Science of Rights,* as Post called his earliest writings (Post, 1867;

and 1872). In them he presented the physical idea that "the world's history is the unfolding of material forces by the specialization of universal types." But as he worked at the problem incessantly year after year he emancipated himself from this idea so that, in another series of writings, he made a very objective compilation of interesting material for a comparative science of law. The subtitles of these works are characteristic of the general course of his ideas. While the first in 1875 and 1876, were introductory contributions to a "universal comparative science of rights," he offers in 1880-81 material for a "comparative ethnological basis" for the science, and in his latest work, in 1884, attempts to construct "a universal science of rights on a sociological basis" (Post, 1875; 1876; 1878, 1881; and 1884). Thus we see that from all sides, ethnology, political economy, and comparative law, scientific ideas tend toward sociology and help to establish it.

However, traces of his "physical" views of the science still appear. In most of his works he advances the idea of "species-organism," an order of structure higher than natural organisms. We cannot accept any such idea, because there is no reality behind it. But we shall not dispute him since he uses the term less and less frequently and drops it altogether in his latest work.

With this correction, we can accept his views of the development of juridical and political life. "There are definite laws for the development of every organic structure within the human race and above individuals," for the development of human communities, we should add: "and they can be discovered by comparing the corresponding periods of development of all the species-organisms which are living or have lived on the earth. It is the first task of the future political and juridical science to determine them" (Post, 1876:7).

He distinguishes several phases in the history of the "species-organism," the first of which he calls a "kith and kin"—or peace—or confederation [Geschlechtsgenossenschaft].

"The most primitive form of organization in the life of the human species is the confederation of kith and kin, a number of men leagued together, on the basis of common blood, for offense and defense."

This forcibly recalls the social contract. We should substitute in its stead the simple primitive horde as the first natural recog-

nizable act. It is neither an alliance, which implies a previous state
or act of separation, nor an "offensive and defensive" alliance, which
would imply a social contract. Yet, with a slight correction, the
"kith and kin" confederation might stand as the most primitive
social formation, if Post's statement of its development into higher
social forms could be accepted. But that is difficult, for he neither
explains development nor shows on what it is based, but presents
it as spontaneously following an inner law.

> "Every form of organization," he writes, "proceeds from
> this and can be traced back to it. The kith and kin confed-
> eration is the normal form of organization in hunting and
> nomadic races and by growth from within outward is often
> extended beyond the narrow circle originally included until
> it has become a system of tribes or a race with institutions
> considerably developed" (Post, 1876:11).

This is not clear. Such development never takes place by
"growth from within outward." Besides Post takes no account of
the motives and factors impelling it. "When the kith and kin confederation adopts a settled life its old constitution decays to a
certain degree." How it becomes settled does not worry him. "It
takes place, the confederation decays," he says, content that there
is some "law" behind the changes. But such statements are unsatisfactory, to the sociologist at least. Although Post's services in the
domain of juridical science must be recognized and although he has
industriously collected suitable material and tirelessly called for
sociological investigations, his treatment of social development is
not thorough. It shows that he has no clear idea of what social
development is. Even his latest work on the *Basis of Rights and the
History of Their Development*, though clearer and indicating progress in every direction, is still unsatisfactory on this point. We can
overlook his old gambit, that "the human race, like every organic
race on our planet, constitutes a biological organism" (Post, 1884:
16). Yet we must reproach him for retaining, even in his latest
work, the fundamentally false views of social development criticised
above, especially as the literature of the subject ought to have helped
him to make many corrections. He says, for instance, that:

> "a number of individuals descended from a common parent
> or parents, affords a nucleus from which a tribe may arise.

As the off-spring grow up, the procreative process is continued and the tribe becomes a union of tribes. After a number
of generations, we speak of a race, then of a people, then
of allied peoples" (Post, 1884:75).

But what scientific proof does he offer? The same naive idea under-
lies the Biblical story and leads with infallible logic back to Adam
and Eve. Or is it a scientific explanation of development to say
that "with the decay of common tribal life the mutual rights and
duties of the individual members are differentiated." And that after
the "gradual decay of original universal common life, the human
individual by degrees becomes endowed with right, which "slowly
develop in times of peace" (Post, 1884:83-87). These are simply
vague propositions about unclear ideas; consequently they make
nothing clear.[9]

But in spite of its defective presentation we must be grateful
for the material which Post has accumulated. He also deserves full
recognition for tirelessly disseminating the idea of a natural science
of law, of a comparative ethnological science of law, and finally
of social science. He conceives the social problem quite in Bastian's
sense however.

"The great fundamental thought of modern social science
is to discover the essential nature of the human mind from
what it has deposited in the several domains of race-life.
Sociological jurisprudence searches for the essential nature
of the human juridical consciousness in what it has deposited in the juridical views and institutions of all races of the
earth."

With Post as with Bastian, the "mind," or "consciousness" is the
primary, the world-moving principle, so to speak, the object of all
investigation; and social phenomena are only means of exploring
this innermost cause of all that happens. We shall soon have an opportunity to demonstrate our view that what happens of natural
necessity is primary and emits "mind" as flowers do fragrance.
Juridical institutions are not grounded in juridical consciousness.

[9] This sentence might also be cited: "Nevertheless, as the tribal state gradually develops, differences of rank also appear." (Post, 1884: 102). If everything developed gradually without our needing to know why and how, we should
be done with sociology at once.

On the contrary, the latter is grounded upon the former. History begets the mind, not the mind history.

11. Philosophers of History

Political economy and the comparative study of law and religion concern particular domains of social life and hence anticipate only parts of sociology. There are other branches of philosophy, however, which have treated the supreme problem of sociology itself, or at least its most important principle, though not under that name.

Here we will mention only the philosophy of history. It deals with the historical development of mankind; its object is to seek the "philosophical idea." It is clear how closely it approaches the supreme problem of sociology; and the sociological importance of its literature is self-evident.

Pretty much everything written on this subject before 1876 is summed up in Rocholl's prize essay. Rocholl has mastered the art of letting all the philosophers of the world speak through him, while he betrays not a single original thought to the acutest reader. A whole volume, and nothing original! He understands how prizes are won. Whoever is curious to see all that philosophers would interpret into the history of mankind should read this book. Either it will make the reader dizzy; or, he will think that Rocholl is exhibiting a fools' gallery. In fact, the philosophy of history had an untimely birth. The "idea in human history" was spoken of before anyone half understood what human history was. What is a fraction of Mediterranean history compared with all the actual history of man on this planet of which the philosophers knew nothing. How childish any opinion on the whole when they knew only the least part!

Yet the stimulus of their sociological ideas is considerable. The most important difference between sociology and the philosophy of history is that the latter would deliver an opinion on that which it did not know; whereas sociology, being aware that the whole can never be known, will judge only of a process which is the same here and everywhere, which transpires in the same way today before our eyes as it transpired thousands of years ago. Sociology declines in advance to interpret the whence, the whither and the wherefore. This is its claim to decided preeminence over the philosophy of history, from whose failure it learns valuable lessons.

The transition from philosophy of history to sociology was more direct in France than elsewhere. In Germany the so-called history of civilization intervened. The history of human civilization from its beginning to the present day is almost, at least might easily become, sociology. Kolb, Henne am Rhyn, and especially Hellwald, have accomplished much in this field, correcting many things that the philosophers had spoiled. They introduced a wholesome soberness into the concept of human development. The indefatigable Hellwald makes use of all sorts of anthropological and ethnological material, extending the horizon of the history of civilization even to the ultimate beginning of prehistoric time. The investigations of Lubbock, Tylor and Caspari in this field are especially helpful; and in anthropology and ethnology, Waitz-Gerland, Perty and Peschel have contributed their share of valuable sociological material.

Thus, there is no lack of material. And with Comte, Spencer, Bastian and Lippert imparting the breath of life to sociology, may it never lack for disciples to labor in it and cherish it unremittingly.

12. LeBon

The rise of sociology in our day from anthropology, ethnology, the study of prehistoric times, and the history of civilization, is easily explainable. First anthropology simply treated physical man and the chief races of mankind. Ethnography constantly added new material from the living human world and raised the number of varieties almost to infinity. Then prehistoric man was studied in order, from his condition, to explain the phenomena of historic man. Making the phenomena of prehistoric civilization the subject of their investigations, scholars passed unexpectedly from this introduction into the history of civilization as a whole, treating also the later period of the same subject. But at last it appeared that all four disciplines were merely descriptive, furnishing material for a science of man which, if it would be a science, must, for the reasons laid down, be concerned not with the individual, but with social groups and societies. In this way it becomes sociology. But the principal difference between these four disciplines and sociology is that the latter is in no sense descriptive; but, based upon materials from the former, undertakes scientific investigation in order to establish scientific laws.

While various authors have severally set forth the disciplines named with more or less significant digressions into neighboring spheres, Gustave LeBon, in a noteworthy book, *L'Homme et les Societies, leurs Origines et leur Histoire* (LeBon, 1881), gives the chief features of them all, together with a thoughtful presentation of sociology in Part Two based upon them, so that his work presents to view the entire course of scientific development beginning with anthropology and ending with sociology.

In the first part LeBon simply gives short sketches of the sciences preliminary to sociology. After an "Introduction" into the changes in our knowledge and opinions, in which the author shows that he is at once a monist and a positivist in the best sense, he subjects the "Universe," in Book I, to a rigid realistic examination. In Book II "The Origin and Evolution of Living Creatures" is portrayed according to the theory of Darwin and Haeckel. Book III, entitled "The Physical Evolution of Man," gives a description of anthropology and prehistory. It treats primitive man, the formation of races and the several prehistoric ages according to the usual divisions. Book IV, "The Mental Evolution of Man," gives a sketch of psychology on a physiological basis. Upon the broad foundation of such treatises on these wide-ranging sciences which have to do with the universal and the individual, LeBon constructs his sociology which occupies the second part of his work.

Aside from Book I of Part Two, which simply contains a special introduction to sociology ("Sociology and its Limits, Uses and Methods"), the substance of what he has to say falls into two books: "Factors of Social Evolution," Book III, and "The Development of Societies," Book IV. However excellent everything LeBon offers us in these two books, however willing we are to subscribe to most of the sociological views and considerations which he advances, still we must say that in spite of the breadth which he has given to his sociology, there is a very serious mistake in its superstructure. He has missed the real subject matter of sociology and has not really found a single sociological law although he set out with that purpose. A detailed examination will confirm our judgment.

LeBon first treats "The Factors of Evolution." What he understands them to be appears from the titles to the several chapters on the influence of *milieu*, of intelligence and feelings, of the acquisition of language, of commercial relations, of the progress of industry, of literature and art, of the struggle for existence, of the development of military institutions, of the knowledge of agriculture and the growth of population, of stability and variation, of race, of the past and heredity, of illusions and religious ideas, of politics and administration, of education and instruction. Without doubt these are very important questions touching the sphere of sociology. But these "influences" are in no sense "factors" acting on them. The factors of social evolution, as has been shown, are the social groups themselves, and they are influenced by the physical and moral agencies surrounding them which LeBon, as shown, enumerates correctly. It is a mistake to confuse these conditions, these influences and agencies, with the real factors or subjects. So LeBon in the chapter on "Factors of Evolution" really says nothing that he had not already said in Part One where, speaking of the development of the individual, he showed the influence of these same agents and circumstances upon it. Hence, the author cannot escape repetitions, in spite of his great literary skill and his evident pains to present the same thing in different lights and to illustrate it by a great variety of examples. They follow necessarily from the faulty design of his sociology, false because too limited and scanty. Thus for example, he elaborates in Part One, upon "The Physical Condition of the First Human Beings." In Part Two, Book II, on "The Factors of Social Evolution," he is forced to return to the same theme and treats the "Existence of the First Human Beings" again in connection with the "Influence of *Milieu* upon Social Evolution." To be sure he strives here in Part Two to relate other details about primitive man. But the subject is the same and what is said in the second part could have been said pertinently in the appropriate place in the first part.

Again another illustration: In Part Two LeBon treats the "Past and Heredity" as a factor of social evolution. But he treated the same thing in part one in connection with the "development of instinct" in the individual, where he speaks of "habits gradually modified and preserved by heredity." In short LeBon knows no factors of "social evolution" to present other than the same agents and forces which influence the individual.

In the second half he does not fare much better. Here too, the

contents do not correspond with what the title promises. The latter
reads as had been mentioned: "Development of Societies;" and what
do the several chapters offer us instead? First comes "development
of language." Is language a society? No doubt language has a great
influence upon the development of society. But can the development
of language for that reason be regarded as the development of
society?

The same is true of the chapters on the development of religion,
morals, rights, industry and agriculture (chapters iv-vii). The last
is an economic phenomenon. The others are simply psycho-
social. Their development is conditioned by that of societies.
Their development presupposes social development and this in
turn exerts a certain influence upon it. Yet the development
of religion, morals, rights, etc., is not that of societies. So Le-
Bon has not offered us here what he wished to and what sociology
ought to provide. He undoubtedly came nearer solving the real problem in the two chapters on the development of the family and of
property (chapters ii and iii). For as we shall see both these institutions are eminently social and immediately connected with social
development, rising directly from it, forming indeed an essential
part of it. Only he should have presented them in this connection
as we shall demonstrate. He has indeed done so in part but not
entirely. Though LeBon does not present each phase in the development of these institutions as the direct result of the contact and
reciprocal effect of unlike social groups, yet he makes a beginning
at seeking the cause of change in these institutions in such transformations as alterations in the relations of the social ingredients to
each other. For example, he inquires (Pt. ii, 294) how maternal,
kinship passed into paternal kinship? How the father became the
head of the family? He answers the question correctly on the whole.
"It seems to me," he says, "that it (this transformation) must
have come to pass at the time when man began pastoral and agricultural life and had need of slaves to aid him at his work. Instead
of killing his prisoners he kept them to aid him and became the sole
proprietor of those he had conquered, of the women especially." Here
LeBon's acumen led him aright, even though he did not take for his
starting point the reciprocal action of unlike social groups as the
only impelling factor in all aspects of social development. Indeed

had he done so, he would not only have hit upon that transformation in the form of the family correctly, but he would also have
turned the right key to solve the no less difficult problem of
changes in property. But as it is, he stands helpless and at a loss before it. This time the lucky idea did not occur to him. He knows
that "property has not always existed in the form in which we know
it today. The idea that soil, air or light could belong to any one
could not have been comprehended by our first ancestors; and mankind had to complete the greater part of its cycle before this notion
could arise." But in what way, what impelling causes did the change
in property, or better the establishment of private property, take
place? LeBon cannot explain. He is confronted with a conception
that arose in the human brain one fine day, an idea that sprang up
suddenly. "When agriculture had become known and mankind
already had an immense past behind it, a very long time had still
to elapse before the idea of personal property appeared. The ground,
like the women, belonged at first to all the members of a community.
Only very slowly did it become the property, at first temporarily
and then permanently, of a family and then of an individual." Thus
we see that without any attempt whatever to explain the causes of
these changes in property, he here simply takes refuge in that phrase
with which we have become acquainted: i.e., "it arose gradually."
Doubtless everything arose gradually, but how? In what way? It is
the task of sociology to explain.

The fundamental failure in the construction of his sociology
is that his framework does give us any explanation. If he
had comprehended that the first and most important sociological
task was to investigate the mutual relations and reciprocal effects
of unlike social groups, he would himself necessarily have
found out that changes in the family and in property are nothing
but the result of these reciprocal relations and effects. He would
have reached another result also which in the beginning of his undertaking he avowedly strives for but completely misses in consequence
of the entirely wrong path onto which he strode. We mean the
discovery of those "invariable laws knowing no exceptions," "fixed
and inexorable laws," which, as he quite correctly assumes, control
historical events as well as the evaporation of a drop of water or the
movement of a grain of sand. We find indeed, the recital of events

and developments conforming to law in the psycho-social sphere (language, religion, rights, morals, political economy and so forth), but of real social laws, of such laws as control the relations and reciprocal connections of social elements, we find not a trace.

In view of this, it is certainly characteristic of LeBon that he treats all secondary social phenomena, like language, religion, rights, etc., at great length but has not devoted a single chapter of his "social science" to the most important and primary social phenomenon, the state. This is indeed a gross and obvious omission, but it is also merely a consequence of the entirely mistaken basis of his sociology.

Nevertheless it must be recognized that LeBon's sociology is one of the most valuable achievements of scientific labor in this field. He is distinguished for thorough knowledge of all pertinent disciplines, a comprehensive view, and above all, for a sober unprejudiced mind. His work unquestionably forms an important landmark in the development of sociology. We greatly regret that in the foregoing discussions we have not been able to appeal to his frequently coinciding views, He would have provided welcome support on many a hazardous point.

Part II

Foundations and Fundamentals
of Sociology

1. The Three Classes of Phenomena

It is an old saying that division and classification are means to knowledge. The more appropriate the means, the greater is the profit that may be expected from their use. To this end all the phenomena surrounding us has been repeatedly classified. But with increasing knowledge, the plan of classification has to be changed. Deeper and deeper grounds of division are discovered, approximating more and more closely the very essence of the phenomena. A superficial examination served to distinguish animate from inanimate nature. According to another very common classification, the phenomena that were perceived by the organs of sense were put in one class and those that were perceived by the mental faculties were put in another; the former were called material, the latter mental phenomena.

As knowledge advanced, inanimate nature was divided into inorganic and organic. Then another class, composed of phenomena which were referred to as the soul of man in origin, was coordinated with the organic and characterized as psychic. Thus three classes, inorganic, organic, and psychic,[1] were obtained. It is apparent from the terminology itself what phenomena are included under each class. And it is just as clear that this classification is intimately connected with a given stage of human knowledge, with the knowledge of the

---

[1] To cite one example among thousands, Rumelin in his essay on the "Laws of History" ("Reden und Aufsaetze," *Neue Folge*: 118) speaks of "the phenomena of inanimate nature, of the organic and of the psychic world." We shall refer to this essay later in another connection.

distinction between inorganic and organic matter. It seemed desirable not to call organic matter simply "inanimate;" for the inorganic inanimate had to be distinguished. There was also a growing conviction that all of man's actions, his whole behavior, at least all the phenomena affected by him, have their basis in a soul (*psyche*) which is found in man and is peculiar to him. If convictions change on this point, if it is discovered that there is no such soul, that man's thoughts, and the whole of his so-called spiritual life is only a manifestation of the physiological functions of his organism, that basis of classification will be dropped. Psychic phenomena will be included within the organic.

Thus classification is a means of promoting knowledge. Knowledge acquired is, in turn, the basis of new and more accurate classifications. But it often happens that phenomena are forced upon our attention which we cannot immediately identify with any class hitherto known; we are not sure how to classify them. In such cases, we include them in some class already constituted, in spite of the differences, or we create a sub-class; or finally, having found some characteristic which is peculiar to them, we proceed to constitute a totally new class. A recent instance is furnished by the "social" phenomena. It was observerd that they differed from other phenomena. There were many reasons why they should be recognized as a special class. But nobody knew exactly what to do with them. They could not be included with either the organic or the inorganic. They presented the characteristics of neither the animate nor the inanimate; they did not seem to be purely psychic, for they did not emanate from the individual soul. Indeed, they appeared to sweep whole aggregates of men, in spite of will and consciousness, along with them. So they presented a problem of classification, the solution of which was attempted in various ways.

It was perceived that especially those phenomena which are manifested in the State, political revolutions, party conflicts, political endeavors, etc., are social. Some attempted to class them all with "organic" phenomena. It is really so comfortable in old quarters, where everything is familiar, that people will cramp themselves a little, if necessary, in order to avoid the trouble of moving! Hence arose the "organic" theory of the State. Schäffle has shown that all the so-called social phenomena are in reality nothing but "organic functions of the social body," which has cells, tissue, nerve, muscle, flesh, bones and blood, just like every animal organism. There are still people, not only in Germany but also in France, who accept this literally. We do not.

There were others who were less imaginative and more reflective, yet abhorred the overthrow of old and familiar arrangements no less than the former. They presented a theory that everything that takes place in connection with the State is manifestly done by man—for who else could do it? But whatever man does issues from the soul within him. Hence social phenomena are psychic. To be sure, a social occurence is different from an individual thought or feeling. But the difference can be disposed of by making a sub-class. Society is "psychic." Thus that estimable scholar, Rümelin (again from many examples citing the one we have first at hand), treats social phenomena as psychic and "social laws as a special kind of psychic law." (Rümelin, 1868:118,134).

But we can no more consent to subordinate social phenomena under the psychic than we can reckon them as organic. Rather it still seems proper to divide the phenomena which we perceive into three classes: physical, mental and social.

We classify social phenomena apart from all others because the ends of scientific investigation will be best served by treating them separately. They constitute a unique cluster, distinguished by several fundamental traits.

It is certain that they cannot be perceived by the senses, and there was thus good reason for grouping them with mental phenomena. But social phenomena happen only through the cooperation of a number of men of an aggregate; whereas mental phenomena, strictly so-called, are inseparable from the mind of the individual. They originate in it and are limited to it. Thus all conditions of the soul, all scientific activity, and each artistic manifestation of the human mind, all works in art and science—so far as the mind perceives them, all thoughts and ideas which, issuing from the human mind, are perceived by the mind, are mental phenomena. But all relations of men with one another, all their economic, political and juridical relations, for example, are social. A number or aggregate of men is its distinguishing trait.Without the group, *social* phenomena are impossible.

As the classification of phenomena is only an aid to knowledge, and since the world around us is strictly one and unitary, so, it is conceived, there is only one scientific method. For, as we have shown elsewhere (Gumplowicz, 1881: Pt. I, sect i; and 1877, sect i), the object of science is to discover the laws that control the sequence and development of phenomena. Yet the division of science into parts devoted to particular classes of phenomena is common and has been recognized as proper. It satisfies the need for a division of scientific labor. The division into "natural" and "moral" (or ethico-political) sciences is the best known and the most usual. It parallels the classification of phenomena into physical and mental.

The natural sciences dealt with the phenomena of organic and inorganic nature and with the physical laws governing them. The mental sciences sought to discover laws controlling the human mind. When Comte and Quetelet classified social phenomena for scientific study and asserted that they too were controlled by fixed laws, the question of defining social laws arose. It was not easy to explain what they were. Yet, if there is a science of social phenomena, if there is such a thing as sociology, we must be able to give a clear positive definition of social laws.

In order to define them we must recall what a natural law is. Applying our idea of a natural law in general to social phenomena, we shall get an idea of what a social natural law, or, briefly, a social law is in the abstract. Finally, we shall test the objections commonly raised to the existence of social laws. If they can be refuted we may enter the domain of social science. For to this we must hold fast: without social laws there can be no social science.

When we find the same phenomena time and again occurring together or in the same order, we say that it is due to a law. Obviously, we are using an analogy. When an act of legislation directs how a thing shall be done, it is uniformly done in the prescribed way. When, in nature, we see a phenomenon repeatedly occurring in the same form, we conceive that it is the result of some higher will incorporated in a "law," and we speak of the law of the phenomena without hesitation. We thus acquire for a series of phenomena an easily intelligible expression, a simple formula. (Mill, 1848: bk. III, ch. iv)

The question then arises: Can such laws be stated for social phenomena as well; in a word, are there social laws? We ought to answer in the affirmative if there are social phenomena which constantly occur together or in the same order, so that we may ascribe them to an hypothetical higher will, to a "law," as we do with physical phenomena. That the mutual deportment of social groups, the formation of social communities, their development and their decay so occur, history and experience prove undeniably. Hence, we may direct investigation in the social domain with a view to formulating the social laws of those events.

This matter is so simple and self-evident that there would seem to be no need of wasting any more words over it. But, unfortunately, it is not acknowledged by everybody. The formulation of social laws, that is, natural laws of social development, is violently opposed by those who are anxious to maintain man's free-will in its integrity. For it is feared that a death-blow would be dealt to it if natural laws of social development were generally accepted.

The struggle between these two principles, whether to apply natural law or free-will to social phenomena, is well illustrated by Rümelin. His candor deserves special recognition. In his earlier years this scholar was inclined to accept natural law in social phenomena which, as we have seen, he made a sub-class of the psychic. He expressed this view in an academic discourse. "On the Concept of Social Law" (Rümelin, 1868). After defining natural law in general to be "an elementary expression of the uniform behavior of force in each and every case," he questioned "whether this idea of law which is taken originally from the processes of inanimate nature is also applicable to the processes of animate nature," and answered in the affirmative, though with no great assurance.

> "As a result, we have found three kinds of forces, physical organic and psychic; no other kind can be conceived coordinate with them. Social phenomena are a sub-class of the psychic. There are two kinds of psychic phenomena, the psychological and the social."

He seems to concede almost without reserve that the phenomena of political economy are social. Since this science:

> "starts, expressly or tacitly, with the hypothesis that man has a strong inclination to supply himself plentifully and at

the least possible cost with the means of satisfying his desires, it seems quite proper that the fundamental propositions concerning competition, the movements of prices and
wages, and the circulation of money should be called laws.
They fulfill the requirements exactly. They indicate the elementary and uniform behavior of psychic forces in a mass
or aggregate."

As to whether the so-called statistical laws should be recognized
as social, Rümelin has serious doubts.

"Psychology considers the psychic forces observable in
typical individuals to be characteristic of the class. Social
science observes the same forces operating in aggregates of
individuals and notices the changes thus produced. Hence
social laws should express in elementary form the behavior
of psychic forces in aggregates."

But he is not certain that statistical laws satisfy these conditions.
Some weighty objections prevent him from recognizing that everything proclaimed by the statisticians to be law is social; and he is
perhaps right. He sees in the reasoning of the statistician, Quetelet,
especially, "significant truths and serious misunderstandings com-
pactly woven together." And in that, too, we will agree with him. He
concludes his *Search for Social Laws* unsatisfied. "The return was not
great." But that is no occasion for reproach. "The youngest sciences
are always the hardest," so he comforts the sociologists. "They treat
problems that others had quite overlooked or did not have the means
to grapple with." He has the "highest opinion of the future of
statistics, of the scientific value of a methodical observation of
facts, if continued and developed." In short, he does not give up
hope that real social laws may thereby be discovered, though he
does not conceal his misgivings. This was in 1868.

Ten years later he spoke again on the "laws of history," and
described the observations he had made in the meanwhile. The
scholar's disappointment is undisguised. The hopes he had cherished
a decade before had been completely dissipated. The serious doubts
he had entertained had been fully verified.

"I thought that there must be social laws, and that statistics
would be especially helpful in discovering them. I have had
the task constantly in mind for many years. I have sought
for them not simply in statistics and in the theory of society,
but in history and in philosophy too. I have fallen upon

numerous cases of uniformity, upon rules of experience of comprehensive import, upon positive causal connections; but never upon any thing answering to the formula for a law, never upon a proposition expressing the elementary, uniform behavior of psychic forces in an aggregate."

Then he explains why his search was futile. He is "inclined" to believe "that the problem was not properly stated and that what he sought is not susceptible of being found." The ultimate cause of failure he discovers in the fact that "physical and psychic phenomena differ from each other even as incomparable quantities."

"Between material existence and motion in space on the one hand, and feeling, thought and volition on the other, there is a chasm which cannot be filled and has not yet been bridged." Hence, "it would be strange if one and the same concept of law were applicable to both."

Thus we see Rümelin returning in his later years full sail into the sea of dualism. And it ought not to seem remarkable that, in tracing out the fundamental opposition between mind and matter, he should dispute the possibility of law in the province of the former since "man's free-will" prevails there. Then come the old arguments on the old theme.

"Whoever denies freedom of the will is bound to show natural laws determining will and excluding choice. It is said by some, for example, that the strongest motive must of necessity determine the human will. If this were something more than a worthless tautology; if it were only explained what besides the will could make a motive the strongest!"

Strange proposition! Why should external circumstances not make a strong enough motive? How can a *deus ex machina* named "will" strengthen a motive, *i.e.*, an external factor? The external factor works with an inherent force in given conditions as steam does in the locomotive. Must it be that will determines the force of steam in overcoming the force of inertia? No more in the case of man is this putative mediation and assistance of will necessary to strengthen a motive which is in and of itself the stronger already. Man differs from the locomotive only in having consciousness, *i.e.*, an inner sense which, like an inner eye, sees the internal processes, becomes conscious of them, observes the conflict of motives, and the victory of the stronger. In common experience this perception is mistaken for free-will; the resultant consciousness of the over-balance of the stronger motive, for the act of choice. All this was long since known. But it will not for a long time to come convert adherents of dualism and free-will. The force of mental inertia and conservatism cannot be so easily overcome.

Those who persistently maintain the dualism of mind and matter cannot possibly accept social laws in the sense of natural laws of social development. Hence Rümelin is thoroughly consistent in discarding them and every "law of history," too. He is perfectly logical when he says:

> "I must characterize the theory as self-contradictory and incomprehensible which imputes to the individual human soul freedom of the will, in the sense of rational or irrational self-determination within the broad scope of given natural conditions, while necessity is recognized in the history of mankind or of single ages and peoples. Psychological indeterminism and historical indeterminism stand and fall together . . . If the complex aggregate of social relations into which I have been put determines all my thinking and doing or allows me only the narrowest scope of individual independence, it is of no use to discuss freedom and accountability further. But if I am able of myself to initiate new series of operations, to mould and assert myself in spite of the opinions and usages of others, then no logic can prevent a community as a whole from acting freely and striking into paths which have no causal connection with the past. Necessity will then signify no more than the universal limits of human activity and will be restricted to the unavoidable influence of the community on the individual."

Persistence in the traditional dualistic view is also largely due to the mistaken idea that "the necessity of natural law" would negate "conscience" and all rational activity.

> "Or we are told" says Rümelin, further, "that the will is determined by necessity, being the product of two factors: the concrete circumstances and the individual character, which is itself the product of inherited faculties, training and course of life. If conscience and reason are included among the inherited faculties and it is conceded that they cooperate in their way in the act of willing the answer

may be accepted. But then it is merely a quarrel about words to speak of the deterministic character of natural law and the necessity of willing."

As if reason and mental effort could not be, were not actually the product of natural processes! As if we could not speak of the natural development of reason, mental effort and will, *i.e.*, of mental effort as the product of motives!

After traversing such errors, Rümelin reaches the principle which, as a true dualist, he believes he has "established," viz.: "that psychological and physical laws are wholly different in form and nature and cannot be expressed by the same formula."

As has been said, the logic is correct; but the premise of free-will and self-determination is false. Possibly Rümelin is justified in saying that the constraint exercised by society upon the individual has not yet been demonstrated to him by obvious proofs.

"I cannot convince myself that investigation into the relations between society and the individual has ever led a single step beyond showing an intimate and universal reciprocation of influences, in which each is giving or receiving, active or passive, all the time, in varying degrees."

But insufficient proof does not alter the fact of unfree-will. And it would be better to have become a philosopher to take the matter in hand himself than to assume the attitude of defense by throwing the burden of proof on others.

Had Rümelin done so without prejudice (his dualism greatly embarrassed him), he would have given up the false premise of free-will and all that it entails. He would not have discoursed at length on the way men of genius make the world's history. Such things should not have to be said at this late date in a German university, and by a lay professor. The standpoint which he maintains is purely and simply theological.

Dualism of mind and matter is a fundamental principle of religion. Religion is a necessity of the masses; their temperament demands it. So free-will and self-determination, the necessary consequence of dualism, are integral components of every religious system; and we have no thought of combatting them here. Moreover, modern philosophy and natural science have spared us the trouble of establishing monism, which is as correct and true as, for the temperament of most men, dualism is necessary. We are not writing for this majority. They may leave our book unread. We turn to the adherents of monism. Our problem is to work out its consequences in the social domain.

2. Universal Laws

Modern natural science has successfully demonstrated that even the "human mind" is subject to physical laws; that the phenomena of the individual mind are emanations from matter. But in the domain of social phenomena unvarying natural laws have not been completely demonstrated. Between "mental" phenomena subject to the laws of matter and the social world, strode the conception of human freedom to distract and confuse. It seemed to order and control social relations according to its own choice. In the domain of mental phenomena in the narrower sense of the word, monistic natural science has in part demonstrated the unconditional sway of natural laws and in part shown the presence of other factors to be impossible. Dualism, driven from this quarter, has retired to the domain of social phenomena, from which it must be dislodged. To this task the distinction which we have drawn between mental and social phenomena is essential; for it is an ancient rule of strategy to divide the enemy and grapple with the scattered sections separately. The critical question concerning monism is the existence of universal laws which are valid for social as well as for physical and mental phenomena. If such laws exist, the monistic theory is true. If such laws cannot be discovered, monism is an unproven hypothesis like dualism.

As we have seen, their existence is hotly denied and doubtless the earliest defenders of monism in the domain of social phenomena give substance to the denial. For with great zeal and less discretion some thought is absolutely necessary to transfer to social phenomena laws that had been discovered in physical phenomena. The laws of attraction and repulsion, of gravitation and the like. Others seemed to see in the shapes which social phenomena assumed, structures similar to animal organisms and they thought that the laws valid for the latter might be accepted as valid for the former also. We have already pointed out the impropriety of these assumptions and we shall criticize them in more detail later.

But in spite of such errors, there are universal laws which prevail in the physical, mental and social domain alike; and the existence of the science of sociology can be justified only by proving their existence and validity.

Before calling attention to some of them, we must answer another question. How far, in general, can we expect to find laws common to phenomena so unlike as physical, mental and social phenomena? Plainly we ought not to go too deeply into the characteristics of species. The fact is that where peculiarities begin common traits end. Where physical nature commences the laws common to the mental and social domain cease to apply.

Of course it may be objected that universal laws will be taken from such a high sphere of abstraction that every idea beyond the concept of mere existence will have been sacrificed. Such laws, though easily found, would lack significance. We shall try to find our universal laws close to where the three classes of phenomena become differentiated, in the sphere of the modalities of existence. Having found them here, we shall consider our task complete. It was the great error of our predecessors that they sought universal laws in the lowest sphere of one class alone, especially among the differentiated physical phenomena. We ought not to commit the same error. We must not seek to generalize the physical laws of organic life and extend them to psychic and social phenomena. We may, and indeed must, discover the universal laws of the modalities of existence of all being. We must be satisfied to possess in them the keys which to use Bastian's expression, "unlock in all directions." Let us now proceed to give examples of such universal laws.

(a) The Law of Causation

The law of causation is just as true of social as it is of physical and mental phenomena. Every social phenomenon is the necessary effect of anterior causes. No special phenomenon originates in the nothingness of individual whims. The principle of sufficient cause is also true. Every social phenomenon, whether political, juridical or economic, must have a sufficient cause in one or more social agencies. The effects must also be equal or at least proportional to the energy of the causes alike in the social, the physical and the mental domain. The deeds of an individual will never create a social condition nor change it, however much appearances may deceive us. One social condition is produced by another. The task which falls to the writer of pragmatic history is to point out the exact connection in each case.

(b) The Law of Development

Parallel with and perhaps emanating from the law of causation is the law of development. Each social phenomenon is a momentary phase in a period of development; though often the end of a period may be beyond the reach of calculation. Every political organization, all rights, every economic relation, undergoes change. We can distinguish the beginning, the process of growth and often the decline and decay.

But of course manifestations of this law in the social and in the physical domain must not be confounded. Cells, germs, stalks and fruit or eggs, embryo, lungs and digestive organs cannot be found in social formations. Such analogies lead away from the truth. They becloud scientific vision and give incorrect results. The order of development in the social domain is from one social phenomenon to another.

If we wish to obtain reliable scientific results in sociology, this distinction must be observed rigorously. No digression to manifestations of the law in other domains can be allowed.

(c) Regularity of Development

Development does not in and of itself involve the idea of regularity. The sequence of like or similar phases might or might not be uniform in all cases. Actual progress is regular and it conforms to law everywhere. We admire the regularity of development in the whole compass of physical nature. It dominates mental phenomena. It is found to be true of the state of law, of political economy, and of language which must also be included with the social sciences, since according to the definition given above, language is a social phenomenon. The great honor of discovering it in the domain of social phenomena is shared by the historical schools in the various disciplines.

(d) The Law of Periodicity

In all domains of phenomena, regularity of development passes into periodicity. Wherever we can watch the whole process we find a period of existence extending from the origin through the phases of growth and perfection to decline and fall. Of course the manifestation is different for each class of phenomena. Sap flows, the trunk grows strong, the organs develop, etc.; or, thought arises, is confirmed, is spread abroad and gains consideration—then loses influence and is recognized as insignificant; or, a social relation arises in small proportions, is extended over larger aggregates, procures ever greater recognition, exercises decisive influence on great masses, is then broken up and supplanted by other relations and disappears leaving no trace. This law is everywhere present and universally valid.

(e) *The Law of Complexity*

In physical nature we always find elements in combination, never isolated from each other. Likewise in the mental domain we meet with combinations only. Our conceptions, our thoughts and our mental powers, are also complex. So too are all social phenomena about us. They are structures composed of simpler parts. Every state, every people, every tribe is complex in a great many respects. Every principle of right is a composite of views, conceptions, ideas and principles. Every common economic interest is made up of conditions, activities, relations. In every language there is an endless variety of philological elements.

But further, what is complex may be analyzed. Analysis of physical phenomena will yield the elements of matter. Analysis of mental phenomena will disclose ultimate concepts and the simplest mental functions. In the social domain it leads to the simplest social structures thinkable, from state and people to primitive hordes; from developed institutional rights to the beginning of actual relations; from the most complex economic interests of the community to the satisfaction of the simplest needs; from a literature in the fullness of bloom to the simplest expression of thought by sound and gesture.

(f) *Reciprocal Action of Heterogeneous Elements*

Another result of complexity is that phenomena of every class reveals the reciprocal action of distinct reacting elements. Although there is an endless variety of cases in each particular domain, yet the law seems to express the first and most important impulse to

development in each and every one of them. The significance of this
force in social processes was surmised long ago, but it was erroneously interpreted by individualists and atomists as the reaction of man
upon man and was designated as love or hate, as sociability or mutual hostility (*bellum omnium contra omnes*). The error in this conception will appear as we proceed. Specific reciprocal influence of
man upon man cannot be affirmed in a universal law. What holds
true between man and man in one group is not necessarily true in
another group. Here it may be love and sociability and there hate
and thirst for strife. First one and then the other relation was assumed to be normal according as attention was confined to one group
or directed to the behavior of group toward group. Neither assumption was correct, because neither was universal. To find a law valid
in all times and places for the reciprocal forces inherent in social
phenomena we must take, not individuals, but social groups
as the elements. Thus the law of the reciprocal action of heterogenous
elements will be found universal. Social groups exhibit reciprocal
effects which are fundamentally the same always and everywhere.
They arise from the same exciting causes and obey the same law,
though manifested in various forms and ways according to time,
circumstances and the peculiar qualities of each.

A more specific expression for the universal action of heterogenous bodies upon each other might seem desirable, but there would
be a danger of getting entangled in empty analogies and of falsely extending formulas valid only in special instances.

Suppose we desired to speak of the "absorption" of heterogenous elements as a general principle. Perhaps the universal law
is manifested in this way in much of the physical domain. But it
is not so manifested in social phenomena. Applied to them the
statement would be an empty analogy. On the other hand, the manifestation of this law in the physical domain, especially in inorganic
and vegetable phenomena, has been described as a "struggle for
existence." Obviously this is an illustration borrowed from animal
and social phenomena. It does not describe physical events. Thus,
if we wish to have a law common to all phenomena we must
modestly be content to speak of the reciprocal action of discrete
elements. The more precise statement of its manifestation in the
respective domains must be left to specialized formulations.

(g) Adaptation to an Obvious End

One thing might be affirmed to characterize this law more precisely, and that is universal adaptation to an end—though in a very definite technical sense. For the universal effect of the reciprocal action of heterogenous bodies is to favor further development of the phenomena concerned; which may be expressed by saying that, universally, phenomena in this state are adapted to the end of further development.

This law has been abundantly demonstrated throughout the physical domain. The botanist knows "to what end" the leaves serve the plant. The zoologist knows "why" the respiratory organs of birds and, in general, all animal organs have their peculiar qualities. Among mental phenomena also, the adaptation of means to the ends produced has been recognized in many cases. In the social domain, to be sure, the law is much questioned. The more warmly it is defended by conservatives, Manchester economists, optimists, the more violently is it opposed by revolutionists, socialists and pessimists. But on one point, at least, there seems to be no dispute: every social growth, every social entity, serves a definite end, however much its worth and morality may be questioned. For the universal law of adaptation signifies simply that no expenditure of effort, no change of condition, is purposeless in any domain of phenomena. Hence the inherent reasonableness of all social facts and conditions must be conceded.

(h) Identity of Forces

The reciprocal action of discrete elements obviously proceeds from forces immanent in them or arising from their contact. These forces never change their character. They are identical, as we wish to say. Those operating in the domain of physical phenomena have always been the same that they are now. So of mental forces; thought, feeling, volition, each has always moved man and controlled his actions in the same way. Likewise the social forces, the causes which we must conclude from the effects that follow on the social domain, have ever been the same. Thus the identity of forces is a universal law. We encounter it in everything.

(i) Similarity of Events

A necessary consequence of the last law is the perpetual similarity of events upon all domains of nature. It has long been recognized of physical phenomena (Gumplowicz, 1883:172). Nobody doubts that the sun's warming powers acting on moist ground, age after age, has produced and always will produce the same effects in vegetation that it now produces. Nobody doubts that ocean waves breaking on a rocky coast have always produced the same effects that we see today. So, too, nobody doubts that man's mental faculties have produced the same effects in all times and climes. Always and everywhere men feel and think and plan; even the sensible products of these mental processes are the same. They differ only in form with changing time and circumstances. The Kamtchatkan sings his native song, and so does the Frenchman. Thousands of years ago the Chinese thinker philosophized just as did more recently the sage of Königsberg; the architect of the pyramids projected his artistic plans and so do the modern European artists. Thus the perpetual similiarity of events in the mental domain is obvious. But people are much less conscious of similarity in the social domain, though it is no less a fact. The identity of social forces could not be discovered because individuals instead of natural social groups were taken to be the true elements of social phenomena. But when the true social forces are recognized, the perpetual similarity of social events must also be apparent. Rights, states, languages, religion, etc., have always and everywhere arisen in ways essentially alike. Economic events are controlled by the same forces; they have always been alike in substance, though often differing in form.

(j) Law of Parallelism

In every domain we find some phenomena which are similar but we do not know the ultimate cause of their similarity. In the physical domain such phenomena are ascribed to identical forces directly. But in the mental domain the tendency is rather to attribute the similarity to some alleged connection between them; and in social phenomena it is considered the result of consanguinity or of some historic relationship. But actually there is something fundamental at the bottom of all these similarities which we must temporarily refer to as a law of parallelism, since we do not know more precisely what it is. By resorting to this law we guard ourselves against obviously false and erroneous explanations.[2]

The reason why parallel physical phenomena are referred without question to identical forces, whereas such an explanation of parallel mental and social phenomena is assiduously avoided as long as possible, is partly found in the widely accepted theory of monogenism. The descent of all men from Adam and Eve afforded a very plausible explanation. But if it is rejected as too absurd, the only course left is to refer the countless mental and social parallels directly to a law of parallelism common to all domains of phenomena.

The existence of univeral laws is one of the most convincing proofs that the whole phenomenal world rests upon a single simple principle. It is a weighty argument for monism, a thorough refutation of dualism. Consideration of these laws shows how untenable it is to refer phenomena to two principles, matter and mind, since the modalities of existence are the same for all and point to one simple principle only. Whether it be called nature, God, or the great unknown world-moving principle matters not. We have presentiments that it is omnipotent, omnipresent, perhaps even omniscient. But we are not in a position to know its essence. Since, however, there are laws which are universally prevalent and valid, we must conclude that this one principle pursues so to say, a consequent and self-consistent policy; that it reveals itself always and everywhere in the same form and in the same character for all kinds of phenomena. This necessary conclusion is of permanent significance to science.

3. Concept, Function and Scope of Sociology

It is almost unnecessary to remark that universal laws like these are not *a priori* cognitions but the result of an exhaustive examination of all spheres of phenomena, inductions obtained by extended mental exertion. In propounding them at the beginning of our dis-

---

[2] "According to the psychological axioms of ethnology, when cases exhibiting similarities occur, strictly universal and elementary laws are applied first. When there is no further possibility of finding the explanation in them there is recourse to such historic relationships as can be established. But the daily swelling mass of ethnological parallels will soon have converted the most obdurate. For since such an interpretation of parallels has come to be reckoned *a priori* reliable, no one can fail to accept it who is not stone blind" (Bastian, 1880: 91).

cussion we are reversing the natural order of cognition, to be sure; but this provisional anticipation of the results of an investigation is simply didactic strategy.

These universal laws govern phenomena of all kinds, it has been said. But for each particular kind they are manifested in a particular way. We might call this quality of special adaptation their "specific energy." An example will make the thought clear. Adaptation to an obvious end is a universal law. It is manifested in plants by the equipment of the several organs and the manner of their growth; and the botanist is able to formulate a whole series of special laws for plants. In the social domain the same law will be manifested differently. For example a horde, before starting on a raid, will organize by choosing a leader. Other illustrations might be given. Hence the sociologist may speak of special social laws to designate the adjustment of universal laws to the peculiar nature and conditions of social phenomena. Obviously special laws will be more numerous than universal laws; for the latter generalize the conditions common to all phenomena, whereas the former take account of those common to small numbers of phenomena.

The function of sociology consists in showing that universal laws apply to social phenomena in pointing out the peculiar effects produced by them in the social domain, and finally in formulating the special social laws.

As we have to deal with social phenomena exclusively in what follows, we must get a clear idea of what they are. We must distinguish the domain of social phenomena, explore and learn the most important groups within it. In so doing we shall come in contact with the special sciences concerned with special groups and which are quite properly designated the social sciences in general.

By social phenomena we mean phenomena which appear through the operation of groups and aggregates of men on one another. The aggregates are the social elements. We must assume that the simplest and original social elements were primitive hordes, of which, for reasons that have been explained elsewhere, there must have been a great number in remote antiquity (Cf. Gumplowicz, 1883:56).

The combinations of the simple social elements into greater associations: tribes, communities, peoples, states and nations, are just so many social phenomena. There are also social psychological phenomena, such as language, customs, rights, religion, etc., arising from the action of social elements with or upon the individual mind.

The province of sociology embraces them all. Sociology must investigate them and show the social laws of their development. Many groups, it is true, have been isolated and made the subject matter of independent sciences. But that should not hinder sociology from subjecting them to a new examination from the standpoint of social science, especially since they have generally been studied from an individualistic standpoint. Sociology should make their social origin and development perfectly clear.

It has just been said that mankind is the substratum of all social phenomena; hence, it is the real subject matter of sociology. But it is clear that the character of the science will be determined ultimately by our conception of the natural history of mankind. According as our conception is true or false will sociology be a success or a failure. The smallest mistake in the beginning will avenge itself in a hundred and thousand-fold greater errors in the end.

Hitherto a very gross misconception has prevailed in social science concerning the natural history of mankind. The character of human phenomena has been completely falsified by conceiving mankind to be genealogically a unitary genus, by supposing lineal descent from a common stock and explaining varieties of race and type as successive offshoots from it. This fundamental misconception set social science as a whole on the wrong track. Not only were all correct points of view, resulting from the fact of original plurality and variety of races, omitted from consideration, but many false ones were presented which produced nothing but mistakes.

Closely connected with this resulting from it, is another error. It was conceived that culture and social relations generally, whether of mankind or of particular peoples, develop spontaneously as a plant or animal develops. It was conceived that one and the same group passed through different stages of culture, from the hunting stage to the pastoral, to the agricultural, to warrior life and so on down to industrialism by simple transitions in virtue of an inner law and tendency to develop. But the law of persistence applies to social groups as much as it does to anything else in nature. Social groups persist in their actual social condition and cannot be made to "pass" into another without adequate social cause.

Therefore, we must remember not only that contiguous groups are diverse in origin, but also that they have been undergoing different courses of development. We must also remember that every social group persists in a given condition until forced out of it and into another through the action of some other group, and such action is pre-eminently called social.

In other words, each alteration in the social condition of a group must always have a sufficient social cause, which is always the influence of another group. This is a law, and can be amply illustrated from history and experience. An important proposition for the methodology of sociology flows from it, *viz.*, whenever an alteration in the condition of a group is perceived we should inquire what influences exerted by another group produced it. It follows, also, that rapid and varied development and frequent social changes, occur only under the continual reciprocal influence of many heterogeneous groups, that is, in states and systems of states.

This brings us very close to the definition of a social event or process. When two or more heterogeneous groups come in contact, when each enters the sphere of the other's operations, a social process always ensues. So long as one unitary, homogeneous group is not influenced by or does not exert an influence upon another it persists in its original primitive state. Hence, in distant quarters of the globe, shut off from the world, we find hordes in a state as primitive, probably, as that of their forefathers a million years ago. Here, very likely, we are dealing with an elementary, primitive, social phenomenon or, better, with a social element, but not with a social process nor with social change.

But as soon as one group is exposed to the influence of another, the interplay of mutual forces ensues inevitably and the social process begins. When two heterogeneous groups come together, the natural tendency of each is to exploit the other, to use the most general expression. This, indeed, is what gives the first impulse to social process. This tendency is so inherent in every human group, so natural and indomitable, that it is impossible to conceive of groups coming together without displaying it, without generating a social process.

The course of the process depends upon the natural constitution of "mankind" and the tendencies peculiar to all human hordes and social communities. Since these factors differ only as one individual or, at most, one species from another, and everywhere exhibit the same generic characteristics the process is essentially the same everywhere.

True, the human race is composed of an endless variety of species; the different hordes and tribes are combined in many ways and produce a variety of social formations or collective entities which in turn act upon one another. Even the influence of time and place yields a diversity of effects, so that the social process nevertheless presents endless variety and individuality of development. But the differences are transient and local. It is the task of sociology —and by no means an easy one—in the midst of diversity to find the controlling social laws to explain the miscellaneous variety of social development by the simplest forces in operation and to reduce the countless shapes it assumes to a simple common denominator.

All social laws, indeed all universal laws as well, have one characteristic in common: they explain the becoming, but never the beginning or ultimate origin of things. This limitation must be insisted upon the more emphatically since the human mind has a propensity for inquiry into the genesis of things. It desires knowledge of the first arising, the ultimate origin—a tendency fatal to science; whereas with all the laws that yield to knowledge it can apprehend only the perpetual becoming.

Hence none of the questions about the ultimate origin of human associations belong in sociology, if indeed they belong in any science whatever! Sociology begins with the countless different social groups of which, as can be irrefutably proven, mankind is constituted. The question how they came to be does not belong within this forum.

As we begin by limiting sociological discussion to the becoming of things, excluding discussion of ultimate origin, may we be allowed to point out that the discoveries which are recognized as the greatest achievements of science all lie in the same field. The Copernican discovery applies only to the motion of the planets in their orbits, without inquiring how they came to exist. Harvey discovered the circulation of the blood, a process continually going on under our observation. And we certainly do the great Englishman Darwin no wrong in expressing the opinion that when, centuries later, the problem of the "origin of man" shall have long since been laid aside, his investigation into the laws of the becoming, into the "struggle for existence," "adaptation" and "heredity," must still be lauded as an imperishable service to science.

We cannot close this section without emphasizing the importance of the knowledge of social laws to historians and statesmen.

The view that history can be raised to the level of a science only by taking account of the natural and social laws of development is still violently opposed though the reasons for it have been presented many times. We could cite innumerable examples to show how very much history has suffered from ignorance of social laws on the part of the most eminent historians. The most common error, one into which almost every historian has fallen, especially if he is treating a single nation, is to regard the phenomena as peculiar to one people; whereas were he to understand social laws he would recognize that they are more general.

How long is it since every history of Germany, in every treatise on the philosophy of German history, political particularism was ascribed to an individualizing tendency inherent in the German people? Particularism was considered a virtue in its day. But Bismarck has thoroughly counteracted the tendency and violently disputed its virtue. If historians were not so absorbed in one aspect of their subject, if they considered the laws governing all historical changes, they would recognize that, as a universal fact, periods of disintegration and particularization alternate with periods of integration. If they recognized that periodicity of development is a natural, necessary and universal law they would come nearer to the truth of many matters. Their results would gain in scientific value.

Or what shall be said when a distinguished historian writes: "The acquisitive impulse deeply inherent by nature in the Greeks, excited them at an early period to a many sided activity," (Curtius, 1892:I:15). Is this tendency natural to the "Greeks" alone? What of the "Semites," of whom Curtius relates that "the Greeks cherished a national hatred against them!" Was the "acquisitive tendency" less "deeply inherent by nature" in them? Had it "excited" them less "to a many sided activity?" Or why did the Spaniards go to America, the English and Dutch to India, if not to "make gain?" Have we not here a general social phenomenon and a general social law? Is it not a scientific error to consider general social phenomena peculiar to the people among whom they have been accidentally recognized? Take another example from Curtius:

> "According to the usual conception of the Greeks, who felt the need of assuming an author for every great historical work, without caring to distinguish what had previously existed from what subsequently ensued, the whole political system was regarded as the legislation of Lycurgus" (Curtius, 1892:I:44).

But to ascribe to a single legislator the creation of a body of juridical and political regulations which have been accumulating for centuries is not peculiar to the Greeks. It is a psycho-social phenomenon common to all peoples. Will not truth and science suffer if no account is taken of the fact?

How much the science of history will improve when historians discern that all alleged individual peculiarities of the peoples they describe are manifestations of general social and psycho-social laws! Similar examples of false and narrow views could be cited endlessly from the best historians. But we prefer to give in precise terms the general cause of error in the conception of historical phenomena. It is asserted that:

> "history, however it may be defined and classified, will never be reduced to a bare natural science or sociological discipline. For it is not simply the product of telluric and anthropological natural forces and the momentum of social masses. There is a third factor, the power of individuality, which is not susceptible of calculation by the rules of either natural science or sociology."[3]

In so far as individuals are concerned, to be sure, history can proceed "neither like natural science nor sociology." But in so far as history portrays the individual it is pure art. For art deals only

---

[3] I may certainly be allowed to cite as typical of the opinion of historians in general the objections made to "history as a natural science" by the distinguished R. von Krones, in reviewing *Der Rassenkampf*. The prevalent conception of the task of historical composition could not be defended more forcibly than in the words quoted.

with individuals, in contrast to science, which deals with what is universal, what accords with law and is schematic. The individual might be typical; nevertheless the historian is generally in error if he thinks that he finds anything individualistic in the history of a people, a nation or a tribe, or in the actions of social groups, however considered. Only single personalities are properly individualistic; when treating them the historian may yield to his artistic impulses. But when he has collective entities to present, where he has to show how they live and move, the effort to "individualize" is shortsighted and erroneous; the science of history can and should "proceed according to the rules of both natural science and sociology." For the behavior of collective units is determined by "natural and sociological" laws and not by the motives and natural qualities of individuals. It will be some time before this is realized but the recognition will come only through sociology.

Important as sociology is for historians, its significance in politics is greater still. For though hitherto politics has not been reckoned a science at all, sociology will give it a scientific character.

At present politics is strife after power. Each state, party and faction, even every individual strives after power with all the means at command. Material means are supplemented with as cogent reasons as possible. Such reasons and arguments are called the theory of politics. But where is the criterion of their correctness? From the standpoint of success, when the fact has been accomplished, the policy which succeeded is recognized as right. Yet it is not so much ideas and arguments as greater might that makes the project prosperous. So ultimately, greater might is the better policy—as things stand now.

Sociology must give quite another turn to politics; though, indeed, it will develop political science rather than practical politics. That is to say, the social laws which sociology is to formulate from its observations on the processes of history include also the laws of the development of political life. When they shall have been correctly formulated from the past, they must be verified in the present and the future. They must control the course of political development now and hereafter as unequivocally as they have in the past. When reliable laws have been formulated, political machinations, tavern politics and ignorant gossip will give place to political foresight and sober calculation based upon positive sociological knowledge.

These words will provoke a skeptical smile—and certainly not without some reason. Similar promises have often proved to be vain talk if not charlatanry and usually people who talk of calculating future politics scientifically are not taken seriously. Did not Auguste Comte speak of a *politique positive,* a positive science of politics, which, "instead of pronouncing absolute judgment and suggesting ameliorations," should rather create "a body of scientific conceptions such as has never been outlined nor even suspected by any philosopher before?" Yet how many false and erroneous notions he held. And Thomas Buckle! How little he recognized the truth about the development of political relations in modern times. Claiming to have obtained final cognition of the "laws of history," he prophesied cessation of war and universal perpetual peace. Yet how has his prophecy been verified?

In one point, however, the old sociologists were clearly right. With presentient mind they suspected the existence of social laws and asserted the possibility of a social science. It is true they did not pass the point of conjecture. They never advanced to the true principles of the science, much less to a knowledge of social laws. They did not even find the starting point of the pathway which leads to the principles. The point of departure is polygenism. The way is the investigation of the natural relations of heterogeneous groups of men to one another. We entered upon it in *Der Rassen-kampf* and here we wish to continue.[4]

[4] It gives me great satisfaction to observe that the reviewers have recognized the great importance of my starting point and have declared it at all events worthy of note. Alfred Koenigsberg writes in the *Neue Freie Presse,* Vienna, August 9, 1883: "His hypothesis that mankind is descended from many pairs is the heart of the matter. It explains almost every historical event in the simplest and most unconstrained way, especially that primitive phenomenon, the conquest of a weaker tribe by a stronger and the organization of society with division of labor. It suggests what Stephenson, the father of railroads, said upon inspecting a good locomotive: 'how hard it must have been to hit upon it; it is so simple!' " The reviewer for the *Rassegna Critica,* Naples, 1883, No. 9, says: "There are two points in this book which especially deserve praise . . . . to wit, the unqualified assertion of naturalism and the fact that, contrary to custom, neither the individual nor the psychology of the individual, but the social group, is made chief element in the interpretation of history." Similar notices of approval appeared in *Globus,* 1884, No. 4; *Ausland,* 1884, No. 2; *Journal des*

Being the science of human society and social laws, sociology is obviously the basis of all the special sciences treating the parts of human society, or particular manifestations of associative life. Anthropology, the science of man as an individual being falls within the scope of the universal science of society as a species within the genus. So do ethnography, embracing the description and comparison of existing tribes and peoples; political science, the science of the state, treating of social communities which are the result of disciplinary organization; comparative linguistics, or philology; the comparative study of religion, rights, art, etc.—sciences of social institutions which satisfy the psycho-social wants of man; finally political economy and other sciences treating institutions which the material wants of man as a social unit have produced. It is perfectly natural that all these sciences should have taken shape long before the science in which they should afterward find their basis. This is the normal course of man's developing knowledge.

It was so in natural science in the narrow sense of the word. Botany, zoology and mineralogy took shape before geology and paleontology, though the latter are the foundation of the former. Similarly the art of healing is earlier than physiology.

The explanation is very simple. Things, institutions, relations encountered in concrete form are the first objects observed and investigated. The most convenient hypothesis or crudest explanation suffices for a time to account for their origin. For instance we live under laws constituting a body of rights. The nature of the phenomenon is investigated; the rights are explained, interpreted, compared with others, and their history is traced out. But provisionally their source and origin was satisfactorily explained by saying that the law-giver proclaimed them. Similarly the explanation of the origin of religion is that God revealed it to His prophet, the founder.

Economistes, October, 1883; Ribot's *Revue Philosophique,* May 1884, and in many other critical periodicals. These critics have caught the idea of my book and it cannot be my fault that Professor Alfred Kirchoff, in Zarncke's *Literarisches Centralblatt,* Leipzig, complains that he does not understand what I mean. However, Professor Kirchoff is a geographer, appears never to have meddled with sociology, and is conversant with neither the literature of the subject nor the questions here under discussion. Judging from the fact that he lists the book under the rubric "ethnology," he considers sociology a geographical discipline.

With the progress of knowledge and reflection, ideas concerning the origin of the subject matter of the respective sciences undergo changes. The new conclusions conflict with earlier explanations. Thus the comparative study of law showed that rights arise
historically in the collective or "folk" mind; and religion, similarly
studied was found to emanate from exigencies of man's spiritual
nature, and so on.

Moreover as knowledge broadened, the germs of all the psycho-
social institutions were eventually found to be in close proximity
to one another and the different social sciences met on a common
ground—though the common designation was not at once applied.
The subject matter of each science in turn was discovered existing in
every people in greater or lesser degree and in a more or less forward state of development. Consequently men were forced to regard
the differences in psycho-social phenomena among various peoples
and to compare psycho-social products.

The first step was the comparative study of law, especially of
customary law, then of religion, language, art and philosophy. This
prompted and aided investigation of the common ground whence the
fountains of all the sciences seemed to spring. This common ground
was at first designated history of civilization, ethnography, or ethnology, Bastian's term. But in fact it may most suitably be called
social science.

It discloses the true source of all those psycho-social products
that had previously been subject matter of special sciences. But it
does this only because it comprehends the substance of human societies. Hence we must recognize in sociology the philosophical basis
of all the sciences claiming to be "social." Therefore, it falls to the
lot of sociology to demonstrate the relation of each of them to their
common basis, and their connection with each other upon it.

4. The Substratum of Social Laws

Laws are revealed objectively. Substrata are necessarily presupposed. It is by the forms in which bodies appear, or through
which forces manifest themselves, that we are able to discover laws.
The law of gravitation cannot be conceived apart from bodies which

fall—in which the force of gravitation manifests itself. To speak of attraction is to call to mind the bodies on which attraction acts.

So the question arises: What are the substrata of social laws? What are the media through which force is manifested when we infer social laws from its behavior? Obviously the medium is not the individual, through whom psychical or physical laws may be manifested, but a social medium. It has sometimes been thought that "mankind" was the substratum; but erroneously, for there must be heterogeneous (*heterogen*) elements wherever reciprocal action and an interplay of forces is expected.

If mankind is conceived to be a unit, the condition necessary for the action of opposing forces is by supposition absent. Besides, nowhere on the earth, and at no time either in the present age or in remotest antiquity has mankind been found to be a simple substance. It always consists in a countless number of ethnic elements. Hence I was led to seek the starting point of sociological investigation in the hypothesis that there was originally an indefinitely large number of distinct (*heterogen*) ethnic elements:[5] and it gives me satisfaction to note that good authorities consider the polygenetic hypothesis established. Indeed, Bastian, the highest authority in this matter, declares that "it is self-evident," and that my efforts, in *Der Rassenkampf*, to "reconcile it with Darwinism" were superfluous.

But since the hypothesis is so fundamental to the whole system of sociology it is not enough to state which authorities accept it. I must also take pains to bring before the reader as much scientific material as possible in support of it.

First of all, I should like to cite Karl Vogt, another authority

[5] "The concept of force," says Caspari, correctly, "presupposes relations to another foreign opposing force which is called resistance. Force apart from resistance of every sort would be a forceless force, unthinkable nothing. Whoever speaks of force must at the same time conceive of mechanical resistance or he contradicts himself. Hence every philosophical investigator who had been educated in natural science, and had studied mechanics, understood that we must continually suppose an original plurality of discrete force-media, force-centers, or force-atoms (Democritus), monads (Leibnitz), reals (Herbert), dynamides (Redtenbacher), etc."—*Kosmos*, (Vol. I: 9).

of the first rank in natural science, to vouch for the "original plurality" and the "constancy" of human races:[6]

"No man would certainly have doubted the specific difference in mankind" says this investigator in his *Lectures on Man*, "if the unity of the human species had not to be defended at any price, if a tradition had not to be supported in opposition to the plain facts — a tradition which has been the more venerated because it runs counter to positive science."

"As far as our traditions go, however far back they reach into the remotest antiquity, we observe that wherever peoples migrated and discovered unknown countries, they found human beings, who appeared to them not less strange than the animals and plants they met with . . . The larger islands, as well as all parts of the continents under the hottest and coldest climates, were always found inhabited by navigators or conquerors (Vogt, 1863:viii:222).

Then Vogt reminds his readers that:

"even religious legends, which have for their object the origin of mankind and the history of a privileged race, even these legends indicate that at the creation of the first pair the world was already peopled, an indication given even in the Bible . . . The only fact from which we can start is that of the original dispersion of mankind upon the earth, and the original difference of races spread over the surface of the earth. However much we may indulge in theoretical speculations on the origin and differences of mankind, however weighty proofs may be adduced for the original unity of the human species, this much is certain, that no historical nor, as we have shown, geological data can establish this dream of unity. However far back our eye reaches we find different species of men spread over different parts of the earth."

"Not merely the difference of races, but also their constancy in the course of time, is perfectly established. We have endeavored to show that these characters may be traced

[6] It may be added that among the earlier natural scientists the following accepted polygenism: Cuvier, Buffon, Lacépède and Burdach. The philosopher Whewell in *Traces of Divinity* holds the Negroes to be a distinct race, of different extraction from the other races of men. Bory and Vierey also accepted polygenism and Perty says: "The far greater probability is that men of diverse natural capacities have arisen in different parts of the earth and at various times, all very remote from ours."—*Ethnographie*, (1859: 386).

back beyond the historical period up to the pile-works, the stone-period, and the diluvial formations. The Egyptian monuments show that already under the twelfth dynasty, about 2300 years before Christ, Negroes had been imported into Egypt; that slave hunts had, as now, taken place under several dynasties, as proved by the triumphal processions of Thothmes IV., about 1700 B. C., and Rameses III., about 1300 B. C. There are seen long processions of Negroes, whose features and color are faithfully rendered; there are seen Egyptian scribes registering slaves with their wives and children; even the down growing in bunches upon the heads of the latter may be distinguished. There are also seen many heads presenting characteristics of Negro tribes inhabiting southern Egypt, which the artist distinguishes as such by the superadded lotus-stalk. But not only the Negroes but also the Nubians and the Berbers, as well as the old Egyptians, are always depicted with those characteristic peculiarities which have been preserved to this day."

Vogt also cites the conclusions of Broca, Morton and Jomard, who identify the modern Fellah-type with the Egyptians of the time of the Pharaohs, and then he continues:

"The same constancy of characteristics can be found in other races with whom Egyptians came in contact. The Jews are as easily recognizable as the Tartars and Scythians with whom Rameses III was at war. In the same way we observe the Assyrian and Indian monuments the characteristics of such races as still inhabit these regions, so that the constancy of racial features is everywhere rendered exident" (Vogt: 1863: 15; 423-26).

Though Vogt concedes a "certain flexibility" to the "natural races" of mankind in virtue of which they "show certain changes when transplanted into different media," yet the change never exceeds a very small maximum and does not obliterate the essential racial qualities. Darwin is not justified in concluding from single demonstrable examples of unimportant alterations due to change of environment that they will continue until eventually the essential traits have been lost and the race has been changed.

"We thus infer that all instances which have been cited of change in races of pure descent by the mere influence of changed media, immigration into foreign countries, etc., are insignificant and do not affect the essential race-characters. These modifications, therefore, which we by no means entirely deny, do not in any way explain the differences in the human species . . . In accordance with the facts," says Vogt finally, "we must assume a fundamental difference of races as our starting-point" (Vogt: 1863: 15:435-36).

We must confine ourselves to these quotations from Vogt. It would lead us too far should we follow the forcible argument in which he not only shows the harmony between Darwin's theory and polygenism but also demonstrates that the latter follows necessarily from the former.

His two most important theses, the constancy and the original "plurality and diversity" of human races, have found striking confirmation in the progress that has since been made in anthropological and craniological investigation.

Efforts were made to find the types of all the known races. It had been assumed upon superficial examination, that each race represented a genealogical unit in which a fixed anthropological type was transmitted from generation to generation. But when scientists undertook to determine the typical peculiarities exactly, it was found impossible to assign a single type exclusively to any one historical race whatever. The investigators would then have been content with a "mean type" for each race. But, says Virchow, "such a variety of individual differences was accumulated among the civilized peoples of Europe that to many it seemed impossible to set up even a mean type for each" (Virchow: 1877).

In his embarrassment he proclaimed, a decade ago, that "science demanded" that the "original type" of each race be discovered and he spared neither labor nor pains in the search. If after all he did not find it among the Germans, where he looked first, it was not his fault. The simple fact is that not a single historical race ever consisted in a genealogical unit. After laborious and unsuccessful investigation he concludes that:

"The assumption of a simple original Germanic type is as yet entirely arbitrary. Nobody has proved that all Germans once had the same shaped skull, or, otherwise expressed, that they were from the beginning one nation (!), the Suevi and Franks being its purest types. If Germans and Slavs belong to the same Indo-Germanic stock, if Slavic brachycephaly and Germanic dolichocephaly do not prevent assuming a common descent of Slavic and German peoples, it might seem that mesocephaly and even brachycephaly among the admittedly pure Germans would be a favorable circumstance. The great hiatus becomes filled and original relationship is more easily comprehended after actual intermediate members have been discovered. If the Germanic nation once had a common fatherland in the far East, it is very probable that these differences were brought thence into the later home" (Virchow: 1877).

We see with what reserve and reluctance Virchow notes that the German race lacks anthropological unity. He demands further investigation.

"Perhaps it will appear that, as the measurements in our schools in my judgment indicate, different Germanic stocks have in fact existed here in Germany for ages, moving side by side from east to west, and spreading out towards the west" (Virchow, 1877).

To the sociologist the "different stocks" which the anthropologist's craniological material leads him to conjecture seem plain and natural from the beginning. To call them "Germanic" is simply national prejudice. There were many different stocks all about; and in time a "Germanic" unit arose as they came into closer contact and took on a common civilization.

But the anthropologist's concession that "the common type" of German "is not so simple as it has hitherto been assumed to be" is of value to us. The farther craniological investigations were pursued, the stronger grew the conviction that even in the remotest tribes, whom the current of migration does not touch, who have no intercourse with others, and who are apparently beyond the reach of every other agitating force of history, there was nothing which could be called a "unitary type." Even among the old Frisians, there are several types. Virchow is forced to assume that "possibly other tribes were there before them, whom they subjected and whose blood was mingled with theirs." Whether the craniologist examines modern Finns and Lapps or wild Veddas from the interior of Ceylon, or the skulls from old Trojan graves, the fact of intermixture appears with equal clarity.

But while Virchow, who started to find an original unitary type, reluctantly notes that there is none and, with disillusioned resignation, concedes an original plurality of types for all the tribes he has investigated, the distinguished craniologist, Kollmann, has proved with scientific certainty that original plurality is universal.

As early as 1883 it was apparent to him that "traces of different anthropological elements can be shown in every race. Many centuries have elapsed since the peoples of Europe were racial units, and now no area, however remote, contains a pure race." But the latest results prove abundantly that racial differences are not due to a later process of differentiation. It has existed unchanged from diluvial times.

"An extended comparison of diluvial and modern skulls, shows that osteological race characteristics have not changed. Since diluvial times the influence of natural selection has not caused man to 'vary' in the Darwinian sense. His race-marks have withstood external influences with great tenacity, persisting in spite of them. These important conclusions contradict the current view that man is undergoing a continuous process of change. But it must be conceded upon closer examination that the evidence I have adduced admits of the construction I have given it, to say the least."

Then he cites the opinions of prominent naturalists to show that not only do many animals have permanent types, but unquestionably the men of the Nile valley also, according to Cuvier, and even mankind since the flood, according to Rütimeyer.

"All the evidence man has left in his burial places," he continues, "shows that he belongs to the latter class of beings, having a permanent type. The osteological characteristics of race and even of variety have not changed in all the time he has wandered over Europe. . . The universality of this rule is forcibly illustrated by the difference between Papuans and Malays, to mention only one example. Since time immemorial they have lived side by side in similar regions without change of habitat. Yet they are different still. As for Europe both prehistoric and modern, it can be shown that the number of different races has always been rather large and that they have always been intermixed. Owing to penetration, representatives of many races live and, for thousands of years have lived, side by side everywhere in Europe. Hence, each people and state contains different races in different proportions. This conclusion I drew after comparing more than 3000 European skulls."

Indeed craniologists who are moved to defend the unity and "purity" of their own races cannot withstand the undeniable facts. Hölder, for example, concedes five different "types" within the "Germanic stock." That is, he finds five among his specimens today. It is not impossible therefore that once there was a greater number and that other investigators may be able to recover more of them.[7]

"Hiss and Rütimeyer, using rigorous scientific methods, have shown that at least three different races have lived in Switzerland since the period of the lake-dwellers began" (*Cf.* Kollmann, 1881, 1883a, 1883b, 1883c).

These same "anthropological differences," to use Kollmann's terms, may also be noted among the American aborigines. "Formerly it was firmly believed that a single race extended over the whole continent from Cape Horn to the great northern lakes . . . Decisive facts to the contrary were first adduced by Andreas Retzius. He showed that there were two different races in America, a brachycephalic in the west and a dolichocephalic in the east" (Kollmann, 1883a).

In Virchow's opinion, also, evidence shows "that the autochthonous population of America is not a racial unit." Kollmann showed from his investigations on American skulls that:

"the various cephalic indices, from extreme dolichocephaly to extreme brachycephaly, are scattered over the whole continent. . . . The autochthonous population, north and south, is composed of the same races, though their relative proportions differ. Hence we must speak of American races. I will add that there is no prospect of finding racial unity even within a smaller region. It might be thought that individual tribes in the north or the south would consist of dolichocephalic or brachycephalic persons only. . . . but the Mound-builders and Cliff-dwellers in their day were composed of the same races that occur later. Even they con-

[7] To social science it is a matter of indifference that craniologists like Kollmann compromise with the alleged Darwinian doctrine of unitary descent by granting that a period of dispersion and of differentiation from a "common stock" may have "occurred in pre-glacial times." It is enough for social science to start with the facts of the post-diluvial period. It gladly leaves the preglacial hypothesis to the defenders of an alleged Darwinian standpoint—to save the "common stock."

sisted of several races, like the men of the first diluvial period in Europe, or the Reindeer-hunters, Lake-dwellers, Germans and Celts" (Kollman, 1883b).

Kollmann's theory of "penetration" is thoroughly confirmed by the observation of his disciple Passavant in West Africa. The first place he visited on the African continent was the French possession of Goree, the black population of which belongs to the Seres and Joloff tribes.

"It is extremely hard for the beginner to distinguish the blacks by their physiognomies," writes Passavant of his first experience there. "At first all the faces appeared alike. Only after several weeks of practice did I really succeed in taking account of individual differences" (Passavant, 1884).

This accords with the well-known fact that the countless differences really to be found in men escape superficial observation almost completely. It also explains the whole previous history of anthropology, especially the circumstance that mankind was at first divided into only three or four races, distinguished by the crudest, most striking traits, such as skin pigmentation, whereas, after a more intimate acquaintance, we become conscious of countless differences.

Cuvier, as is well known, divided mankind into three races: Mongolians, Negroes and Causasians. Blumenbach distinguished five types and made five corresponding races. Lacépède and Dumerit added a sixth. Bory discovered even fifteen races and Desmoulins sixteen. But Waitz found this number insufficient and declared that theoretically there ought to be no division into races lest he be compelled, in spite of ethical scruples, to recognize a great number— several hundred in fact. Fortunately, the American investigators were not influenced by such insipid considerations. They carried the subdivision courageously forward unconcerned about the Bible and European ethics.

The catalogue of human races accepted by Morton, Nott and Gliddon ran into the hundreds without being complete. There is nothing to prevent the increase of the number as anthropological knowledge increases. Passavant's investigations among the Negroes affords further proof that this may be expected in the nature of the case.

The first subdivision of the African Negroes into four grand races: Negritos, Congo Negroes, Kaffirs and Hottentots, he says

> "is the fruit of our exploring expeditions; it is connected with the progress of ethnographic knowledge. Undaunted explorers have gradually brought a population which may be estimated at 151 millions so far within our knowledge that we can now distinguish several large ethnic groups" (Passavant: 1884).

There are "at least three Negro races" in Africa, in addition to the Berbers and the Bedjas or Ethopians.

"There are, besides some intermediate tribes between the Negroes on the one hand and the Berbers and Bedjas on the other. There are some also in which different stocks and types are so mingled that they cannot longer be ascribed to any one in particular" (Passavant: 1884).

According to Passavant, instead of the one black race, we should have seven ethnic groups in Africa. But what of the material of each group? The Negroes "differ so among themselves," says Hartmann, "that the current conception of the black men with woolly hair, flat nose, thick lips and raven black skin must be entirely disregarded."

Endless differences still! But it is well understood what they consist in and why closer observation makes it necessary to increase the number of "races." "Racial characteristics are pre-eminently anatomical," says Kollmann. Thus "physical or material traits must be apparent on the bones." Relatively few races were recognized by scientists because "laborious investigation is needed in order to show specific characteristics on the bony framework of the skull."

But is it worth the trouble? Are not all these "differences" capricious sports of nature, endless and ever changing, without rule or law? Modern craniology answers the question decisively.

> "The skeleton," says Rütimeyer, "seems to preserve its acquired shape more tenaciously than any other organ; so much so that a cross does not produce a third form, but the two elements persist side by side. The effect of crossing on the skeleton might be called mechanical rather than chemical."

Vogt also maintains that racial characteristics are permanent on the skeleton, and Passavant considers the "shape of the skull to be a constant and inheritable race-characteristic."

"There is a mass of evidence, showing that race-types are maintained continuously or reappear by reversion. If the characteristics of different varieties did not resist external influences with such extraordinary obstinacy," says Kollmann pertinently, "complete uniformity must have long since prevailed among men everywhere; for intermixture has been continuous and prolific. But craniological evidence shows that there is no uniformity and every unprejudiced observer confirms it." Elsewhere he says: "Life in the drawing-room may reduce the ligaments and the muscular strength and make the hands and feet small; but the characteristics of his race which the individual bears in himself as heir to an ancient heritage, remain undisturbed in spite of tall hat and patent leathers" (Passavant, 1884).

If, then racial characteristics are constant and the number of human races or varieties is still undetermined, it follows obviously that when man's existence on earth began and before races had mingled and "penetrated," there were countless distinct human swarms, differently representing the various racial characteristics which have persisted unchanged in penetration.

The conclusion is imperative. If racial characteristics pass from generation to generation only by inheritance; if no new ones arise and only the old ones appear over and over again; if they are countless to-day and penetration and inheritance are still spreading them (though many may have disappeared forever); if they prove to be as permanent and ancient as the tombs; must we not conclude that there was in the beginning a countless number of distinct human hordes since even the anthropologists and craniologists who accept warped by Biblical traditions and modern conceptions of the family would insist on substituting first "pairs" instead of hordes.

It may be said that it is exaggeration to speak of countless hordes since even the anthropologists and craniologists who accept polygenism use modest numbers. But to how few traits they limit themselves or are confined by necessity! Who will believe that the racial characteristics are all confined to the skull and skeleton though that is almost the only place where anthropologists may look?

Obviously there should be corresponding differences even in the finest features of the face and in the minutest convolutions of the brain, which are as yet wholly unknown. Some are entirely inaccessible to such investigations as we apply to the bones; others are too delicate for our sense-perceptions; others still are on organs and parts of the body, like the nose and ears, which suffer complete decay so that no comparison can be made with the past. Yet nobody doubts that the racial differences in these members are important. So it is not too rash to suppose that a far greater number of human varieties now exist (and since types are permanent always have existed) than anthropology has any means of knowing. These considerations, we hope, will still further justify us in starting upon our sociological investigations with the polygenetic hypothesis.[8]

5. Concept and Essence of Social Law

The facts cited show plainly that existing "races" are not simple and mutually exclusive in the anthropological sense. Moreover, every means of investigation fails to disclose racial purity in prehistoric times. Yet, reasoning deductively from the mixed to the unmixed and from the composite to the simple, we must infer that races once were pure. The logical conclusion must be accepted as the working hypothesis, at least, of a scientific investigation. But anthropological changes have not affected the social relations of either ancient or modern human groups. Sociologically they are still distinct groups. Sociological dissimilarities are independent of the structure of the bones and skull. They consist in very different factors. Once the distinction between native and alien may have answered to differences purely anthropological. But ever since the dawn of history the native has been distinguished from the alien simply by social status and relations which he and everybody else recognizes as necessarily

---

[8] It has already been stated that Bastian considers such a justification superfluous since polygenism is "self-evident." But the fact that Alfred Kirchoff professor of geography who calls himself a "wicked Darwinian," writing in the *Literarische Centralblatt*, declares this theory irreconcilable with Darwinism, proves that the correct conception of Darwin's theory has not been so widely diffused as might be wished. Hence the above explanation seems to me still necessary.

correlative with, and consequent upon, sociological or simply social factors.

Birth and training are social factors. The latter, especially, imparts the language, morals, ideas, religion and usages of the group and causes the individual to appear to himself and to others to belong to it. Together they bind the members to each other by a common interest, which is patriotism in its earliest form.

The simple syngenetic groups are effected by a great variety of interests—political, economical, national and intellectual—in such ways that several elementary groups become united into one; primary social complexes are followed by secondary and these by others of successively higher orders. The same regular processes which took place in the simple groups in virtue of their social nature occur in all the others. Combinations and cultural changes only modify or complicate them. These processes, which we shall call social since their source is in social elements, are the content, as the groups, simple and compound, are the agents of social history.

Social processes exhibit great uniformity. Though time and circumstances modify them they remain essentially the same. So for each instance of uniformity in the social domain, as elsewhere, we formulate a law of the cause and call the law social.[9] Hence a social law is an inference from concrete social occurrences presenting the norm of the development and reciprocal influence of social elements, *i.e.*, of the syngenetic groups.

The only way to conduct social science is to discover social laws where ethnic and social elements intersect and to demonstrate their validity. So long as the investigation was conducted in

[9] De Tocqueville was impressed by the thought that peoples, however distant and unrelated, must develop according to some law. "When I perceive the resemblance," he says, "which exists between the political institutions of our ancestors, the Teutons, and the wandering tribes of North America,—between the customs described by Tacitus, and those of which I have sometimes been the witness,—I cannot help thinking that the same cause has brought about the same results in both hemispheres; and that, in the midst of the apparent diversity of human affairs, certain primary facts may be discovered, from which all the others are derived" (*Cf.* De Tocqueville, 1838: 441-42). The ethnographical horizon has been much extended since, and De Tocqueville's conjecture is confirmed. Sociology may attempt to distinguish the *faits générateurs*, the primary facts. "Ethnology has irrefutably proven that certain phenomena of

any other way, no attempt to discover or formulate a social science could succeed.

It was recognized that there must be regularity of development and that the laws of development must be demonstrated, if a philosophy of history or a social science were to be constructed. Comte and Carey insisted upon this repeatedly. But no one knew where to look for conformity to law. Some, like Voltaire, sought for laws of the development of mankind. But if mankind is taken as a unit, it is obvious that development must be either upward or downward; that there must be either progression or retrogression. Rousseau and others accepted the latter alternative. Assuming a primitive happy state of nature, they went on to prove man's growth in corruption. The greater part, including nearly every writer on the history of civilization, taught the contrary however, laboring to show upward progression from original savagery to successively higher forms of civilization. Both parties were wrong. Both erred in treating "mankind" as a unit of development. The mistake was general but the position cannot be maintained unless the scope is materially limited. Generally it is confined to the narrow stream of European civilization running through Greece and Rome, to France or Germany. The development discovered here is attributed to mankind as a whole. Comte, for instance, locates a period of polytheism between primitive fetishism and modern(!) monotheism and asserts that "it was under its reign that mankind rose to a settled monogamy" (Comte, 1881: II, 230). It is clear to what a tiny fraction of mankind the statement applies. Comte took no thought of the rest. It would have vitiated the orderly development of "mankind" and its elevation to monogamy.

But a few sagacious statisticians led by Quetelet escaped the self-deception. Unsatisfied by this fancied regularity, they sought to discover laws of orderly development by other means. Quetelet is conscious that there can be no science of man unless man's whole conduct depends on fixed laws just as the phenomena of natural science do; and he regrets that philosophers have never perceived it.

---

associative life are perfectly similar among peoples who are entirely unlike and who have never been related in any demonstrable way whatever. Hence . . . the nature of the human race (species) is manifestly one and universal in spite of all differences" (*Cf.* Achelis, 1881).

"Either from a distrust in their own strength," he says, "or a repugnance in supposing it possible to reduce to fixed laws what seemed to flow from the most capricious of causes, it has hitherto been deemed expedient by learned men to abandon the line of inquiry employed in the investigation of the other laws of nature as soon as the moral phenomena of mankind become the object of research." (Quetelet: 1835b:5).

He also correctly surmises that if we would discover the laws controlling man's behavior we must disregard the individual.

"It is of primary importance to keep out of view man as he exists in an insulated, separate, or in an individual state, and to regard him only as a fraction of the species. In thus setting aside his individual nature, we get free of all which is accidental, and the individual peculiarities, which exercise scarcely any influence over the mass, become effaced of their own accord, allowing the observer to seize the general results."

After giving-the well-known illustration of the particles of chalk-dust which form a circle only when seen from a distance, he continues: "it is in this way that we propose studying the laws which relate to the human species. For, by examining them too closely," by examining the individuals, he means, "it becomes impossible to apprehend them correctly, and the observer sees only individual peculiarities, which are infinite" (Quetelet, 1842: 5). That is, in place of the false and discarded subject, the individual, he substitutes a vague and incomprehensible "human species," "society," or "social body." This is his error. He never discovered what the real subject matter of observation should be. Consequently all his efforts to found a science were a failure.

How could Quetelet discover conformity to law? His concept suggests nothing concrete, nor even anything measurable. But every concrete object in nature is limited, and none but limited objects can be observed scientifically. His terms suggest something unlimited, undefinable, as unfit for concrete observations—the foundation of all science—as time and space. It must be resolved into concrete units first. He wisely discarded the "individual," but he failed to find the real unit.

He resorted to the "great number," as has been pointed out. It is the magician's wand with which he conjures a finely plastic scientific subject matter out of the unyielding "human species," "society," or "social system." Using a "great number" of cases, he finds laws prevalent where formerly blind confusion reigned. The operation is very simple; if it were only as sound!

Any convenient phenomenon may be observed and a record made of the frequency of its recurrence in equal periods of time. If the several totals are compared, either they will seem to conform to law or they will not, one or the other. In the former event, the statisticians proclaim the "law of the great number;" in the latter they keep their silence. Generally some law is discoverable. For everything in the world is amenable to number. Anything can be counted. At some limit, which must eventually be reached, numbers always give certain proportions. This property of numbers seems to have been communicated to the enumerated articles.

Take any rare occurrence in ordinary life. Say a lunatic climbs a tower and jumps to the street. Within the memory of man the like had not happened in that locality. It stands alone. No law can be discovered on the basis of it. If it is never repeated it eludes all statistical treatment. But possibly it may recur. If we could find only one other instance in a long series of years, even that would be enough to show "conformity to law;" the event will occur once in so and so many years.

Obviously the opportunity for making ratios is far greater when the events enumerated occur daily and hourly, as many in human life do. Births, marriages, deaths, in fact the majority of demographical phenomena must occur with great regularity and statistics win an easy triumph. But have the laws governing natural phenomena been explained with the regularity of their occurrence? Here number is an indication or proof that there is conformity to some law and that is all.

Statistical results are wholly insufficient for formulating and explaining the least law of "mankind," "society," "the social system." In a word the "law of the great number" is a law of number and not of the phenomena enumerated; whereas social science wishes especially to learn the laws of social phenomena. Granted that statistics are a very important means of investigation yet counting phenomena and computing ratios is a purely arithmetical process.

It has no identity with the discovery and explanation of the laws of the behavior of phenomena.

Quetelet's statistical investigations are a great boon to science. But he did not demonstrate social laws as he proposed. He mistook the laws of number for the laws of social phenomena. His self-deception originated in his unclear concept of the subject matter of social science. His indefinite and incomprehensible "mankind" could not be subjected to rigid and exact scientific treatment.

In one of his later works, the *Natural History of Society*, he tried to improve by distinguishing several social communities from one another. But he got no clear idea of "race," "nation," and "state." On the contrary he did what would not have been expected of him. He assumed the individual to be their source and so prevented apprehension of their true substance as effectually as the individualistic and atomistic tendency in politics does.

Spencer's philosophy and sociology is, as we have said, a significant advance upon Quetelet, Comte and the historical philosophers. He too argues that social science is both necessary and possible. (Spencer, 1874). But he does not insist, as Comte does, that the subject matter of social laws is mankind developing as a unit; rather he always speaks of the development of social aggregates. Nor does he, like Quetelet, use the "great number" to solve the problem of regular development. He thinks he has found the solution in his formula of evolution.

As evolution stands in a certain though distant relation to social phenomena, it might be accepted as a "universal law." But we cannot accept it as a "social law." In every science, according to Spencer's theory, if we trace the history of particular things backward we shall find that their constituent parts were once in a state of diffusion. And if we trace their history forward from any point we shall find concentrated instead of diffuse conditions. Hence he concludes that the formula for the law of evolution must include both processes, concentration and diffusion. Every perceivable thing, as he states it, is in a state of continuous change; it is either becoming or passing away. The former state consists in the integration or concentration of matter and the dissipation of motion, which he calls evolution. The latter consists in the disintegration of matter and the absorption of motion, which he calls dissolution (Spencer, 1864:94-97).

He demonstrates its validity for all classes of phenomena with great acumen. But the connection between the universal formula and the concrete phenomena is so loose that we gain no explanation of them from it. Applied to everything it explains nothing. It is not really a law of the phenomena. It says no more, at bottom, than that motion is universal without disclosing why.

In the social domain the defect is particularly glaring. The formula fits the social processes in a certain figurative sense, but does not explain them.

> "While there exist nothing but small, wandering assemblages of men, devoid of organization," he says for instance, "the conflicts of these assemblages with one another cannot work changes in structure. But when once there have arisen the definite chieftainships which these conflicts themselves tend to initiate, and especially when the conflicts have ended in permanent subjugations, then arise the rudiments of political organization" (Spencer: 1880:I).

The process uniting social aggregates into political organizations is remotely analogous to his law of evolution to be sure; but we must still have recourse to the law that solicitude for the means of subsistence [Lebensfürsorge] forces each social aggregate to try to make every other social aggregate coming within its reach serve that supreme end. This law fully explains why the stronger of the "small wandering hordes" aim to subject the weaker and exploit their services and it shows the necessity for all the "structures" or variety of organizations which culminate in the state." The universal law" of evolution applies to the process but Spencer fails to emphasize the "social law" which explains it.

But Spencer offers many just observations upon social phenomena and processes. The formula of evolution does not prevent a correct conception of them and in so far as it is harmless and superior to other universal formulas. The most significant part of Spencer's sociology however is his demonstration that psycho-social phenomena develop with regularity. Herein he displays a natural talent and masterliness unequaled save by Bastian. Let us note this feature of his social psychology briefly.

Ethnographic and prehistoric investigations conducted in all climates and regions of the earth have established the remarkable fact that changes in social phenomena from period to period are consequent and logical, in a word, are evolutionary. Thus the investigation of the prehistoric material showed a developing series of utensils from bone to stone, to bronze and to iron. The entire series could not be illustrated in the history of one people but had to be constructed out of the relics of peoples from all regions of the globe. Many groups, moreover, had continued permanently on some one stage without any development whatever. In all the domain of social life, religious, moral, judicial or cultural, it is the same.

The philosophizing human mind finds a logical and strictly regular development from fetishism through anthropomorphism, polytheism, monotheism to the atheism of free thinkers. But scarcely would any one group illustrate the whole series. How many groups still pray to fetishes, conceive their God in human form, people their heaven with throngs of deities or recognize only one Jahveh as they did thousands of years ago! While, on the other hand, there were occasional free-thinkers and atheists even in antiquity.

Spencer's "sociological" and Bastian's "ethnological" works abound in examples of apparent psycho-social development reconstructed out of the contributions of various peoples, times and lands. The first available explanation might seem to be the hypothesis that mankind is a unit and this explanation has often been offered. But man's actual condition is unlike historical constructs. Take any series of psycho-social phenomena whatever and the several phases prevail as generally to-day as at any time in the past. Yet how inviting it is to a nineteenth entury European to construct a "social development" from the condition of unregulated "free love" to polyandry, polygamy and, finally, to the "most beautiful flower of human development," monogamy.

Not only is this method relied upon by Spencer repeatedly and used by Bastian in compiling his "manifestations of race-thoughts;" even Lippert uses it in his thoughtful presentation of the family and the priesthood, etc. Indisputably such series exhibit logical sequence and (logical!) "conformity to law." But the development is not social and must not be taken for it. The development of social institutions ought not to be confounded with the development of mankind itself, with social development in the stricter sense. Psycho-social progress never takes place uniformly throughout mankind. Rather

there is always such a great variety of human conditions that types
may always be found for a logical series. Not only thousands of years
ago but today there are communities living in unregulated free love,
and tribes and races in which polyandry, polygamy and monogamy
continue to prevail. Bastian wants to base a "science of man" upon
a law of the manifestation of "race-thought," upon a case of social-
psychological development, as we should call it and Spencer constructs his sociology out of similiar cases (Bastian, 1881a). To a
certain extent they are justified. Social-psychological investigation
furnishes valuable material. The "examination of the mental creations of aggregates to find the laws of the human mind's growth,"
may be considered an integral part of sociology, or ethnology, the
word Bastian prefers. "Whenever the local surface colorations are
penetrated and analysis is vigorously prosecuted, uniform fundamental conceptions are disclosed" (Bastian 1881a:178). But sociology, the "science of man," is something more. Social and psycho-
social must be sharply distinguished. The former comprehends the
relations between groups and communities of men. The latter, the
manifestations of "race-thought" in the domain of religion, morals,
rights and civilization. Only the laws of the relations of distinct
aggregates of human material to each other are social. In distinction,
the laws of the "mental creations of aggregates," to use Bastian's
language, may be suitably designated psycho-social.

6. The Method of Sociology

After the principal sociological works of the nineteenth century
had been published, including Ratzenhofer's political writings, a
dispute arose concerning the method of sociology. The cause of this
was first of all the strong opposition which developed sporadically
against the so-called "organic" method that was being followed by
Schäffle, Lilienfeld and then by Worms.[1]

---

[1] Schaffle first published his principal work (in 1875) under the title: *Bau
und Leben des sozialen Korpers. Enzyklopadischer Entwurf einer realen Anatomie, Physiologie und Psychologie der menschlichen Gesellschaft, mit besonderer Rucksicht auf die Volkswirtschaft als sozialen Stoffwechsel.* Among this
multitude of titles, the expression "sociology" does not appear and the detailed
biological and physiological excursions that are contained in the work, as well
as the repeated assurances that "real analogies" are concerned, necessarily

At the international congress of sociologists in Paris 1898, a long discussion was held on this subject (*Annales de l'Institut de Sociologie*, Vol. IV). At the session chaired by René Worms, there was no lack of advocates of the "organic" method. The defenders in the forefront of the "organismic" were all present. Besides Worms, the youngest "organicists," Lilienfeld and Novikow were present. If there had been an election campaign the defenders of "organic" method would have won—especially since the philosophic historian, Ludwig Stein from Bern, readily acknowledged its "great scientific merits." Fortunately, the ingenious philosopher Gabriel Tarde was also present and he did not hesitate to vehemently send the "organicists" about their business and confront them with the truth about the complete worthlessness of this "method."

"You compare the State with an organism" (this is a paraphrase of his wording) "but the State does not quite coincide with nationality. Where then is the organism: in the State or in the nation? In the first case, Germany consists of many organisms, while in the latter lives the organism of the political nation, although it is split into three pieces. What kind of organism is it that can live in this bifurcated way?" Then he continued as follows: "After all, if one wishes to treat mankind in a natural scientific way by means of organic theory, then one should consider nationality as the only authentic social organism."

In 1898, this method had to be disproven. Even though it was the year when even Schäffle, on principle, retreated from his "organic method" by stating that he did not mean his analogies to be used as "homologies." If then, at that time, this method had still to be disproven, Gabriel Tarde surely dealt the death-blow. Only old Lilienfeld did not give up in defeat and in his last book *Zur Verteidigung der organischen Methode in der Soziologie* (1898) he

---

leads to the assumption that he seriously considers the "social body" as an organic being. At a later period, Schaffle guarded himself against this interpretation and repeatedly called his work a *Versuch der Soziologie*. In later editions he erased the flat physiological analyses and finally assured us in his memoirs, that he "does not merge sociology and biology" and that the attacks that were aimed at him were unjustified. The result of all this was that in later years he realized the weakness of the organic method. This was not the case with Lilienfeld.

once more although unsuccessfully, defended his life's work. This "method" is abolished once and for all.

It is actually incorrect to speak of an "organic method." For generally only two methods exist: deduction and induction. In scientific researches one either proceeds from facts or pre-conceived notions which means from non-facts. There is no third way. Nevertheless, if following the bad example set by quarrelsome professors of political economy, one speaks of diverse methods, as for example of speculative, historical, psychological, naturalistic, organic method, etc., etc., one must do so by the logic of deduction or induction—for a third procedure is inconceivable. The other so called methods simply indicate the field from which the facts serving as a basis for the research have been taken. Thus, at their best these descriptions (historical, naturalistic, organic, psychological) only represent a sub-species of the two methods: deductive and inductive. The supposedly organic method is deductive because it proceeds from the incorrect presumption that "society" is an organism. This is in fact an inadmissable method, for instead of referring to social facts in order to explain the social world it refers to facts of a very different level, the biological. But the historical method is properly inductive. In order to explain social phenomena it proceeds from corresponding historical facts and avails itself of these facts.

If the sociologist takes the facts, or anchors his theories to conclusions drawn from the life of primitive races, which means from ethnography and ethnology, one may describe them as ethnological for the purpose of characterizing this inductive method more precisely. The "psychological method" with which some political economists tamper, can also be the proper inductive method in psychology if, in order to explain psychological phenomena, it relies on the facts of individual psychic life. If it serves as an explanation for all political-economic phenomena, as some political economists assert, that would constitute an illicit use. It is not at all useful for explaining social phenomena since they did not have their source in the individual psyche.[2]

[2] Durkheim, quite correctly said in his methodological paper (1895): "A purely psychological explanation of social facts is therefore not able to avoid the elimination of everything specific, that is to say, the social." But inasmuch as economic phenomena are also basically social, Durkheim's above mentioned

If we now grant a concession to this perhaps exaggerated and doctrinaire disease of defining a discipline, and we must define the method in sociology more precisely, then we can only define it sociologically, that is as an inductive experimental method which, to explain social phenomena relies on social facts. This approach to sociological method, which clearly has to be inductive, embraces both the concept of the scientific and the historical, as well as the ethnological method. It is scientific for it proceeds inductively like science, and historical, since it uses historical facts to explain social phenomena. But it can also be ethnological if it draws its material from ethnography and ethnology, which means from the life of primitive races, which offers, just as history does, abundant data. Consequently, each and every sociology (following the example set by natural science methodology) has to proceed inductively. The sociologist can proceed either historically or ethnologically, according to his subjective inclination and his assessment of the requirements of particular investigations. Nevertheless, he will always stay within the framework of the sociological method. Each of these methods can of course be applied incorrectly or abused. Nothing can be done about this. There is no cure for dilettantes and pretenders and no branch of science is immune to them. This is the reason why recently the "ethnological method" has frequently been abused, inasmuch as the attempt has been made to prove all sorts of things, i.e., the correctness of Lewis Morgan's ideas on evolution by quite arbitrarily and uncritically assembling quotations from travel books. Thus Richard Hildebrand (1894) made an abortive effort to prove that "development has essentially been the same with tribes and nations who live on different, and even separate continents" and that this development, always and everywhere, takes place in a quite uniform way. Fortunately, the second volume of *Recht und Sitte* was never published. Richard Mucke remarks correctly: "It is quite naive when Hildebrand refers to alleged periods of development (from hunting to cattle-breeding to agriculture), as if these periods had been recognized from antiquity to the recent past. Recently however, strong doubts have been raised from the point of view of

---

sentence might refer to those as well. There is altogether too much exaggeration in the "psychological method" of political economists.

economic history. Instead of *proving* the three periods of development, Hildebrand regards them as a matter of course and accordingly
pre-determines the conditions of law and customs in their succession
by inserting diverse travel notes whenever they can be of use to him"
(Mucke, 1897: 257). The sociologist Steinmetz (1901: 438) also
turns against this "childish and naive abuse" of the ethnological
method, a methodology that "has nothing in common with scientific
research." He writes that "these fanatical adherents to evolutionism
believe that all they have to do is place a few arbitrarily selected
primitive races in a sequence that corresponds to their scheme of
imagination in order to furnish proof of unilineal evolution. Indeed
does it suffice to give a casual reading to the social history of races
and peoples which often reduces itself to an uncritical description of a few dozen arbitrarily joined primitive races? Is there no
better method? Why should we always study the hundreds of cult-
ureless (uncivilized) peoples in such a simplistic way?" By all
means, do we have to treat the study of primitive peoples as awkwardly as possible? The excellent sociologist from Leiden (Steinmetz) may console himself with the thought that such bungling does
not occur only by using the ethnological method—so heartily recom-
mended by him. The historical method also has to endure such abuse.
And the same Richard Hildebrand succeeded in doing both in the
volume mentioned. Obviously ethnology was not sufficient to confirm
Morgan's idea of evolution. He also sought out historical sources
(Tacitus) and used them badly. The historian Eugen von Below
pitifully laments this abuse of history. He writes: "One grants unconditional trust to the comparative method in order to ascertain laws
of evolution that are valid for all people and downgrades in favor
of such abstract analogies, statements from immediate sources about
the behavior of the old Teutons." Von Below here means that famous
ambiguity that Hildebrand takes up in discussing Tacitus' *Germania,*
which Mucke also rejects with justified indignation. (1897: 141).

At present, sociology has to suffer more than the other sciences
under the invasion of such dilettantes and pretenders who compromise all the sciences. They are never concerned with the problem area
itself but about writing a book. And even if there is only a "volume
one," to consecrate it with very trivial purposes. There are always

enough fools, even in professional circles, who are impressed by every printed book, even if it contains the worst trash.

Part III

The Interconnection
of Social Elements

1. The Primitive Horde

As individual consciousness, long dormant, does not awaken until the mind has passed through the early stages of development, so also political reflection is not aroused until after stock has been taken of other complex social phenomena. In natural science we are confronted at the very outset with composite units which have to be analyzed. And so, too, modern social science has to work laboriously back to the primitive horde, reconstructing the originals of modern social communities out of scattered vestiges in traditions and survivals, but deriving great assistance from living examples of wild, "uncivilized" hordes.[1]

So-called "mother-right" is an instance. There are vestiges of it still among civilized peoples, and its former diffusion is confirmed by its presence among contemporary uncivilized races. It is the Ariadne's thread of sociology, leading through the complex social communities of present and historical times back to the primitive horde.

The type of "family" presided over by the "father" existed in Europe even at the dawn of history. The Greeks and the Romans considered it the pristine form established by nature, the true

[1] Darwin gives the following graphic picture, from personal observation, of a politically unorganized horde: "The astonishment which I felt, as I first saw a troop of Tierra-del-Fuegians on a wild and rugged coast, I shall never forget. For the thought flashed through my mind at once: Thus were our forefathers. These men were absolutely naked of clothing and covered only with paint. Their long hair was twisted together, their mouths-bedriveled from excitement, and their expression wild, amazed and suspicious. They possessed scarcely any skill at all, and lived like wild beasts on whatever they could catch. They had no government, and had no mercy toward those not of their own race" (Darwin, 1871: II, 312; Cf., Gumplowicz, 1883: 195).

germ of all later social forms. They followed the tradition of the Asiatic races and European science accepted the current view.

Only recently has ripened reflection and acute observation discovered that the "father-family" was preceded by a period in which a very narrow consanguineous group flocked about the mother as its founder. The evidence collected by Bachofen, Giraud-Teulon, McLennan, and more recently by Lippert, Dargun and Wilken, must be considered conclusive. Even in Germanic law, Dargun has recently shown undoubted traces of a former "mother-right."

Hitherto it has sufficed to prove that historically, or rather prehistorically, there was a "mother-family" and resulting "mother-rights," which survived for centuries. But it is more important, in our opinion, to show that the "mother-family" is the necessary consequence of the constitution of an earlier group. Not only is this necessary to a proper conception of the "mother-family," it will also help us to understand the nature of what for the present we must assume to have been the primitive horde. The very fact that the former existed confirms the existence of the latter.

Such a horde cannot be conceived of simply as new, or as proceeding directly from the hands of "a creator;" for in distant parts of the world there are hordes that are primitive still. It is a group of men who are still dependent upon the simplest animal impulses, whose conditions of life and social constitution show no social change. Its life moves upon the plane of the simplest and most common impulses inherent in man.

The satisfaction of hunger and thirst, the first necessity, engages the men of the primitive horde and constitutes a great part of their life work. The satisfaction of the sexual impulses is the next strongest factor.

The simplest form of sexual relations is promiscuity, transient connection within the horde according to accidental encounter or stronger momentary attraction. It is still exemplified in the conduct of contemporary uncivilized tribes (Post, 1875:16).

No fathers are recognized because, as a rule, they are unknown. The bond of kinship between the men and their own children is lacking and the only tie of blood other than kinship with the common stock, which binds the whole horde together, is through the mother. Under this primitive system there could be no other family than the "mother-family." The children were hers; she exercised authority over them and over the "family"—hence "mother-rule" and "mother-right."

This type of family organization had nearly disappeared at the dawn of written history. But numerous traces of it persisting have been collected. Further proof is furnished by the "ethnological" explanation of the subordinate position of woman where the opposite system prevails.

A conspicuous case is the Biblical narrative, which treats woman as a secondary creation of God since she was made of the rib of the man; a circumstance tending to justify his authority.

This is perhaps one of the earliest examples showing that no actual ruler is ever at a loss for a theoretical explanation of his "right." When woman lost her authority, she also had to make the best of a descent from the insignificant rib of a man, as the political philosophers in the new order of society alleged. They who suffer the injury must also endure the ridicule. Later the subject classes were traced to an inferior descendant of Noah; while the ruling classes were called the descendants of his privileged, first-born, son. These are all genealogical tricks and etiological lies of the historian.

It is recognized that mother-rule everywhere gave place to father-rule; but the natural forces which produced this revolution in the original constitution of society have never been pointed out so far as we know. Yet marriage by capture or, more exactly, exogamic connection explains it fully.

The universality of woman stealing both in the present and in the past is fully established and the custom has been well described by ethnologists. Too little weight has been given to the circumstance which constitutes its real essence: the wife must always be stolen from another horde.

This is self-evident when we consider the condition of a horde living in primitive promiscuity. Within the horde woman stealing is impossible. It must be from without; and to this form of it the gynecocratic [matriarchic] constitution gives abundant incentive.

In the raids of unrelated hordes the woman has been and in many cases still is more valuable than cattle or any other form of food-supply. In the gynecocratic horde an exceptional position can be claimed for her, for the captor can hold her as his individual property; whereas the native women are common and occupy a ruling position protected by custom.

The foreign woman has to share in their privileges; belonging exclusively to her "lord," she must serve as his slave. This is greatly to his advantage; it was the beginning of his "emancipation" in the primitive horde. No wonder that the advantages which this invocation secured caused it to spread so that, when the historical period opened, traditions of woman stealing are universal. Recollect, for example, the rape of the Grecian Helen by a prince from Asia Minor, with which Grecian history begins; and the rape of the Sabine women, from which Roman history starts. Herodotus, the father of European historiography, begins characteristically by reciting the rape of Asiatic women by the Greeks, and of Grecian women by the inhabitants of Asia.

Woman stealing readily developed into the institution of marriage by capture, the universality of which is fully attested to by the countless survivals still persisting. (Post, 1875:54: Dargun, 1883: 78).

But as the custom spread the mother-family and mother-right necessarily declined; the native women could not maintain their position in competition with the foreigner. The charm of the new and strange alone would have assured the latter a certain preference but it also afforded the man an opportunity, certainly not unwelcome, to escape from a condition which had become unnecessary, burdensome and "unreasonable," though the innovation must have been a rude offense against old and sacred customs.

Thus mother-rule was overthrown, and with it fell mother-right and the mother-family, while the sovereignty of the men was extended over the native women also. They had to adapt themselves to the inevitable; the good old custom disappeared and a new ethico-legal institution prevailed: father-hood, father-family, father-right.

But its significance for the social development of mankind was increased by one of the attending circumstances, the mingling of unlike ethnic groups. The process has been continuous and universal and the intermixtures are interminable in number, variety and degree. Together with political, judicial and other institutions, they have produced an endless number of differentiated social unities.

However, rape was not the only occasion of early intertribal hostilities; the plunder of property must also have been an incentive just as it has always been and still is, and not among uncivilized tribes alone.

Simple plundering raids are carried on at irregular intervals as necessity dictates and circumstances allow. But they generally lead to expeditions for the permanent subjection of the foreign horde and the acquisition of territory.[2]

These latter conditions are the most favorable for the development of civilization, as has been explained elsewhere (Gumplowicz, 1883: 231). Yet the proximate basis of evolution is the institution of property which develops in connection with them.

We have already seen that property developed concurrently with the control of one group of men over another is in fact, a means to uphold it (Cf. Gumplowicz, 1881:344). But a few remarks must be added here, partly for the sake of greater clarity, and partly because of some recent works which were written in ignorance of our explanation.

In the first place property in land is, in our opinion, the only form which serves as an instrument of control. "Property" in movable goods should be distinguished from property in immovable goods. What is there in common between the unlimited possession and free disposal of chattels and that juridical relation in virtue of which a person may keep a piece of land exclusively for his own benefit? Yet for these fundamentally different conceptions the European languages use but one term, with consequent indistinctness and confusion of ideas in science.

Common property (*Eigentum, proprium*) is a contradiction in terms. Yet even separate or private "property" has been discussed as a simple concept. What might be true of property in movable goods has been applied without distinction to property in land, a very different thing. This is certainly a great mistake.

---

[2] Some idea of the behavior of primitive stocks can be gotten from the modern Bedouins who, however, have made considerable progress. A recent French traveler writes: "To fall upon caravans of strangers, to drive off flocks, capture goods, kill and massacre the defenders, especially if they are inhabitants of cities, such are the virtues which he rates highest. All these ignoble heroes of Bedouin legend we would send to the gallows as highway robbers" (Charms, 1881).

To justify private property as the natural right of the individual to the fruit of his own exertions sufficiently explains property in movable goods including the product of the land which a man's own labor has tilled, but does not explain property in land or in the fruit of another's labor. While to trace its origin to the actual possession of weapons, ornaments, etc., an attempt which Dargun has recently renewed, leaves a gap between movable goods and immovable which no analogy can bridge, for they are totally different. No doubt individual property in movable goods has always existed, for the conditions of human life require it. But the conditions of property in land are quite different. Land is not the product of human labor and its use is temporary; it can be occupied, detained or possessed only in a limited and figurative sense. It might be possible to defend a small portion of land against a trespasser but it would be impossible to defend the larger tracts which alone are under consideration here. Property in land is not a physical fact and cannot be explained by physical facts: occupation, labor, etc. To say that land is occupied or possessed, as is currently done, is to use a metaphor or a legal fiction. Land, by its nature, admits of only one relation to man, the enjoyment of its use, the common enjoyment of its use, the common enjoyment of many.

Hence the first form of property in land must have been its common use, and further, it must have been used by such a group or horde as we everywhere encounter in the beginning of social evolution. The evidence supporting this conclusion is abundant. Even the primitive hordes of modern times use land in common.[3]

Thus, in the nature of the case, common property in movable goods is impossible but so-called common property in land is real and original. What is commonly called private property in land is never real, much less original; it is purely a legal relation presupposing a complicated social organization. It presupposes, first of all, an organized control, with power to compel obedience. This is necessary so that the individuals of the ruling class may procure from the subject class the labor power to till their lands and make them useful. Thus they prove their "ownership." Without power to dispose

[3] "Man does not have property in immovable things in this stage" (Lippert, 1883: I: 35).

of the labor force of others it would be merely a name; with that power property becomes valuable.

A second presupposition is the possibility of excluding some from the enjoyment of the product in favor of others. The organized whole must protect the movable goods thus acquired; for if they were left exposed to every aggressor it would not be worthwhile to raise them. In a word, property in land is a legal relation which necessarily presupposes governmental organization and the guarantee of legal protection.

Thus the "common property" which the primitive horde is said to enjoy in the land on which it has settled is simply common use and not real ownership, for the word "own" contains originally the idea of separateness. Laying aside our complex, advanced legal relations, and speaking of primitive conditions, we must take "ownership" to be separate ownership and its antithesis is unseparated, non-owned, *i.e.*, common. It was a much later and highly refined jurisprudence which transferred the idea of separate ownership to a juristic person composed of a number of natural persons and it would be an unseemly transfer of modern legal conceptions to speak of the common property of the primitive horde.

Passing on from the use of the land in common, we first recognize the beginnings of separate immovable property when one horde has overpowered another and uses its labor force. As soon as there are subjects who are excluded from the enjoyment of certain goods which their own labor contributed to produce, in favor of the ruling class, and when the members of the ruling class are protected in their enjoyment of them by the well-organized whole, then there arises separate or private property in immovable goods. Not only did this form of property arise with the organization of control and by means of it, it was at first the sole object of the organization, which, moreover, contains the germ of the State. So long as organization continues in a nomadic condition, and lords and slaves alike have no abiding place, we do not call it a State. We apply that term only when a permanent dwelling place has been adopted and the organization asserts its sovereign right of property over the land it occupies against all other social communities.

2. The State

The State is a social phenomenon consisting of social elements behaving according to social laws. The first step is the subjection of one social group by another and the establishment of sovereignty; and the sovereign body is always the less numerous. But numerical inferiority is supplemented by mental superiority and greater military discipline. There is a double life in the State. We can clearly distinguish the activities of the States as a whole, as a single social structure, from those emanating from the social elements.

The activities of the State as a whole originate in the sovereign class which acts with the assistance or with the compulsory acquiescence of the subject class. The movement is from within out. It is directed against other states and social groups. Its object is always defence against attacks, increase of power and territory, that is, conquest in one form or another. And its motive in the ultimate analysis, lies in human providence, in the impulse to secure conditions favorable for existence [in *Lebensfürsorge*] to use Lippert's apt expression.

The activities within the State are seen in the several social elements and arise naturally from the positions which they occupy in the State and in relation to each other.

The motive of each is essentially the same as that which animates the State as a whole. They seek conditions favorable to existence and therefore endeavor to increase their power. In particular, the superior class seeks to make the most productive use of the subject classes. As a rule this leads to oppression and can always be considered as exploitation. The subject classes drive for greater powers of resistance in order to lessen their dependence.

These are the simplest and most fundamental efforts and they account for the internal and external development of the State. While differences in the history of different States are due to different local and ethnic conditions. As the commonest things of life are often the most difficult to understand so it is that political scientists to this day have no clear conception of the State. Each has his own definition and scarcely one is correct.

Modern scholasticism has made the theory of the State endless and fruitless. "Volume I" of a work on the definition of the State

has appeared in Berlin already and there is a "history" and a
methodology of the subject. Who will write a theory of the history of
the State? Some use general terms, calling the State a "politically
organized national person" (Bluntschli, 1885:23) or the "highest
form of personality," or the "organism of freedom." Others solve the
problem by using a metaphor, by calling it a "living being," an
"organism," etc. But Knies justly remarks that "it is a sad proof
of unclear thinking to discuss scientific conceptions in metaphors."
Schulze made great progress in the method of defining the State by
insisting that "it is a question of separating the essential from the
unessential in the plenitude of social phenomena;" and after methodically searching for its historical characteristics he concluded that it
is the "association of a settled folk in an organic community under
a sovereign power and a definite constitution for the purpose of
securing all the common ends of a folk's existence, above all for the
establishment of law and order.

   But his definition can be improved by eliminating superfluous
parts. The idea by no means clearly expressed in the words "an
organic community" is included in the preceding phrase; for a
"folk," and much more, a "settled folk," is "an organic community."
Indeed a "settled folk" is a State. No further "association" is needed
to make it one. It is superfluous also to mention a "constitution,"
for a written constitution is not essential and an unwritten constitution is a prerequisite of a "settled folk."

   If nothing but the universal and essential characteristics of
every State were incorporated into the definition, an agreement could
be easily reached for there are but two. First, there are certain institutions directed to securing the sovereignty of some over the others.
Secondly, the sovereignty is always exercised by a minority. A State,
therefore, is the organized control of the minority over the majority.
This is the only true and universal definition; it is fitting in every
case.[4]

   ---

   [4] Elsewhere in his book Schulze gives almost the same definition. In section
41 he says that "it is observable that in all actual States men are subject to a
sovereign power and that, as members of the body politic, they are even held
by physical compulsion to certain lines of activity." And in section 49: "The
presence of a supreme controlling power is essential to the notion of a State."
(Von Ihering, 1877: I: 130) defines the State to be "society as a possessor of an

But many definitions of the State predicate its end, declaring it to be a union or community for securing the common weal, for realizing justice, etc. All this is wholly inadmissible. No State was ever founded with one of these ends in view and there are many which are States though they have never exhibited even a trace of such a purpose. The truth is that in the course of time under favorable conditions every sovereign organization necessarily acts in harmony with these ends. Thus any State may serve them. Indeed after reaching a certain stage of development every State does endeavor to advance justice, welfare, etc. The definition must not be confined to States at one stage of development only. It must apply regardless of the stake which has been or ever will be attained. Moreover, the affirmation of such ends conceals the fact that the single object in organizing a State was to establish the sovereignty of some over the others, and that the results which necessarily followed were not foreseen, much less intended. They cannot be referred to the intention of the founders who followed their own immediate advantage, as all men do. High above egoistic human efforts social development is the product of natural law.

There is still another universal characteristic of the State, although it has hitherto been wholly overlooked; there are always ethnic differences between the ruling class and the ruled.

We called attention to it for the first time in our former publications. "Authorities" in political science solemnly ignored it but they could not refute it. The world moves, nevertheless.[5] States have never arisen except through the subjection of one stock by another, or by several others in alliance. This is not accidental; it is essential, as we have already proven. No State has arisen without original ethnic heterogeneity. Its unity is the product of social development.

---

orderly and disciplined power of compulsion." But he tries to define the "State" by the less clear term "society" and, besides, adopts the untenable French view of "popular sovereignty." Continuing the argument, he again defines the State as "organized social compulsion." Properly understood this is nearly correct. But we had already defined the State to be "the organized sovereignty of some over the others;" and as "sovereignty" is more specific than "compulsion," our definition is the clearer of the two (Gumplowicz, 1877).

[5] Playing on the words attributed to Galileo while under ecclesiastical sentence for his astronomical views.—*E pur si muove.*

Spencer without especially emphasizing ethnic heterogeneity confirms our position when he says that "no tribe becomes a nation by simple growth." Instead of the naive conception that a family gradually grows to be a tribe and the tribe becomes a folk, he holds that there must be a combination of several tribes. To which we add that, with perhaps a few unknown exceptions, tribes are united only by the forcible subjection of one to the other. Spencer also goes on to say that "no great society (nation) is formed by the direct union of the smallest societies" (Spencer, 1880:I). By which he evidently means that a great nation necessarily comprises several smaller ones and includes a multitude of ethnically compound groups. It is a group of the N*th* power, so to speak.

Let us observe the necessary result of founding a State, *i.e.*, of subjecting one community to another or to a union of several others. It has already been pointed out that it is due to the effort to secure conditions favorable for existence. But the efforts which men naturally make to better their condition require the services of other men. If this were not so, States would never have been founded and mankind would have developed along quite different lines or not at all. It will be readily conceded that civilized men cannot live without the services of others. But there is no man known to history nor can any be thought of so uncivilized as to be able to renounce the co-operation of his kind.

The services which are needed are not easy and the farther back we go the heavier they necessarily were. Their alleviation is an infallible characteristic of progressing civilization. We can observe it in the development of current industrial relations. The struggle for power is the real subject matter of so-called social legislation (*Social politik*). How men must have had to labor and indeed must still labor without the knowledge and the means of civilization![6]

[6] The naval captain, Pantero Pantera, said of labor in the galleys in *L'Armata Navale*, 1614: "High wages will supply a galley with soldiers and sailors, but freemen cannot be persuaded to submit to service at the oars, to be fastened to the chain and to take without possibility of resistance the bastinading and other inflictions incident to labor in the galleys." Yet, if the galley was to move with precision, the rowing must be controlled by chain, bastinado and all. Therefore he advised that convicted criminals be sentenced to this slave's work. Such was labor in the galleys even so late as the seventeenth century (Gravière, 1884).

Many governments still commute death sentences to labor in the mines expecting to profit by this act of grace. Earlier, the conquered were similarly condemned to slave-labor in the interest of the victors. Men never have treated their fellow-men (using that word in its most primitive sense) so severely. And why should they do violence to their natural feelings when strangers have never been lacking whom it has always been meritorious to prey upon. United under the leadership of the eldest and the mightiest they have imposed the yoke of servitude upon the stranger in hard fought battle.

Thus nature laid the foundation of ethnically composite States in human necessities and sentiments. Human labor being necessary, sympathy with kindred and tribe and deadly hatred of strangers led to foreign wars. So conquest and the satisfaction of needs through the labor of the conquered, essentially the same though differing in form, is the great theme of human history from prehistoric times to the latest plan for a Congo State.

Notice the condition thus established. The one party commands; the other labors and accommodates itself to superior force. As every war must cease raging and the weaker party must give up fruitless opposition, so nature helps to make the situation peaceful and lasting. But peace and permanence is the cement of order, out of which come habit, custom, and law.

The hostile contact of different social elements of unlike strength is the first condition for the creation of rights; the conditions established by force and accepted in weakness, if peaceably continued, become rightful. Inequality of power is essential, for contestants of equal strength would wear themselves out in mutual conflict or, more naturally, would unite and subject a weaker. Moreover inequality is stamped on every right: the husband orders his wife, the parent in the strength of his years commands his children, the owner excludes all others from enjoying the fruits of his property. All these are rights expressing the orderly relations of unequals. It is an error and a delusion to think that rights have been or can be equally distributed. They arise only in the relations which exist in the State. They express them and measure their inequality.

Let us now examine more closely the nature of political relations. Universally there is a ruling minority and a subject majority, this is the essence of the State as it is the essence of sovereignty.

But what is the ruling minority disposed to do? There is but one thing it can wish, *viz.*: to live in better circumstances with the services of the subject majority than it could without them. The result is a common industrial enterprise conducted under compulsion in which the greater burden, all the unfree service, falls upon the subject class though the rulers freely contribute their no less valuable share in support of the political community. Thus compulsory labor is organized through the organization of sovereignty and the whole body of rights.

The kind of industrial labor depends upon the nature of the soil, the climate and the material resources of the State. If the subjected population was roving over rich agricultural lands it will be compelled to till the soil and the conquerors will settle among them so as to exploit both land and people to the best advantage. The agricultural States of Europe still bear traces of such a compulsory organization of labor wherever an exclusive nobility has settled among a numerous agricultural population, spreading itself like a net over the whole land.

But a huge swarm inhabiting an extended prairie and pasture land will adopt a different social organization. The captives taken on many a plundering raid will be distributed among the members to perform the heavier work of tending cattle, transporting tents and the like. The nomadic State thus organized will fulfill its political functions as truly as the settled State of the large property owners. In the latter case the lord over his manor or in his castle manages the peasants and vassals settled about him, satisfying their simple necessities from the produce of the fields and reserving the surplus for himself. In the nomadic State the master from his chieftain's tent rules over his numerous following who tend his herds and enjoy a simple subsistence out of the increase; the rest of which, after the richer yield for his family is deducted, is added to his accumulated wealth and capital.

The organization will be different still where a narrow strip of coast like Phoenicia, or a group of islands like Venice, make agricultural or pastoral pursuits impossible. The superior speculative talent of the ruling class must suggest another method of utilizing the services of the subject class. They will be put to ship-building and employed as sailors, so that the ruler may seek distant coasts and win wealth and power in navigation and foreign trade.

Labor must always be organized under compulsion; the training and the discipline for the State are necessary. It demands of the laboring class, in the beginning at least, untold sacrifice of life and health; but finally in a rising civilization they become participants in the material and moral possessions.

The life of the State is summed up in this common though unequal labor. In it the state performs its task and fulfills its mission, if task and mission can be spoken of where blind impulse rules on every hand. Out of it comes the highest moral possession of mankind, civilization (Gumplowicz, 1883: 231 *et seq.*)

3. *The State as Industrial Organization*

The motive force in the establishment of primitive political relations was economic. As has been seen, higher material welfare was sought. But this force never fails; the innermost nature of man keeps it in ceaseless operation, promoting the development of the State as it laid its foundation. Investigate the cause of any political revolution and the result will prove that social progress is always produced by economic causes. Indeed it cannot be otherwise since man's material need is the prime motive of his conduct.[7]

This necessity incited men to exploit the services of their fellows. Nature supplied a great many different groups whose natural antagonism is still an important factor in developing political relations; for human labor could not be exploited without violence, and ethnic and social contrasts promote the disregard of all human considerations, facilitating the satisfaction of human needs and maintaining the everlasting struggle. Thus the two fundamental social processes are satisfaction of needs and exploitation of the services (*Dienstbarmachung*) of foreigners. Two apparently unimportant means with which nature accomplishes so much. Moreover this evolution cannot cease. For nature has provided that man's needs shall not stand still. Higher and "nobler" wants are constantly awakened. At the very point where natural ethnic distinctions would disappear,

---

[7] "The real motive force is actual need. The only reason for formulating it in written law is to give it recognized legal basis," says Bruns on the Development of the Roman Law, 11 Holtzendorff's *Encyclopaedie*, p. 91.

artificial, "social" distinctions arise to perpetuate the antagonism of human groups. Human desires never fail and there are groups differing in stature, color and odor, in diet, morals and religion, or in possessions, conditions, calling, occupations and interests.

Only in the course of social development do they rise to higher stages and meet us in new forms as the need for the bare means of subsistence at the most primitive level is transformed in the higher stages into the necessity for satisfying ambition, love of glory, the interests of a dynasty and various other ideals; and the life and death struggle between hordes anthropologically different becomes a contest between social groups, classes, estates and political parties. The great sociological difficulty in describing the course of development arises from the fact that there can be no leaps. Though social development like every other case of evolution is gradual, the transitional phases are innumerable and imperceptible and overtax the resources of science. The only alternative is to treat a small number of examples chosen more or less arbitrarily, which is all we can endeavor to do here.

It must not be forgotten that here, as elsewhere, the same phenomena are found sometimes contemporaneously, sometimes in sequence. There is a social development in time from the simplest satisfaction of necessities and the rudest struggle for existence up to the highest needs of a refined civilization and the system of rights developed in political strife. While its counterpart with all the imperceptible gradations and vivid contrasts can be seen in the cross-section, so to speak, of a State on the highest plane of development. If we look at its inner structure we see the proletarian toiling for his daily bread in the sweat of his brow, and all the countless stages to the uppermost rung of society, to the statesman struggling for position or for principle. Moreover what is true of the desires is true also of the means of satisfying them.

This is said in passing. Let us now turn to a closer analysis of social evolution founded upon and promoted by organized sovereignty. Equality prevails only in the most primitive hordes. In them alone are needs satisfied without the subordination of one man's labor to another's ends. In them alone there is neither command nor obedience, lordship nor dependence, chieftain nor subject. Equal misery is the common lot.

"When Rink asked the Nicobarians who among them was the chief they replied, laughing, how could he believe that one could have power against so many?" And there are many similar examples. Among the Haidahs "the people seemed all equal." Among the California tribes "each individual does as he likes." Among the Navajos, "each is sovereign in his own right." (Spencer, 1880:II: sec. 71: 466).

> "Groups of Esquimaux, of Australians, of Bushmen, of Fuegians, are without even that primary contrast of parts implied by settled chieftainship. Their members are subject to no control but such as is temporarily acquired by the stronger, or more cunning, or more experienced, not even a permanent nucleus is present." (Spencer, 1880:I: sec. 228;II: sec. 456).

Plainly the subjection of some to the service of others is opposed to the feeling of equality, of solidarity, of consanguineous relationships. Even the ruling classes of Europe exhibit the same feeling. "The nobleman in a peasant's cottage is the peer of the commander of the Palatine's army." "*Szalchcic no zagrodzie rowny wojewodzie,*" say the Poles. This is the equality of the syngenetic group (Gumplowicz, 1883:40).

The primitive horde emerges from this condition of uniform independence and uniform misery only when a strange horde comes within its reach as the result generally of migration or a plundering raid. If it subjects the strangers its wants are more easily satisfied and its economic life is raised above the primitive condition. The "extra" labor of some for others begins.

If the rulers should remain content with the higher stage of economic life; if they could isolate their State from external influences, development would cease. But Lycurgian plans can never be realized. States can never be "isolated" even with Chinese walls about them.

Stagnation in development is prevented by the steady growth of the wants of both rulers and subjects, for the law that wants increase with the opportunity to satisfy them is universal, and the isolated State is also an object of desire to its neighbors near and remote, so that as they grow powerful it must increase its means of offense and defense. Even the least aggressive State will be drawn in spite of itself into the stream of "history. Evolution cannot stop.

As strivings increase, the State, which was called into being to satisfy them, is driven to further conquests of territory and power. But the same tendency which animates the State as a whole also animates each social division within it. The only difference is that its manifestation is confined by established political relations to a struggle for control by peaceful means; while outside the State it breaks out in bloody and destructive wars.

However unavoidable war may be, it cannot last forever; for it produces physical and mental exhaustion and if it becomes chronic the end for which it is undertaken is thereby defeated.

Peace is as necessary as occasional war, for both are the result of a natural law of strife. Thus it was possible to establish States, since otherwise the more powerful would have had to exterminate the weaker. Peace is useless without the opportunity to satisfy the wants which war was undertaken to secure. However, only one party can triumph. One party secures the better satisfaction of its wants; and the other is circumscribed and oppressed. Some force is necessary to maintain the unequal condition in peace. Suitable institutions must be set up and sedulously sustained. This the ruling and possessing class does while the other class accommodates itself to the law of the victors. But it jealously guards the established limits, now staking everything on preventing any further circumscription, now striving to enlarge them.

So apparent peace is only a continuous latent struggle. What is its object? What are the means employed? What is its essential characteristic? The immediate object of dispute is the body of reciprocal rights. The less privileged oppose every limitation whatever asserted in the interest of sovereignty: restricted connubial rights, exclusion from office and positions of honor, incapacity for holding landed property and others only relatively less important and less common. Sovereignty cannot be maintained without them. The peaceful struggle of the underprivileged is directed to breaking them down and eventually removing them.

In the common interest, the subject class must be assigned some privileges and functions, for Spartan severity cannot be rigorously enforced. Even the superfluous Helot population was not always exterminated; neither do the Australian colonists hunt down the natives everywhere. In Sparta, to be sure, the contest of the Helots could not be conducted by peaceable means but the sovereignty over them was not shortlived on that account. It succumbed to another course of development.

Yet wherever in the interest of the whole the least concession is made to the subject class it serves as a lever to enlarge their privileges. Two conditions, however, are necessary to success: well-being and enlightenment. When the ruling class is well off, the condition of the subject class will necessarily rise too; otherwise the desires of the sovereign class cannot be fully satisfied. But appetite comes with eating and the initial progress creates the desire for more.

Thoughts cannot be hermetically sealed, and as social facts even more than any other facts provoke reflection, the subject class, if relieved from external pressure and direct need, will experience mental growth. The ruling class is influenced less by the outside world and by social relations. Their lives are easier and they are lulled to sleep mentally. It is otherwise down in the seething mass of the "people." Huge numbers of them may succumb to the hard conditions of life and languish in ignorance and stupidity; but if the pressure ever relaxes, or if it falls on unusually strong natures, the psychological reaction is all the more violent. On the whole the life of the subject classes is more fruitful in ideas.

Some degree of well-being and some ideas are the necessary leaven, as even Aristotle knew. It only needs a favorable opportunity, an external danger or defeat, a permitted popular gathering, a tumult of unusual dimensions, to make the first breach. Further development in the market-place and on the forum is unavoidable. The same factors are active. The method is the same, the result is the same. Woe to the conquered, was the cry in the beginning and woe to the conquered is often the cry to the last.

4. Development of Rank and Political Organization

The social struggle however is not so simple as it is here represented. Economic development and historical facts create a multitude of classes equally endowed with political tendencies and the result is a complexity of political rights. Intermediate classes intervene between the master and the slave which may hold the lower classes in dependence and be in subjection to the upper, or be superior to all in certain spheres of activity and dependent in others. They may be both rulers and ruled.

The simplest political organization consisting of lords and vassals, the simple *civitas* of the Romans, receives the first fatal shock from the foreign merchants. The effect of their visits upon the primitive political constitution is vividly portrayed by Caesar in his *Commentaries*. The Belgians were the bravest of all the Gallic tribes, he says, "because they are farthest removed from the civilization and culture of the Province and the merchants visit them least often bringing things which tend to effeminate." The merchants seeking gain penetrate the primitive political organization and disturb its monotonous course. Their "fine articles" charm the uncultivated man.

But these "missionaries of commerce" are the pioneers of culture. They visit the most inhospitable shores and impenetrable regions of unknown lands, staking both property and life; and the thousands who fall are followed by other thousands fearless of death—all for the sake of "business." This is a universal fact, attested to by classical witnesses, by the history of European colonization in all quarters of the globe, and, above all, by the living present. The clever salesman, the trader of wares seeking gain, is the first to enter the Congo and the Niger valleys, braving the difficulties of the dark continent and visiting tribes who receive the stranger as they would a wild beast. Then, if his venture succeeds, come the "chivalrous lords" and "patriotic statesmen."

The merchant, coming as guest and offering his wares for sale, is personally free and knows how to maintain his freedom. Identified neither with the lords nor with their vassals, he soon becomes necessary to both, for the "articles" which he brings from a distance delight them and awaken new desires which must be satisfied. The one class labors more, the other saves more in order to get the new means of satisfying the new wants. They begin to grow "effeminate;" but it must be added that they also grow in "civilization" and "culture."[8]

[8] Tacitus also understood that civilization is promoted by trade and it is clear that he meant trade with foreigners. Thomas Aquinas speaks of the merchants as strangers in the State. He considered it desirable that the citizens should refrain from mercantile pursuits leaving them to "foreigners" lest "by the practice of trade" they "grow covetous." Thomas Aquinas, *Opusulae Venitiis*. 1587, p. 298. (*De Regemine Principum*.)

They learn to value and to tolerate the stranger, and he in turn discovers the virgin treasures of the land. Things are gladly given to him which before his time had no worth and without him would still have none. Occasional visits are followed by permanent settlements and the first settlers are followed by more numerous followers. A middle class forces itself between lords and vassals, personally free and having no direct share in the government; instituting its own corporation in its own quarter—the later city. By compromise with the lords it creates for itself rights within an assured sphere limited and defined both from above and below. (Gumplowicz, 1883: 332). Thus a new factor arises in political evolution and social strife. Changes proceed more rapidly than before. Foreign commerce makes domestic labor more productive and awakens handicrafts and industry, while those who follow the new branches of economic labor are consolidated by their common interests into compact groups demanding their rights.

But such rights are only the realization, the unhindered exercise of acquired power, *i.e.*, supremacy within politically recognized limits, which, however various the means of acquiring it, consists essentially in the free and disposable possession of whatever will satisfy human wants.

Prominent in the list is the possession, or better, the disposal of human energy and labor. Without human services every other possession is valueless unless indeed by means of it human labor can be instantly secured, which amounts to the same thing. The power varies in greatness with the coefficient of disposable human energies and not with the amount of other possessions, though generally the former is proportional to the latter.

There is one method of utilizing human services directly, that is without the intervention of other possessions. It is the one by which the founders of political order assure themselves of the services of their vassals and slaves. They rely upon physical and mental superiority, strict military organization and discipline and innate tact in governing. Power thus acquired may be strengthened by various material and moral means or it may fall into decay through weakness, lack of discipline and energetic opposition.

Other means of facilitating and assuring the uninterrupted application of human services is the possession of supplies and of institutions for promoting production. The most powerful moral means is a purely natural factor, habit. Having elsewhere (Gumplowicz, 1877: sec. 23) emphasized its overwhelming power in political and legal relations, it is a great satisfaction to find our views confirmed.

"The power of habit is mysterious as witchery. It sways the insignificant life of the individual and the great history of mankind. The dark impulse of all material things pauses in the midst of change. In the midst of ceaseless motion it becomes stable for a moment. By the pendulum's uniform swing it gives constant vibration the appearance of regular motion; and essentially the same impulse gives equipoise to all the mental activities of our race. First the natural inclination to repeat the same act, then the incorporation of the repetitions in regular habit: how much conscious thinking and willing thus gradually becomes the unconscious function of an unthinking machine! Rule, order, custom and law transmitting civilization from generation to generation would be unintelligible without the incessant action of this mysterious force."

Thus nature itself is the strongest ally of the rulers. Habit becomes an element of their power and its incessant action produces the other moral factors, order, custom, rights, and also the moral bonds that unite men of the same language and religion. For however unlike the rulers and ruled are in terms of power, the former have understood how to adapt themselves to the latter, at least outwardly (Gumplowicz, 1883:253).

Thus do the founders of sovereignty sustain their power, but the power of the new middle class is built up differently. It starts from the possession of material goods and the more necessary they are, the greater is the equivalent offered for the surrender of them, whether in labor, services and goods, or in the right to demand services. In any case the equivalent can be reduced to terms of human labor. Thus, the middle class also acquires political power. By labor, industry, inventiveness, speculation and thrift it can even attain the balance of power in the State.

That the possession of material goods can be a source of power only in the State is so self-evident as scarcely to need mentioning. Where the law of the club and anarchy prevail they fall to the physically superior; no power-producing energy is inherent in them. Within the State however, purely economic power, as we may briefly call it, has secured recognition and has its part in sovereignty.

Let us consider how the middle class exercises its authority; who performs the services to which their authority, like every other, may eventually be reduced. The rulers as a class do not perform them. They must be performed either by the subjects as a class or by wage-laborers drawn from other sources. The rulers therefore cannot recompense the middle class directly by them. They offer treasures of the land over which they exercise "eminent domain," products of the fauna which are also the "lord's property," agricultural products produced by the labor of the subject people, and finally the concession of rights to have exclusive sale of articles of universal necessity: to hold markets, to claim certain services from the unfree, etc. In so far as the lords must acquiesce as a class and each can be complelled by law and right, it is proper to speak of the power of the middle class over the rulers, although up to a certain point in political evolution the balance of privileges, prerogatives and power is decidedly with the latter. The power of both can be expressed in services of the ruled class which, being superior in numbers, represents the greatest amount of human energy in the State and is the great reservoir from which the whole political apparatus is fed. In a word, the whole State is supported by its lowest and most numerous stratum.

Later we shall inquire whether the burden becomes greater as the classes increase in number and variety. At present we must consider the course of political evolution. Though material wants created the middle class, even at the dawn of social life wants of quite a different character laid the foundation for another class which should eventually affect the evolution of the State considerably.

We have elsewhere shown how the human temperament worried by the riddle of its own existence, peremptorily demands to be soothed, how this is found in religious ideas and how these lead to religious ceremonies (Gumplowicz, 1883: 137 *et seq.*) We will not here enlarge upon the psycho-social process involved (Lippert, 1883). Universally these religious needs sooner or later produce a priestly caste inspired with the desire to sustain and increase its power.

Now its power also must consist in the ability to command men's services. The only difference lies in the form of the power and the manner of securing it corresponding to its peculiar means of satisfying human wants.

The nobility commands human reserves immediately by its superiority. By establishing an organization it confers an undeniable benefit upon the whole. Furthermore, the merchant brings material goods to both the lords and the subjects, receiving payment from both. The priestly caste for its part, conducts the religious ceremonies, thereby satisfying a peremptory need of human nature and fortifies its position by acquiring material goods and human services. The classes differ only in their functions. The equivalents received by all can be reduced to the same terms: a greater or lesser sum of human services rendered in kind or in goods or in the grant of privileges, rights and "royalties."

The rationalist might object that the services of the priest are imaginary and no real equivalent for what the recipient of them gives in the sweat of his brow. The same might also be said of the services of the ruling class. But what are these objections against the fact that men's religious wants are as peremptory as their material wants and that the ruling class also fulfills its function in social economy and has no substitute. In addition to which sociology must avoid criticizing nature. It is interested only in facts and the laws of their behavior and it cannot raise the question whether the thing could be accomplished differently or better. Social phenomena follow necessarily from, and must meet the requirements of, the nature of men and their relations.

Sociology is coming to recognize that there would be no rulers if there were no servants; no priests if there were no believers; no traders if they could find no buyers. The phenomenon of class-building can be referred to a universal law: each want produces its own means of satisfaction. Insofar as a class is able to satisfy a social want it first is indispensable, and, secondly, receives an equivalent which can be expressed in terms of human services, the instrument of power. In exercising its acquired power it participates in government.

As new wants produce new professional classes and castes, the more progressive a State is and the higher its civilization, the more numerous they are and the more complex must be the mutual dependence of the several social circles which jointly possess the elements of power.

Material and intellectual (moral) wants, it has been seen, are rooted and grounded in human nature. They might be called primary. But civilization continues to develop other secondary wants. The uncivilized and those in lower stages of culture do not feel the need for; of such a variety men become sensitive to only as a result of their higher culture.

On a low stage of culture, for instance, the priest is at the same time medicine-man and no need of a lay (*weltlich*) physician is felt. By a process which might be called differentiation, there arises out of religious needs a demand for medical care and treatment which in an advanced cultural complex is supplied by the medical profession which is organized, has social standing and enjoys legal protection.

The necessity of legal assistance has grown out of the intercourse and the legal relations of men in the civilized State. It is well known what great influence the legal profession wields in the modern State. But its power is no greater than the great and universal need it satisfies.

The necessity for an administrative department as the State becomes large, for distributing governmental duties among a number of functionaries and maintaining facility of communication between them and the people has produced the official class, which has its own interests, possesses power and exerts a controlling influence in its own sphere.

The trading and industrial class has been subdivided into very many different classes and callings, because a division of labor became necessary as the demand increased for many products which commerce brought to hand or trade and industry supplied.

In the modern civilized State, large industries are opposed to small, the laboring class to the capitalist and the entrepreneurial classes, agriculture to manufacture, and so forth. Each has its own interest which it represents, its own power, which it strives to increase. Each bears down upon the others according to its strength and their resistance. In other words each participates in sovereignty solely and exactly in proportion to its power. Wherein this power consists we have already seen.

Just as the middle class was subdivided to correspond with the division of labor and the development of specialties so also a military class was differentiated from the simple ruling class as methods of warfare changed. It assimilated portions of other classes and developed into the modern military profession. Though in deference to passing doctrines, some efforts have been made to sink this independent profession in the universal obligation of all citizens to bear arms it is a question whether they can succeed, whether nature will not prove stronger than doctrine, finally producing in spite of them a military class.

5. The Twofold Origin of Classes

We have seen that some classes, the ruling, the peasant and the merchant classes for instance, arose from the union [Zusammentreffen] of different [heterogen] ethnological elements; that their characteristic differences are original. Such classes antedate the State and are the more easily maintained in it because their differences are both anthropological and moral.

But there are others, as we have seen, the priesthood, large industry as contrasted with small, scholars, jurists, officials and so forth, which arise from the others by a process of differentiation. When they have become fully separated they in turn devote their whole conduct both active and passive to guarding their peculiar interests and take on the nature of the original classes.

These phenomena depend upon a universal law which we must explain before we can show its application in the social domain. Corollary to the distinction between original and derived classes is that between heredity and adaptation. Organic types seem to arise in two distinct ways and the solution of the whole anthropological problem depends upon setting aside the one or harmonizing the two. Is the principle of perpetual growth in organic bodies heredity, or adaptation, or what?

The wisdom of the ages, which must not be scorned, answers heredity. Modern materialism answers adaptation. "The man is what he eats." Darwinism to reconcile the difference says: both. Let us see which answer is nearest the truth. A superficial glance at organic structures is enough to show that heredity is the mightiest principle of their growth. It is clearly the rule that such structures are as their progenitors were. However there are some exceptions, for which the cleverest and at present the most widely accepted explanation is Darwin's theory of adaptation. What cannot be explained by heredity must be referred to the property of adaptation to external conditions, which organisms possess and to which the struggle for existence forces them to resort.

This theory would scarcely have found acceptance if Darwin's genius had not pointed out many cases which show that organisms do adapt themselves to external conditions in their growth and so change the hereditary type, though he was less successful in showing that changes produced by adaptation would become hereditary.

So the law of adaptation is still a hypothesis in spite of the particular instances cited in support of it. Though it is our belief that the law of heredity is established beyond a doubt.

It is a fact however, that natural structures arise in two ways; they are either primary or secondary. There are two universal and so to speak opposing tendencies in nature. One we might call originality, the other imitation. That is to say, what nature made originally in some unknown, "creative" way, is also frequently produced under the influence of external circumstances which may be easily comprehended. The latter origin is called by Darwin's school evolutionary.[9]

Autogenesis and evolution always cooperate and we are often in doubt whether a particular organism is genetic or evolutionary; while in many cases in fact it may be either.

Nature's processes are after all one and the same, like those by which an artist produces an original and a replica. As it is not impossible for a painter to produce an original because he has made copies, it is a fallacy to conclude with the Darwinians that the

---

[9] We are able to comprehend the secondary or evolutionary origin while that which is original in the realm of organic nature is incomprehensible to our faculties. Accordingly we are always inclined to prefer the former process; as Darwin and Haeckel do in the domain of organic and the sociologists in the domain of social phenomena. But it does not follow that because this is the only way we can explain matters there is no other.

many instances of evolution prove all organisms to have originated in that way.

Some human types originated in adaptation and evolution but not necessarily all. If the geographical character of the habitat is sufficient still to modify a type of organism how much greater must its influence have been upon the origin of varieties. For once it produced, so to speak, genetic differences, though still active, the original genetic effect proves to be more permanent. This might seem to justify one argument used in support of evolution, viz., that if the period be indefinitely extended the supposition of an original method becomes superfluous. But this is only arithmetically correct. It is insufficient to refute the supposition of an original genetic origin when so many other considerations support it.

Both forms of origin, the primary and the secondary, the genetic and the evolutionary, are common in social as well as in organic phenomena. Social inequality arises originally from the union [zusammentreffen] of distinct ethnic elements of unlike power. It also arises by evolution, by the slow development of some elements at the cost of others which recede in power owing to unfavorable conditions.

Though the original means of State formation is subjugation, it might happen as an exception that a period of peaceful development should result in the differentiation of the population into classes, the stronger gradually separating themselves from those who are weaker and need protection. As a rule, classes arise originally out of different ethnic elements or by the permanent organization of such as are at different stages of development at the time of their union. But there are instances of secondary origin also. As we have seen, people turn to this or that calling, according to conditions and inclinations, and those of each calling congregate in a class.

But whether a social group arises one way or the other, its character as a group, as a factor in social development, is not affected. It tends in the direction of its own interests, tries to protect and further them, increase its power and acquire a corresponding influence in the State.

These efforts are always the same and all groups necessarily had to adopt the same policy respecting them. The natural differences between the original classes and the syngenetic coherence within them helped in maintaining and extending their power; and the secondary groups in turn must acquire like differences and cohesions. Hence comes the strong tendency to divide into classes and to maintain the power of each by endogamy; or by celibacy to sunder all connection with other social groups and prevent the weakening of power by division.

6. Society

The great number and variety of mutually related groups within the State considered as a whole is called society in contrast with the State. In this wider sense society is not different from the State. It is the same thing viewed from another point. But in the narrower and more accurate sense of the word each group centering about some one or more common interests is a society. This double meaning often leads to confusion which is made worse because social groups are not always separated by a hard and fast line. They overlap and intertwine so that the same men are bound to one group by one set of interests and to another by another set. Thus a government official may own a large estate, be a zealous adherent of a religious sect, and be a sugar manufacturer as well. In the social struggles over material and moral questions his position will be finally determined by his relative interests.

On the other hand with the development of civilization, certain interests have become broader than the boundaries of a single State. And some societies embrace the subjects of several States. Religious beliefs, the ties of kindred, socialism, *e.g.*, have produced international groups.

Until these relations are thoroughly and scientifically analyzed the notion of a society will remain confused. Such unclear Hegelian definitions as von Ihering offers explain nothing.

"Society," he says, "may be defined as the actual organization of life on the plan of mutual assistance. And since the individual is at his best only through the others it is at once indispensable *per se* and in reality the universal form of human life" (von Ihering, 1877:I:95).

For society substitute State, political economy or anything else and the definition is equally good or equally bad. In fact the State has actually been called "the form" or "the organization of human life," general phrases fitting anything and explaining nothing. Ihering's use of them is not surprising. For instead of seriously studying the phenomena themselves, he inquiries as a Romanist, what the Roman jurists say about them and frames his definition to correspond. His meaningless definition of society is derived from *societas*. But others have failed without this excuse.

How helpful in contrast is Spencer's clear explanation of society considered as a unit. "It is the permanence of the relations among component parts," he says, "which constitutes the individuality of a whole as distinguished from the individualities of its parts." (Spencer, 1880:I: sec. 212).

The "permanent relations" between men unite them into a society, and since there are different kinds of relations there are different kinds of societies. And a man may be bound to several at once, as we have seen.

Much would be gained if we could use "society" simply to designate a concrete number of men united by "permanent relations." For this is perfectly clear. The broader use suggests nothing real. It is only another way of looking at folk life. Schäffle, who calls these narrower social circles "cohesive masses or tissue" (*Massenzusammenhönge oder Bindergewebe*), remarks that it is:

> "singular that social philosophy has as yet been unable to assign even the most insignificant place in its system to these elementary tissues which are neutral as a rule, but at certain times extremely sensitive. They are thrown with much other rubbish into a heap called 'society,' which is alleged to lay midway between that State and the individual. In reality no such miscellaneous society exists." (Schäffle, 1875:I:292).

He fails to note that a "society," something less than the State and more than the individual, had necessarily to be assumed as the starting point of a social philosophy which began with Schloezer's and Hegel's "society of burghers," and later was powerfully influenced by the broader conceptions advanced by Mohl, Stein, and Gneist. (Gumplowicz, 1877: sec. 12; 1881: 158 *et seq.*). But nowadays when people ought to know that there is no concrete reality behind the idea, the use of the word in its broader significance has no further justification. If it should be objected that all the social groups in the State are united by "permanent relations," such as those of common territory, government, etc., hence in turn forming one "society," we reply that the word "folk" is a sufficient designation. There is no further use for this expression in its wider connotation. It should only be applied to the simple social groups in the State, or to those united by interests transcending State limits.

7. Societies

We cannot be expected to enumerate all the societies which occur in the State and still less to discuss the historical development of each. Lippert in his *History of the Priesthood* has described one successfully. To do as much for every other would take us far outside the limits of this sketch. We can only explain the social "relations" which bind the members of the several groups together and the general principles underlying their power in the State. For here also the description of what is individual must be reserved for history. Sociology can only state the general modes of behavior, the laws of the phenomena. It is clear that the societies both in their origin and in their development are controlled by "laws" since human nature is the same everywhere and social differentiation corresponds to the growth and development of human wants as we have discussed. Social structures thus arising from a common basis require the same efforts and have the same aspirations. Whether they shall develop power and sovereignty depends simply on the greater or lesser resources they have at the beginning or acquire later. They differ in degree; they are alike in plan and tendency.

To discover what ties bind a number of men into a society we must start, as elsewhere in sociology, with an original or primary condition, one which we cannot analyze further, the origin of which we cannot observe. Such a bond is association in the horde.[10] It seems to be natural. In contrast, all others are evolutionary, arising with social development. Of course they too are natural in a sense. The

---

[10] Spencer too has recognized the necessity of this point of departure in sociological studies. He says that: "Social evolution begins with the small simple aggregates" (Spencer, 1880: I: sec. 239).

difference is that we know their origin and do not know that of the former.[11] To those who feel this bond it suggests a contrast with the "stranger." Later reflection based on experience adds the etiological explanation of common descent from some god or hero.

Analysis shows that the positive binding force is association and simple consanguinity with the resultant community of language, religious ideas, customs and mode of life, while the contrast with the stranger lies in his lack of participation in them.

In reality, all socially binding forces are represented in the primitive horde: association and consanguinity, similar material and intellectual needs and similar interests in satisfying them. There are no social constrasts which cannot be referred to dissimilarly in one or more of these respects.

Social development presupposes the function of heterogeneous or the differentiation of homogeneous elements. In the former case the combining elements are united by common interests and fall into conflict for lack of them. In the latter the differentiating group develops certain common interests which hold it together and separate it from the rest. The first is the case when political relations are established between foreign elements, or a middle class is gradually developed. The latter, when the various priestly, military and professional classes slowly appear.

The establishment of the first political relations calls two social classes into existence at once: the lords and the slaves or serfs. The social bonds which unified each group and created feelings of tribal loyalty will be strengthened by the common interest of rulers and the common lot of subjects respectively. Class feeling will be added to tribal but it does not follow that mutual opposition will be intensified. The centrifugal factors will be offset by local association and all the ties which habit and adaptation develop under such circumstances. The psycho-social functions: language, customs, religious ideas and ceremonies will gradually become assimilated.

The subject class may even acquire a feeling of respect for the ruling class, and all factors together may be strong enough to make the two classes at times appear as one in contrast to outsiders. But the difference in rank, the separate consanguineous circles (while

[11] For the distinction between "natural" and "artificial" social institutions, see (Gumplowicz, 1881: 329).

intermarriage is prohibited), and the difference in political interests will keep them divided in the long run.

So when a foreign merchant class takes its place beside the others all are strangers at first in every respect. Language, customs, religion, descent, everything which binds the members of one group together separates it from the others. Some of the dissociating factors may disappear in time. Local association may develop love of home and folk and assimilation of language, customs and ideas may follow. But in spite of all and in addition to differences in descent, rank, customs, and class ethics, the interest of the traders will be permanently opposed to the interests of the other classes.

When classes are differentiated from a homogeneous element the course of events is different. There is simply some one interest which distinguishes the dissociating class from all the others and brings its members together. Besides, such classes are not composed of the members of one class exclusively but generally attract members from different sources. The sacerdotal, military, official and learned classes are recruited from the older classes indiscriminately. For the inclination, fitness and capacity for such callings is not distributed with regularity.

Though the peculiar interest of one calling distinguishes all who follow it from others, still the individuals stand in the greatest variety of relations to the classes from whence they sprang. New complications arise and social classes become wholly exclusive. These conditions often exert a decisive influence upon their position and power in the State and on the outcome of the social struggle.

8. Group-Making Factors

Let us now attempt a scheme of the forces or "relations" which classify and unite men into societies. On a former occasion, I distinguished three "natural" bonds: consanguinity, local association and common interests (Gumplowicz, 1877). They are very comprehensive, especially the last. But I now think a double classification according to fundamental principles and permanency is plainer and more to the point.

According to fundamental principles they may be divided into material, economic, and moral. Material factors are: like places, of residence, sociality or common social life, consanguinity and relationship. The economic factors are similar and equal possessions and common occupation, agriculture on large or on small estates, tenancy, manufacturing, skilled trades, commerce and so forth. The grouping into nobility, burghers, priests, artists, scholars, writers, etc., is partly economic and partly moral. That according to language, religion, political allegiance, birth, citizenship and nationality, is wholly moral. Accidentally sharing the same fate, as in a common migration, is a moral factor also.

Most of these factors are of varying duration and their permanence must be considered. The influence of a common place of residence may continue from generation to generation or no longer than a visit at a watering place. Its effects vary accordingly. The effect of common religious views differs according to whether they have been inherited generation after generation or are the result of proselytizing.

The following table illustrates this double classification.

			Through Generations	For a Lifetime	Temporarily
Material Culture	Common Living Quarters {in immediate or remote neighborhood} Common Social Life Consanguinity Relationship				
Economy	Rank	Nobility Bourgeoisie Peasantry Priesthood, etc.			
	Possession	Farmland Urban property			
	Occupation	Land owners Tenant farmers Industrialists Merchants Artisans, etc.			
Morality	Language Religion Science Art Accidental fate (emigrants, etc).				

Each relation enumerated may endure for a longer or shorter period. The greater the number of group-making factors binding men together the more intimate is the social bond and the greater its cohesive force and power of resistance. Strongest of all is a community united by permanent material, economic and moral forces. It is a unitary race and in the struggle for existence is superior to all lesser social combinations in endurance if not in power.

In the primitive horde, in the "small simple aggregates" with which, according to Spencer, social evolution begins, we find, generation after generation, all three classes of factors permanently active: common place of residence, common blood, common means of subsistence, common language, religion and customs. When such social groups are politically organized they retain their compactness and cohesion. But the union grows weaker as language, religion and other factors became common to several social groups. Membership in the same political system is sure to produce this result in the course of time.

Without doubt the consanguineous social group always retains something of the elemental power of primitive hordes, treating all strangers as hostile beings. The division of European nations into lords, middle class and peasants would not have produced such rigid social distinctions if the three classes had not, generally speaking, represented distinct consanguineous groups. For economic differences would have been counteracted by the assimilation of language and religion. However it is also the tendency of each economic group to become a consanguineous unit.

9. Social Circles and the Social Struggle

It has already been pointed out that it is not the size of the social group which determines its power. The lords were always in a minority and in modern States with millions of inhabitants, power rests with the "upper crust." The intimacy of the union and the resultant organization and discipline, together with mental superiority, complement numerical inferiority giving the minority the preponderance. The minority applies the strategic maxim: march as individuals, strike as one. The masses always lack unity and organization, as a result partly of their great bulk, partly of indolence.

Since the result of the social struggle depends on discipline the minority has the advantage because it is small. Besides there will be greater intimacy and common interests. The group-making factors will be more numerous, more intense and more permanent.

The more indolent a man is the less appreciation he has for the ideal goods of life. As he has fewer wants he has fewer interests in common with other men and is less energetic in defending them.

The power of a social group increases with the number of common interests among its members irrespective of its size. When success depends on numbers, it relies on uniting with other social groups. This is very important. It is the key to social politics. The number of common interests necessarily varies inversely with the number of individuals in the social group. For though the number of interests increases as conditions improve, it is the condition of the minority especially that improves since the majority must labor and serve to produce it.

Prosperity is the natural lot of the minority. With improved conditions the number of interests increases; with these the intensity of social cohesion and this gives more social power. In the final analysis the intensity of the union depends upon the personal character of the individuals. But as their mutual intercourse is made easier by custom, and as good customs grow with common welfare and culture the union is strengthened too.

The highest and smallest aristocratic circles are mightier than the other social groups in the State though a thousand times larger. The masters united in a guild are stronger than the journeymen and laborers.

In times of revolution everything may depend on numerical strength and then the small groups are at a disadvantage. Their power can be realized only under normal conditions of political organization. But this must be considered the normal condition of civilized man.

Each group exerts whatever power it normally possesses and tries to have its relative position recognized in the State in the form of rights. But every right is made the basis of renewed efforts. Human desires are constantly growing and no social group ever rested content with what it had obtained. On the contrary, present attainments are used to increase power and satisfy new desires.

From this fundamental law the conduct of each social group can be definitely predicted in every case. It will strive, like the State, to increase its power. But the result of the struggle does not depend on the individual. Though there are always individuals who deviate first one way and then the other, they, like meteoric stones which are loosened from their orbit and fly off in all directions, are abnormal, and do not influence the behavior of the group as a whole.

In its political actions each social group is a perfect unit. It opposes other social groups in behalf of its own interest solely and knows no standard of conduct but success.

The struggle between social groups, the component parts of the State, is as inexorable as that between hordes or States. The only motive is self-interest. In *Der Rassenkampf* we describe the conflict as a "race-war" for such is its inexorable animosity that each group that is able, tends to become exclusive like a caste, to form a consanguineous circle. In short it becomes a race.

What is the character of the struggle between the social groups? What are the methods and the means? No general answer can be given. They differ with the position which the groups occupy in the State, with the amount of power and the instruments which they possess.

The refusal to perform religious rites is an instrument in the hands of the priesthood. The higher nobility can make certain lucrative and influential offices exclusive. The guild-masters require "proof of competence." Attorneys restrict the privileges of practicing law. Manufacturers insist on free trade in grain. Laborers strike, etc., etc. The social struggle consists in establishing appropriate institutions for increasing the power of one social group at the expense of others. However it may be with the individual, society never errs in seizing and applying the right means. Its instincts are always right.

If this seems to be a contradiction consider the actual experience of history. At every step it shows the mistakes of even the cleverest individuals and the demoniacal cleverness of society infallible as natural law. (Gumplowicz, 1883: Pt. iv: sec. 9). Theories and passions often confuse the individual. But society never fails, for it never reflects and never chooses but simply follows the powerful attraction of its own interests.

10. The Field of Combat

It is a peculiarity of social struggle that it must be conducted by a collective whole. Previous organization into assemblages is necessary and every society must secure some suitable organ for conducting the social struggle. Thus the ruling classes through their parliaments exercise the legislative power and are able by legal institutions to further their own interests at the cost of others.

In the cities, the middle class very early resorted to the use of guilds and representatives. The priesthood also organized into hierarchies and created synods and councils, advisory and representative bodies. The fact that the great mass of people in the very nature of things could not thus organize made the conduct of the struggle in their interest more difficult. It is in consequence of having entered upon this struggle that laborers now organize and wily agitators even originate peasant unions. The procedure is logical.

Yet the difference must not be overlooked. The prosperous and property-holding classes perfect their organization more easily because the greater number and intensity of their common interests make it easier to unite and act as a body or by representatives. The weaker social connection of the masses prevents a sound and strong organization. Such as occurs is generally the ephemeral, artificial work of selfish leaders seeking selfish ends. But this much is certain: without organization, without united collective action, the social struggle is impossible.

The proximate end of organization is to establish a legal norm for the mutual relations of the groups, to confirm by right the commanding position which has been acquired or is striven for. Hence it is clear that the organization which has acquired the right of legislation in the State occupies the most powerful position, and that it is the aim of every other organization to participate in the same right.

It is well known that the history of European politics generally turns upon the struggle of the lower classes for participation in legislation; that it has been partly successful and that it is still in progress. Indeed, it can never end, for after the third estate comes the fourth. The real object is to be able to wage the social struggle with equal weapons.

11. The Moral Character of the Struggle

Nothing impresses thinking men so seriously as the contemplation of the social struggle, for its immorality deeply offends their moral feelings. Individuals can consider ethical requirements, they have consciences, but societies have none. They overwhelm their victims like avalanches with irresistible destructive power. All societies, large and small retain the character of wild hordes in considering every means good which succeeds. Who would look for fidelity, veracity and conscience in the intercourse of the "most civilized" States of the world? Lying and deceit, breach of confidence and betrayal is on every page of their history. And saddest of all, no one can foresee whether it will ever be different though the noblest of men with the highest intentions may stand at the head of affairs. What self-deception it is to believe that monarchs rule the social world! They are not responsible for all the moral lapses that occur daily in politics. How trivial are royal assurances that the friendliest relations exist with all the neighboring States. Often they have scarcely been uttered before bloody war breaks out. They were not really perfidious. The current of history, the rivalry of States, is not under the arbitrary control of rulers.

However cordial the personal relations of the monarchs not one will cease arming. It is felt instinctively that with the first favorable opportunity any State will pounce like a wild beast upon a defenseless victim. Indeed, it is generally recognized that States oppose each other like savage hordes; that they follow the blind laws of nature; that no ethical law or moral obligation, only the fear of the stronger, holds them in check; and that neither right nor law, treaty nor league, can restrain the stronger from seeking its own interests when the opportunity is offered.

The same is true of the struggle of the social groups in general. It is conducted not by individuals but by societies and communities. The lack of moral principle is nowhere more conspicuous than in the alliances into which societies unite for the sake of assuring success. The overmatched horde makes terms with its recent enemy in order to fall with superior force upon the present foe. Civilized States consider only their advantage in making alliances. No consideration of principles, intimacy of relations or community of ideas avails. Republican France and America ally themselves with Russia without scruple. Constitutional and liberty-loving England upholds Turkish rule and aids American slaveholders. Social units behave in the same way. The extreme conservatives fight side by side with the social democrats today for the sake of defeating the middle classes, and tomorrow perhaps will join their defeated foe to overcome their expedient ally.

But these "perfidious" struggles do not reveal individuals to be utterly base. They only prove that in the struggle of whole entities, individual opinions play no part; that here social groups struggle inexorably to satisfy their own interests, to demonstrate their own power. Blind natural law controls the action of savage hordes, of States and of societies.

12. The Struggle for Emancipation

Though the exercise of legislative power, as we have said, is indispensable to carrying on the social struggle, those who do not possess it are not condemned to perpetual passivity. The unique method which they employ against the ruling classes is aptly called the struggle for emancipation. The might of ideas is on their side, a significant statement which needs careful explanation.

The superior classes, as we have seen, cannot rest content with the fact of superiority. Political relations need to be confirmed. Might must be turned into right. It seemed simple enough for them to say: let this be right. But every right has its obverse obligation. However comprehensive, there are limits at which their obligations begin to those who hitherto have had no rights. So the rights of the rulers led to the rights of the ruled. The germ was there and it must develop.

But more than this; the human mind probes to the foundation of things seeking the principle of causation and analyzing the changing phenomena to find their eternal, unchanging essence. Now in the changing phases of right the enduring principle is the idea. Thus rights not only led to obligations but also to the concept of law.

If the obligation could be called the consequence of right in space, the idea was its consequence in time. Whoever asserts his rights can not escape their consequences. Thus the rulers themselves forge weapons with which the ruled and powerless classes successfully attack them and complete the natural process. The egoism of the powerful prepares the way for the uprising of the weak.

The idea of right is not a purely fanciful notion. It has power to influence men and can be practically applied. Men grow accustomed year by year to submit to laws. They use legal forms constantly and learn to respect rightful limitations, until finally the conception, the very idea, of rights pervades and controls them. In this way the idea of law becomes the proper weapon for those who have no other.

But its application is not simple. The legal buttress of the powerful will not yield to a simple appeal to ideas as Jericho's walls fell at the blast of trumpets. And, besides, the propertyless and powerless are unable to use such intellectual weapons immediately. Again we see. the egoism of one class promoting the social evolution of the whole. The bourgeoisie in the struggle with the other property classes is the first to appeal to universal human rights, to freedom and equality. It claims to be contending not for itself alone but for the good of the whole people. And it succeeds not without the support of the masses whom it flatters and to whom it reveals the splendrous goal of freedom and equality. Its might, like that of the upper class, is now based on right, and though for the moment what it has won seems to be clear gain, it has found a yoke of legal logic about its neck and must submit to its concepts.

For the lowest classes, participation in the struggle was a profitable experience. Even the slight amelioration of their condition was an advantage. It taught them many a lesson. But it is hard for them, relying simply on ideas, to conduct social warfare. For political regulations are firmly based on the possession of material goods and are defended by the middle class also. Moreover as time goes on some of their ideas prove false and indefensible. But in spite of exaggerations they are logical consequences of principles which the ruling class asserted in its own interest and from which the middle class profited by then declaring them to be universal. They cannot be wholly eradicated. They powerfully aid the struggle for the emancipation of the fourth class. They inspire the masses with fanatical zeal and the struggle for emancipation succeeds.

Meanwhile, however, an unsocial compound of societies has taken the place of the primitive horde. The principles suited to one

condition are unsuited to another and cannot endure. The fatal consequences must be corrected by retracing those steps back to the point
where might of its "own right" as a spontaneous factor of public
life assumes control of a society tired of revolution. This completes
the period of evolution in the social struggle: from the freedom and
equality of the anarchic horde through might and inequality, right
and law, to the freedom and equality of revolution and State destroying anarchy. From this unbearable condition to the despotic
strength of reaction and the beginning of a new period of evolution.

13. The Growth of States

Semper Augustus, always augmenting the empire, the characteristic title of honor borne by the Roman and German emperors, is a
naive recognition of the nature of the State. For its most natural
tendency (here predicated of the ruler) is incessant increase of power
and territory.

It is inherited from the horde and characterizes every social
community. A roving horde subjects strangers and uses as many of
them as possible for servants and slaves. After permanent settlements
have been made and States establised, the object of the raids must
be either to levy contributions and exact tribute or to annex territory.
As the latter is more successful in augmenting the State it is the
most desirable and frequently resorted to. It is the general rule of
history that all States have attained much of their greatness in
this way. So long as inherent strength and external circumstances
allow, the process is continued. But there must be some natural limit
to the tendency, otherwise the whole inhabited world would long
since have become one State.

The first condition precedent to external growth is relative
stability of political authority within. If political authority is not
firmly established, if there are no firm bonds of reciprocal interest
between rulers and ruled, or of common interest in the State, the
rulers cannot pursue foreign conquest without risking their position,
as many historical examples illustrate.

A State can undertake foreign conquest with prospects of success
only when, by shrewd and strong political organization or through
community of interests, it has succeeded outwardly at least in giving
its constituent parts the quality of a social element. It must emerge

into action as a unit. Hence follows the social law that a State's ability to undertake foreign activity grows as the process of unification proceeds within it. Since every new conquest adds a new element no conquest can be undertaken successfully until the spoils of the former have to some degree been assimilated and social unity is re-established.

It is a simple outcome of this law that statesmen have always regarded internal divisions in neighboring States as security against attack upon their own. For as soon as the State is strong internally it must utilize its power externally though in some cases an enterprise which promises advantage to all will even relieve considerable internal friction. So necessary and so strong is the tendency to foreign conquest that no State can escape it whatever may be the disposition of the ruler at the time. Methods will vary with circumstances and unfavorable circumstances will be circumvented or overcome.

So long as a compact and powerful body politic finds itself encircled by weaker States it will continue its policy of conquest and annexation to the last possible limit, as Rome did in Italy and as Russia is doing in the East where its neighbors are weak and loosely organized.

If all are equally powerful, so that no one can hope to overthrow any other one, then two or more will form alliances in order to conquer the selected object of attack. If a weaker State happens to be neighbor to several more powerful, it must supplement its strength by alliances or they will not fail to partition it among themselves. No code of private morals can successfully oppose it. Even the men who are individually the most exemplary are forced to acquiesce to the milieu. The scruples of individual feeling and sentiment are unknown in politics. As Emperor Francis said: "The State has no daughter."

Political conditions are peremptory. Natural law prevails though the will of the individual seems to be "free." Those who suffer speak of "crimes." You might as well call an earthquake by which thousands have perished a crime, for the only difference is that in the one case we think we see the responsible agents while in the other we can find none.

But the conditions of the party attacked may present serious obstacles to the policy of conquest. For a nation, which is the product of a long period of development, is such an exclusive unit that the attempt to incorporate it must tax the strength of the conquering State and render it for a long time incapable of future external activity. That is to say, it is neither simple nor does it promote humanism and healthy morality to subject a foreign people by violence. Though simple conquest and annexation cannot be treated as "crimes" without characterizing the whole history of mankind as one long crime, yet every violent attempt to destroy a nation, which is a product of history, is after all immoral and inhuman.

To profit by the conquest of a neighboring folk, a State must sometimes resort to war indemnities. Plundering expeditions, conquest, annexation, incorporation and war indemnities: these are the various forms in which the natural tendency of the State to augment its power and extend its authority is manifested.[12]

It would not be hard to set a limit to the increasing size of a State. But in fact the tendency is ceaseless and may lead to destruction as history proves. Every great State has striven to increase its authority and the greatest have striven to rule the world. The end has come only in their sudden downfall, in a historical catastrophe.

---

[12] To illustrate the whole range from the most primitive to the most modern manifestations of this tendency I compared (Gumplowicz, 1883: 166) the Apaches and the Kirghese, who are content to capture a few horses or asses or a herd of cattle, with the modern "European victor" who knows how straightway to force the payment of several milliards. This passage offended some of my honored German reviewers, though it is plain that no exception could be taken save on the supposition that Bismarck was referred to. But he is neither the first nor the only "European victor" who has won his milliards. If he were the only one still the insinuation is unjustifiable considering my contention that historical events are subject to natural laws and independent of individuals. But they should not have applied to the German war, of which I said nothing, what should be applied to false idealism which I have always attacked. I confess that in politics I fully accept the realistic standpoint of Prince Bismarck. He has never spoken of the great indemnity with false pathos, and in his report to Herr von Mantuffel, from Frankfurt in July, 1853, he said: "The other German States have the same interests that we have, to be left in peace where there is nothing to be gained," and weighing the chance of war he added: "If we can profit by it then the case is different." If those who today write about politics would study the works of Prince Bismarck there would be much less pathos, fewer chauvinistic phrases and fewer political quarrels.

The social law thus illustrated is not peculiar to the growth of States but is manifested in all other social domains. The periodical crises of economic production, for instance, are due to it. Each lucrative process of production is repeated until the limits of present need have been far exceeded and business breaks down for lack of demand. The experiment though often tried is constantly repeated. Admonitions avail nothing and "wise moderation" will at most influence a few individuals. The tendency of social communities knows no limit but "crash." In trade and commerce, everywhere, social strife for power or for wealth and property lasts until all energy is exhausted. Disruption, crisis, panic are then unavoidable.

So long as the State has aggressive power it strives to augment, to increase its territory, to conquer, to colonize, etc. This continues until strength fails from internal or external causes or until it is surpassed by other states and crippled. Only when strength fails does strife cease.

14. State and Nationality

Since each political organization creates a civilization and each localized civilization is, with the aid of such spontaneous moral agencies as language, religion, custom and rights, transformed into a nation, it follows, that with the development of a number of States, side by side a number of nations must arise also (Gumplowicz, 1883:23 et seq.; 253 et seq.). If the mere fact of common allegiance is sufficient to bind the subjects into a social unit it is clear that as the number of mutual relations between the subjects increases, the unity will be more pronounced. In this way the nation-state acquires greater offensive and defensive power. But in the course of time the nation-States will fall into opposition. The original contest will be repeated in higher form and as the perpetual strife for power animates them it cannot fail to happen that some are disrupted and others grow.

As the impulse to increase power is not checked by the establishment of any political or national relations whatever, a great variety of social and political combinations are bound to arise in the course of history and it cannot fail to happen that there will be political organizations consisting of different folk and parts of nations.

The greater difficulties which the conquering State must encounter and the scruples it may entertain at annexing foreign nations in whole or in part we have already discussed. But if the margin of superiority is not too narrow the foreign folk-elements will eventually be assimilated by the conquering race and blended into a social unit, a new nation. There have always been composite nation-States. They are the necessary result of the historical process which is constantly breaking down the old and establishing the new. To deny their right to exist or to justify them less fully than folk-states would display crass ignorance of history. Social relations tend to develop; and as surely as history produces only what is reasonable, this higher order of political organization will overcome the internal struggle of the composite folk elements and justify itself.

The struggles are severe; they are, so to speak, higher powers of the simple social struggles. To the social contrasts of the unitary nation-State the contrasts between the different folk are added. As the most conspicuous difference is in language the contest centers about the right of one or the equal right of several in official business. But the essential point is the struggle for authority. The contest over language is only an excuse to rationalize this tendency.

The question at issue is whether authority shall be monopolized by a privileged folk speaking a privileged mother-tongue. The struggle becomes justified when the unprivileged folk-elements possess sufficient social and political power and have acquired sufficient mastery of the official language to oppose the ruling successfully. Other things being equal the folk which can use more than one of the competing languages will win, the polyglots will overcome the ruling class which remains monoglot.

But once the victory has been secured the impractical idea of the equality of tongues must yield to the real needs of State. Either there must be one official language of the whole people, or at least the ruling classes, must speak several. In a composite nation-State there can be no serious question over which should be the official language. As it is simply the means for promoting general intercourse throughout the State, the most accessible one plainly must be chosen. This must be the one in most general use or rather the one most widely diffused among the educated classes of all the different folk-elements. Generally this will be the language of the older civilization. Only living tongues of course can be considered. But its rank will be questioned so long as its natural representatives enjoy any political advantage or other national minorities suffer political prejudice. In a word, the struggle which begins with the battle-cry "no discrimination on account of language" will continue until the actual relations are so altered that the complete equality before the law of all the elements is no longer imperiled by the official preference accorded to the language of the oldest civilization; or until a general polyglot condition of all the folk-elements serves to put an end to the struggle.

Part IV

Social Psychological Phenomena and the Individual

1. Individualism and Collectivism

The point of view from which social phenomena are considered has oscillated between two opposite principles — individualism and collectivism. Not only the attempts at explaining "the social world," but also all propositions that aimed at shaping it in virtue of its accepted nature and all the differences and disputes in the domain of social science turn upon the antithesis between "mankind" and the individual. There was no third standpoint, no middle way known to the theorists.

Smithian economics and materialistic philosophy considered egoism and self-interest the source of social development and the sole motive of human behavior. Others pointed to the self-sacrifice of the individual and contrasted egoism and self-interest with "charity" and "altruism." While some sought to explain social phenomena by the egoistic nature of the individual, the statisticians pointed to the "community," "society," "mankind" and its nature and development according to "law" for explanation. The real truth was overlooked. Neither one alone and neither to the degree supposed is the cause and motive of social development. If we preface each with the adjective "social," giving it the meaning not of the abstract whole but of the limited social circle, like the syngenetic group, we shall have found the middle way which social philosophy has hitherto missed.

Not personal but social egoism is the motive of social development. No devotion to the world at large, nor "charity" in the broad sense of the Christian theory of universal fellowship and feeling. Rather, it is social understanding and self-sacrificing devotion to the

238

natural social community. Man is not so bad as crass materialism pictures him; neither is he so big hearted as Christian philosophy in vain requires him to be. He is neither devil nor angel, simply human. Fettered to the community by natural ties of blood, habit and mode of thought, his egoism is social, his sympathies are social. To demand more than social sympathy is to demand something unnatural and superhuman. But to credit him with less than social sympathy, social him wrong. But social egoism includes social sympathy, social sympathy is social egoism. Let us call their union syngenism and we have identified the motive of all social development and the key to its solution.

Those who conceive the whole social world from the individualistic standpoint, who explain all development by reference to the individual and look upon his development as the highest goal and simple object of all that transpires in society, want to heal all the hurts and ills of the social world by freeing the individual and proclaiming his rights.[1]

Doctrinaire liberalism and abstract constitutionalism both occupy this position. Every individual as such must have every possible right and enjoy every privilege of the "most favored" individual—that it may be well upon the earth. The plan has been tried in Europe repeatedly and has failed, for the individual profited nothing from all these rights; relying upon them alone he hurled himself against the unyielding barriers of social institutions which no proclamation of individual liberty can displace.

At the opposite pole is socialism, communism and every other form of collectivism. The collective whole, preferably the largest at hand, must labor for and protect the individual. Worry and care fall upon the collective. Labor must be performed in common. The individual must be directed and utilized [but also supported].

Unfortunately legislative conditions have never been adequate for an experiment or it would appear that a collective whole caring for the individual so providently is as Utopian as a self-determining individual.

---

[1] Marx was quite right when he said: "The real insignificance of the individual is in strong contrast with the importance conceded to him in scientific speculations. His insignificance is apparent, not only in political affairs but in economic" (Marx, 1867: 235-36).

In truth, everywhere and from the very beginning, the social
world has moved, acted, fought and striven only by groups. Legislation to be wise and true must take account of the actual conditions,
neither being blind to them like the "constitutionalist" nor imagining
with the collectivist that it can change him. The only possible solution of the social question lies in the harmonious cooperation of the
social groups so far as that is possible.

2. The Individual and His Social Group

The great error of individualistic psychology is the supposition
that man thinks. It leads to continual search for the source of
thought in the individual and for reasons why the individual thinks
so and not otherwise. It prompts naive theologians and philosophers to consider and even to advise how man ought to think. A
chain of errors; for it is not man himself who thinks but his social
community. The source of his thoughts is in the social medium in
which he lives, the social atmosphere which he breathes,[2] and he
cannot think anything else other than what the influences of his
social environment concentrating upon his brain necessitate. There
is a law of mechanics and optics by which we compute the angle of
refraction from the angle of incidence. In the realm of mind there
is a similar law though we cannot observe it so precisely. Every ray of
thought falling upon the mind is reflected in our views. What we
think is the necessary result of the mental influences to which we have
been subjected since childhood.

The individual simply plays the part of the prism which receives the rays, dissolves them according to fixed laws and lets them
pass out again in a predetermined direction and with a predetermined
color.

The influence of environment upon the human mind has always
been recognized by psychologists and philosophers, but it has been
considered a secondary factor. On the contrary, the social medium
which the child enters at birth, in which he lives, moves and has his
being, is fundamental. Toward this environment the individual from
childhood to ripest old age is more or less receptive. Rarely can the

[2] "To think is to be conscious of the growth of psychological activity." (Bastian, 1880: viii).

maturest minds so succeed in emancipating themselves from this medium, as to undertake independent reflection while complete emancipation is impossible. All the organs and modes of thought, all the organs for constructing thoughts, have been molded or at least thoroughly imbued with it. Granted that very mature and independent thinkers have passed the age of receptivity, still it is questionable whether the most eminent and original philosopher in the world can so far dissociate himself from acquired modes and organs as to substitute independent creations in their place.

Consider the mental make-up of the ordinary or "average" man. The child gets his first impressions from his earliest surroundings. His earliest ethical ideas come from the conduct of his nurses and early tutors. Praise and blame, reward and punishment, the hopes and fears that are imbibed, the fears which he is given, all go to make up his first impressions and educate his mind. Before long the little "world citizen" has become the exact mental image of his "family," giving the word its broadest Roman meaning. His childish mind corresponds to the many-sided mold in which it was cast. The mind bears the impress of every hand which impresses itself upon it.

Thus prepared, the youngster comes in contact with the "world" in the shape of a troop of playmates and companions for the most part cast in the same mold. Their impressions are much the same. All have been inspired with the same admiration for certain things and persons and filled involuntarily with the same hate and abhorrence for others which prevailed about them. Even for food and drink they have received the same tastes and distastes. They are mere clockwork, which runs as it is regulated. Who is it who feels, thinks, tastes? Not the individual but the social group. Its thoughts, feelings, tastes, impressions, hence its plans, purposes, and conduct live again. As the elders sing, so chirp the young.

Who can grasp everything that has accumulated in the mind of this new individual? The mental precipitate of generations long gone is condensed in the mind of one person. There are experiences thousands of years old which have been inherited for generations as completed intuitions. Destinies, historic and prehistoric, have their effects upon mental character and inclination, with their forms of thought and mode of reasoning: sympathies, prejudices and prepossessions deeply seated and concentrated in the mind of the "free" individual like countless rays in a focus. They live in him as thought, though the crowd imagines that he thinks freely and has feeling, though the crowd imagines that whether right or wrong, praiseworthy or not, it is he that cherishes them.

For the great majority of men so-called intellectual development strictly ends with this. The educative impressions of childhood and youth suffice for the whole life. Only an insignificant minority continues its education by absorbing mental impressions and influences from outside their social group as they have opportunity. How much we overrate the efficacy of classical antiquity and the accumulated culture of other nations in this respect! How insignificant it is in comparison with the inherited and inculcated culture in which the spirit of the social group is manifest.

Unprejudiced consideration will convince us that all the "education," especially that of our schools, is scarcely sufficient to varnish over the heritage of each. None of it ever plumbs the depths of the soul unless the pre-existing conditions are favorable. What do the so-called educated men, doctors, teachers, officials, etc., generally get from their education, whether acquired in school or not, save a little knowledge? But knowledge is not thought, neither is it feeling. What does knowledge profit if it cannot alter thought or influence temperament? It does neither. Hence the sad sight of people who with a little knowledge so much the more easily conceal from the world the vulgarity of their ideas and their inborn baseness; who varnish over rudeness by pretending special knowledge and vainly cloak a coarse nature in "education." Even if it were as Buckle contends in his great work, that mankind is improved by knowledge and by that alone, it must first improve the mass or at least the group which in turn would ennoble the individual.

Though paradoxical it is true that the knowledge of the mass, of the social environment, benefits the individual, while the knowledge which he acquires comes too late to affect him. Like a coin he is complete when he steps out into the world.

A mature young man is bound to his family, class, or social group by ties of common interest. He is treated by the world, that is by the other social groups, simply as a member of his syngenetic circle and so feels that his identity with it is involuntary and often a misfortune. However much he may know he is only what his social medium makes out of him, he is subject to modification by the heterogeneous social elements that confront him. Though there are rare and exceptional cases where individuals, whether living in isolation or separated from their own circle by force, have been thoroughly absorbed by a strange group or have intentionally submerged their identity in it, a complete transformation of character taking place, they simply confirm the rule.

The fate of youth determines man's destiny in his broader sphere. Hard conflicts of interests arise and struggles with powerful currents which the individual can neither cause nor control, but by which he is tossed to and fro, with which he must swim lest he sink. Does he choose? The current beats him back. Of what avail is his knowledge? He must struggle, but if he would not sink he must swim with the favorable tide and his freedom consists only in holding himself as much above it as possible and warding off the opposing flood as best he may. To get into an entirely different current or to change his course is a matter of accident, not of choice.

The struggle of life brings the individual to self-consciousness. In this way he obtains an unobstructed view of the field of conflict. He has acquired personal knowledge, not simply adapted another's. But it cannot transform him for he is at the end of his career and cannot begin life anew. Like the youth of Sais he has drawn the veil and knows the secret. He knows what he was and must make his exit. His own knowledge is his only comfort—or disappointment.

Between the cradle and the grave one thread is spun which once broken cannot be reunited. A chain is extended whose every link is wrought into the preceding. Man may choose to break it by violence but not to re-weld it. He may die by his own hand but can never be born again although even the determination to die must be conditioned by the whole life-span.

The whole belief in the freedom of human action is rooted in the idea that man's conduct is the fruit of his thoughts and that his thoughts are exclusively his own. This is an error. He is not self-made mentally any more than he is physically. His mind and thoughts are the product of his social medium, of the social element whence he arose, in which he lives.

Those who doubt whether the influence of the social medium can be so powerful must consider what is more remarkable; that the social element in which a man moves exercises an undeniable influence upon his physical features. The fact is well known to physiognomists and is too apparent to be seriously contradicted. Who does not recognize an Englishman, a Frenchman, an Italian, a north or a south German among a hundred different nationalities? It is difficult to say exactly how we recognize them. Only the artist's sketch can express it. But we recognize John Bull, the "honest Swabian," the Frenchman polite and tractable and even the Parisian, the Italian somewhat uncanny and Mephistophelian, and so on. Who has not observed how living for years among a people of a pronounced type of culture changes a foreigner's whole external appearance and bearing to theirs? Does not the German become a perfect John Bull after living a decade or two in England? Who has not observed the remarkable orientalizing effect of life in the East upon the European? We have known Poles, offspring of old Polish families, who after a long residence in Turkey have assumed the oriental type completely. But it is useless to cite further instances. Those who have no experience can neither comprehend nor believe it; but those who have will certainly corroborate this.

To these alone we turn with a logical demonstration. That which works upon the greater may also work the lesser. If the social element changes a man's physical features surely it has already changed his mind, has more easily transformed his thoughts and opinions and exerted upon his feelings and disposition an influence which betrays itself in his whole outward bearing. For this is nothing but the expression of the mental man, the mirror in which his soul is reflected.

Human speech may never be sufficiently discriminating nor our thoughts clear enough to express what we recognize as characteristic in the different types, though the artist's crayon already does it in the illustrated comic papers. Still we must confirm the fact that there is something by which we recognize the members of various nations, peoples and social groups, etc.; that it is transferable to the individual by means of the social influence regardless of descent or relationship. This influence seizes upon and transforms the human mind quicker and easier than the body. But after a time it seizes the body as well, and transforms it by its power.

While we are considering the action of the social factor on the individual whom it surrounds, we must not fail to notice that the character of a social group is developed by the continuous assimilating action of the whole on its parts. We distinguish different nationalities not so much by physiognomy, figure, complexion or proportions, for our eye is not sensitive enough to perceive all this without practice and without the aid of scientific apparatus. But what strikes us is the type—something inexpressible and indefinable—which is the effect of social influence, *i.e.*, of the influence of the social factor.

It is of the utmost importance that this should be widely appreciated for it shows us that the character of the social group depends more on its mental than on its physical constitution. In a word the type or physiognomical character of a folk or social group is not anthropological but social. On the one hand this explains how it is possible for a foreigner to assume the type of the group into which he has fallen. On the other hand, the transformation of the individual by the group proves that we are dealing with purely social and sociological facts. For if the type were anthropological the transformation and assimilation of the individual through the group would be inconceivable.

After the influence of the social medium upon the individual has been established it only remains to investigate the nature of the factor which exercises it. If it is not anthropological what is its character?

After what has already been said no one will expect a precise answer. The most that can be said is this: between each conscious thought or desire and the accompanying act intervenes man's involuntary responses (*physis*). We know that violent thoughts and efforts are expressed externally in the *physis,* because we see it constantly in cases of sudden anger, joy, pain or despair. The effect follows the cause immediately. But a natural result which is real and true where we can observe it is no less so where our eye is too slow to notice it. If an internal emotion, thought, or effort, exercises an influence upon our body, upon our deportment and bearing, it may exercise it in such infinitesimal degrees that our sense is too weak to perceive the separate and distinct effects. Our perception does not begin until, after a long series of effects, the completed type confronts us.

But can we designate the effective agents more exactly? Thoughts and desires produce the type, we said. Life in turn, social life, produces them. As it differs from area to area and land to land among men of different races and different ethnic composition so their thoughts, their entire conceptions and their efforts, are different and difference of type follows necessarily. As a people's conceptions and thoughts stand also in the perpetual stream of evolution and alter from time to time, there arises the well known variety of types among members of the same folk in successive generations.

3. Influence of Economic Status on the Individual

Our assertion that thoughts and opinions are created by social life can be made still more specific. A man's behavior is determined immediately by his economic status, which constrains him to follow a certain mode of life and awakens the corresponding mental response within him. In all freely organized States amid the multitude of divisions and subdivisions there are, as we have seen, three great social circles distinguished by economic status: the ruling class, the middle class including merchants and tradesmen, and the peasantry. They rear their members differently by educating them to their respective opinions, customs, legal usages and principles and, by offering and even imposing upon them a particular vocation, compel them through self-interest to continue in the path traversed by the whole circle.

Thus the nobleman is accustomed to rule and command and to have his life made comfortable for him by others in the traditional way. Higher appreciation of personality arises naturally, and self-assurance, depreciation of others and the thousand and one traits which, independent of land, folk, nation, religion, race or individual peculiarity, characterize aristocracy universally.

The peasants and slaves of every land and people harbor deep, suppressed ill-will towards the lords. It is inherited from generation to generation, and is held in check by the consciousness of mental inferiority and economic weakness. But when opportunity offers, it bursts into flame with the abandon of a barbaric horde.

Neither persuasion, kindness nor advances can uproot it. In

stolid resignation the peasant closes his social circle to the higher classes (which likewise do not open theirs to him), listens to the consolations of religion as a matter of routine without the least reflection, and heaps the blame for all the misery of his life upon the lords. Yet if habit and inherited notions have taught him to bear his hard lot patiently, inculcated feelings of respect make it easier for him to do so; though all together they would be insufficient to maintain the political organization were it not protected by the strong arm of State power.

The member of the middle class is educated in "business" traditions. Trade, commerce and business profits are his ideals from childhood and he sees many examples of accumulated riches. Fortune-hunting, a notion that the peasant never divines and which seldom excites the nobleman, is the great guest which attracts the middle class. They soon learn that skillful labor and inventiveness lead to success and every thought turns in that direction.

Seldom can the peasant, bound to the soil by law or by the force of circumstances, think of leaving his hereditary pursuit. As a rule he is unable to conceive of such a thing. So overwhelming are the legal and political regulations that it does not even occur to him to oppose them. As a result of his inertia his horizon grows narrower and narrower, not extending beyond the neighboring village. He must either surrender to labor and adapt to the circumstances or pine away and die in misery—or in prison. There is no alternative.

It is different with the city-dweller. Trade extends his horizon. The world lies open before him. His plans are ambitious. Yet the narrow limits of political regulation hold him in check. What is more natural in such circumstances than the effort to break through or circumvent them! This is what causes the ferment and ignites the social struggle. In such an atmosphere the quickwitted townsman's thoughts and opinions germinate and grow. His eternal discontent resists the contented conservatism of the ruling classes. He is the first to stir up the resigned conservatism of the "masses."

Lord, townsman, peasant: these would be the three main types of individuals if the State had not progressed beyond the primitive stratification of society. But we know how complex the social structure has become and how the different types have multiplied.

It is impossible for the scientist to distinguish them all. Art alone can present the typical. The sociologist must yield to the delineator. We will only add that as civilization advances and the sphere of the State enlarges, the ruling class subdivides into the civil class, the military class and the large landholders, transferring its various functions to particular organs.

Each of these smaller circles has its particular interests, its peculiar calling and its corresponding views and style of life. The subdivision into classes determines also the method of participating in the government of the State. Compare the general who remains a solider and stakes his professional honor on fulfilling the royal orders even against his own convictions; the minister who feels honor bound to hand in his resignation on account of some difference of opinion with his monarch, or incident which does not please him; and the "great lord" who will accept a royal invitation to hunt but will politely decline a minister's portfolio in order not to sacrifice his freedom. How different the views of life's duties and principles! What different ideas in one and the same ruling class through the social differentiation of pursuits!

With the middle class it is the same. What a difference there is in the artisan's line of thinking from that of the merchant or shipowner! How different the sort of mind among merchants themselves according to whether one stays in a shop, another is engaged in foreign trade, and a third trades on the exchange. Yet these are not individual fortunes, but social destinies, social fates.

What must be the psychological make-up of the workman's child, accustomed to uninterrupted labor in the family, meagre earnings and the monotony of the small tradesman's life. Yet how different is the circle of the traders on the exchange, with abrupt alternatives of wealth and misery and the continual excitement of speculation, where success depends on the turn of events the world over.

How many educated professions are differentiated in the middle class: doctors, attorneys, judges, teachers, officials, master mechanics, engineers. Each circle creates its own peculiar spirit, so to say, a moral atmosphere of principles, ideas, views and conceptions, in which its members dwell and in which their posterity is born and educated. The number of types is endless. But it must be pointed out that in every case the individual's thought and conduct, feeling and effort, is not created in him but in his social circle. Least of all is it created by him freely and independently. It is laid upon him without his knowledge. Sociology must stress some of the fundamental factors in this process.

It follows from what has already been said that it is moral force alone which transforms the individual. The group affects him through his moral nature, his thoughts and views. He is only a part of it, growing up in its moral atmosphere, drawing his intellectual life from it. In this process ancestral descent and long lineage is not the decisive factor. Whatever the anthropological material, if a newcomer enters a group, however strange, and he is uninfluenced by any other, and he is treated like other members, he will be as completely assimiliated as though he had been born there. Hence it is that while anthropologists assure us that no race in the world is pure and while experience daily shows us the greatest variety of anthropological types in one and the same society, the members of each group show a unitary moral type. Anthropological variety and moral unity is characteristic of every social community, not simply in Europe, but of the whole world. Yet so predominant is the impression made upon us by the latter that the impression of the former disappears in comparison. As we are in general more impressed by what is human in man, *i.e.*, by his intellectual and moral faculties, than by what is animal, so we are most impressed with a man's social type and the anthropological escapes observation. Thus when an individual has certain outward marks denoting membership in a group, such as costume, head-dress and the like, the moral type of the group is still more striking in him and we do not notice his anthropological type or deceive ourselves about it unless it is very conspicuously unusual.

The notorious fact that all Chinese seem alike to us is due to the fact that, being struck with the well-known outward characteristics, queue, clean-shaven crown and the like, we observe nothing else except the moral type, although there are different anthropological types among them as in many other folk. Similarly, to a Negro all the soldiers in a regiment of European grenadiers will look exactly alike because in addition to the similarity of costume, head-dress, etc., he notices only the moral type, the expression, mien and bearing. Nevertheless an anthropologist or craniologist would certainly find in such a regiment sufficient data for a classification into many races and anthropological types.

But some social circles, as we have seen, are very firmly bound together, compact and cohesive, while others are loosely connected and less cohesive. The degree of cohesion depends, as we have further seen, on the number of group-making factors, on the interests holding the group together and on their duration. For some are inherited and will endure while others are temporary, ephemeral and momentary.

The difference in the degree of social cohesion has great influence upon the creation and the endurance of moral types and we do not hesitate to formulate a sociological law that the tenacity and endurance of a moral type is directly related to the degree of cohesion and firmness of social structure and so to the number of group-making factors.

It is as if their greater number put the individual under better control. Highly cohesive social circles are well adapted to create firm characters. The individual members seem to be cast from one mold, to be flesh of its flesh and blood of its blood, nothing more nor less than pieces of it. Hence the elemental moral power of men contending for their class, their rank—their folk, to which every group-making factor and every heartstring binds them.

Contrast the vacillation and wavering when one of the forces binding a man to his own group is dissolved with the surface artificiality of the individual who presumes to relate to a group with which he has only a loose, ephemeral connection—most of the group-making factors being absent. Therein lies the perpetual absurdity of the parvenu, which greets us not only where the "upstart without family connections" puts on airs on account of his intimate relations with counts and princes (who is not familiar with this type), but also where the townsman among peasants would demean himself like a peasant or the aristocratic candidate explains his political and industrial program to his agricultural constituents. The ridiculous effect in every case derives from the absence of every natural bond of union between the individual and the group which he pretends he belongs to or represents. Affectation is always ridiculous. With such comic figures compare the man who embodies his own social group. His appearance commands respect everywhere. Its very naturalness is imposing. Even someone of little importance must be taken seriously for his behavior is natural and consistent.

But social life is not confined within the exclusive social circles. In the very nature of political and social development there is an incessant movement of individuals back and forth, up and down, so that social circles touch and overlap in great confusion, while individuals stand in the greatest variety of relations to their own and to foreign groups. Thus life is richly provided with every degree of variation from cheerful pleasantry to bitter earnest, from delightful comedy to shocking tragedy. It is a barren task for science to distinguish the countless shades of individual style and situation, though not for history and art.

4. Morals

We have tried to explain how the moral type of individual is produced by the group, having already pointed out that the social group not only creates the individual's thoughts and opinions, sentiments and feelings but builds up what we call morals. For morals are nothing but the conviction implanted by the social group in the minds of its members of the propriety (*Statthaftigkeit*) and manner of life imposed by it on them. This conviction, the individual's innermost thought concerning his whole conduct and that of others, is the second factor in the development of morals. The first being acquired and customary habits, the manner of life and conduct. There are certain rules and principles which the individual absorbs from his group applicable to all spheres of life and possible situations.

Consider a man who is firmly rooted in his group. In no situation which is accessible to it considering its nature and position is he in doubt as to his procedure. He has acquired a standard of conduct and possesses a moral code which guides him everywhere.

While the simple unitary group (Spencer's "small and simple aggregate") constitutes the individual's whole world, in the primitive horde and wild natural stock, he knows what is right, proper and permissible toward his fellows and toward strangers. But as soon as two or more groups have been united and sovereignty has been organized the different moral views begin to contend in the larger social circle. The primitive moral codes are useless and must be formed anew if the union is to continue. Not only do the relations of sovereign and subject peremptorily demand thus, but they provide it for themselves. The members of the new union become habituated to the new institutions which become necessary to sustain sovereignty. New conceptions of what is right, proper, permissable and good, emerge. As the new political organization grows and is perfected the new moral code establishes limits, *i.e.*, statutes promulgated by the State, the transgression of which is punishable by the State.

Hence there is a fundamental difference between rights and morals. The former is a product of the fusion [*Zusammentreffen*] of different social elements, the latter is the product of the relations between the simple social group and the individual. Rights never arise except in a union of societies however simple it may be. Organized sovereignty is always presupposed. Morals arise in the most primitive social element, in the simple aggregate or horde.

Every complex community, consisting of parts which are united by certain group-making bonds, constitutes a social unit aside from the social circle comprised within it. Necessarily the very fact of the existence of this social community will create a common moral code binding on all its members. But on account of the weaker cohesion of the whole it will of course not have the effective power and intensity of the moral codes of the several social elements and will frequently conflict with them and sometimes be broken down by them. It may be confidently asserted that probably the greater part of the crimes and offenses occurring in the State arise from the conflict between the general and the particular moral codes. Thus the poacher does not offend the morality of his group when he hunts game in the mountains—although in so doing he violates not only the rights but also the moral code of the political commonweal.

Many infractions of law in the mercantile world, such as usury and the like, result from the antagonism between its moral code and that of the political whole and prove that the higher unity, the State, has not succeeded in reducing the social elements to a homogenous community and imbuing every individual with that higher morality which is as needful for the welfare of society as the primitive morality of the horde is for its welfare.

It is the State's supreme object to do this. Consciously or unconsciously it strives toward homogeneity in morals. Although this is never accomplished, no higher sanction or more complete justification of the State can be given then the determination to educate mankind to a higher moral place. But the ideal moral code must never be limited to national sentiment which is nothing more than a symbolic love of the horde. It should at least embrace mankind so far as it is civilized or capable of civilization. The way to its realization has been entered upon by the construction of political systems like the European, which will in time reduce Europe to a social unit, however loose. The process may then be extended to other portions of the world. Although its realization may lie in the unseen future, civilization must hold fast to it if it would be anything more than a blind natural process. It is certainly the noblest function of social science to illumine the wearisome path along which mankind, dripping with blood, yet yearns for the distant goal.

5. Morals and Truth Perception

It has undoubtedly already become clear that morals are not the result of human reflection, the conscious product of the human will and understanding, but art, like all social institutions, the result of natural development. It is a product of the natural feelings and thoughts of man in connection with the active impelling forces of life, the resultant as it were of the mutual action and reaction of nature and human life.

Hence we can distinguish two elements in the result, the natural and the human. The former is everlasting and unchangeable and is constantly and universally repeated. The latter is perpetually changing because it represents the ways in which individuals react upon natural realities and forces. In the morals of all ages and peoples we find something similar and typical, and also something changing and individual. While the social process that produces morals is always the same, its various contingencies make the psycho-social result different.

Placed by nature in a sequence of necessities which he cannot alter, man naturally strives to adapt himself to them as best he can and to make life as pleasant as possible. Habit helps him over the worst difficulties by deadening his sensibilities. He gets accustomed to the rack on which he is stretched and ceases to feel it. He attributes his sufferings to a higher necessity and, knowing the uselessness of protest, gives up the futile fight and looks instinctively for means to alleviate his hard lot.

In following this natural tendency, or rather in being driven to do whatever his nature and conditions compel, he reflects (which again is a part of his nature) and believes that he acts freely, finding a proof of his freedom in the individual shading of his acts, though this happens simply because reflection, in essence the same, is individualistic in form.

If, acting as he must, though reflecting as he acts, he hits upon a mode of behavior which long experience proves to be the most suitable and appropriate to his conditions, he takes this to be the right, the only good and moral way. Whatever is contrary is held to be immoral.

Thus man acquires moral ideas which correspond to the larger or smaller extent of his needs and experiences, the higher or lower stage of his civilization, the more or less complex relations of his life, growing, broadening and developing with them.

But, as we have seen, an individual's moral feelings all develop within the sphere of his social group through its influence upon him. Take a primitive savage, a gregarious human being; what are his moral ideas? He is bound to his fellows by the natural feeling of connection. They help him in his need; to hold to them, help them and stand by them loyally is one of his moral ideas. But strangers from another horde waylay them, try to steal their property, invade their hunting ground, slay them occasionally and kidnap them. Therefore to kill these strangers and rob them is another of his moral ideas.

Now the element in these ideas which is natural and eternal inheres in the mind of man, surviving savagery and appearing in changing garb and more refined form throughout the whole period of human existence. Today, as thousands of years ago, there is the struggle with the foreigner for lordship. Between strange social groups today as always there are only two possible relations: conflict or alliance against a third. After century upon century of development, in the midst of high civilization, the primitive moral idea of the savage meets us in the form of patriotism, heroism and bravery.

The savage feels more keenly than the civilized man that he is only a part of the community, for without his own horde his life is every moment exposed to the superior force of hostile beasts and alien hordes. It cannot appear immoral to the savage to satisfy hunger and thirst and to feed the helpless children of his own horde. This must seem to him good, profitable and a moral duty.

Between young and old, helpless and strong, arises a mutual relation of protection and gratitude which with the changes of years becomes reversed. Protection of children and the infirm creates a moral idea. However, if times, circumstances and individual dispositions cause a horde to put an end to the misery of old age by violent death, this practice also becomes, locally and temporarily, a moral act. And the same is true, locally and temporarily, of fostering or exposing children. The essence of the moral idea is the same: practices springing from natural tendencies take on one form or another. Whichever one lasts and proves to be suitable comes to be considered moral.

The relation of the sexes and the division of industrial labor between them is regulated by time and circumstances, the temperament of the particular horde, and its physical and mental constitution. Whether the result is promiscuity, polygamy or polyandry, whatever practice persists and is recognized as suitable becomes a moral duty and command, a part of morals.

When one horde establishes lordship over another, when two make offensive or defensive alliance against a third, or finally when captured aliens are reduced to servitude and slavery, the circle of life's relations broadens, a new series of practices begins and a new sphere of moral ideas arises.

The best method of handling captives, slaves and servants, and the best conduct toward allies offer new grounds for moral opinions and the most reasonable and appropriate government of subjects becomes the only moral one. Fidelity towards allies produces a new moral idea. Differentiated treatment of members of different social circles in time makes moral principles, conforming to the usage, eventually settle into rights.

As a different treatment seems wise and appropriate for each condition of life, so different moral standards grow up according to the different social position of the younger or older generation, of healthy or infirmed men, of women in different periods of life, of

masters and dependents, of the rich and the propertyless. Unconditional obedience is recognized as moral in servants and slaves;
inflexible energy and strict discipline in masters. The killing of a
master is recognized as immoral conduct in a slave. The killing of a
slave is by no means immoral in a master.

Men are never satisfied simply with actual occurrences. It is a
peculiarity of the reflecting human mind to ascribe to events, causes
which have no relation whatever to natural causes and to give the
most far-fetched explanation possible. A myth-maker and poet by
nature, man ascribes poetical and generally anthropomorphic mean-
ings and derivations to natural phenomena and he treats social
occurrences in the same way.

As man at first ascribes his own existence to the creation of a
supersensual being so he traces all social differences to different
creative acts of the same being. Social organizations which the force
of circumstances has produced, men prefer to ascribe to an original
arrangement of the creator of the world, being led by an unconscious
desire to give a higher sanction to his various moral ideas. Thus when
social relations have been so far developed that murder is interdicted,
and to spare a fellow-being's life is a moral commandment, the myth-
making mind has a god appear in flames and deliver to the law-giver
in the midst of thunder and lightning a table on which stand the
words: Thou shalt not kill.

Every code of human morals from earliest times to the present
has this thoroughly characteristic peculiarity. The product of actual
occurrences and real relations is everywhere explained by and derived from imaginary circumstances, and men cannot comprehend
a moral idea otherwise.

Whether theologians base morals upon divine commandments,
or philosophers derive them from ideas inherent in man, fact and
fancy are blended together until one seems incapable of existing
without the other. As morality takes root in men's hearts, gains
control of their dispositions and becomes a part of their mental ego,
the myths which support them take root there also; until it appears
as if morals could not be maintained without myths and every attack
on the latter must cause the former to fall.

Socrates was accused of undermining virtue and morality, the
real forces of life, because he questioned the existence of those

creatures of the imagination, the Olympian gods. And so today, whoever ventures to criticise and doubt one of the myths which have been put forward as the explanation and foundation of our morals, whoever denies the "universal and eternal truth of inherent, moral ideas," and seeks to represent them as the product of actual social relations—changing with them and taking manifold forms and shapes, is considered a dangerous enemy to the myth-makers.

This fight of naive ignorance against truth in the name of morality still lingers in very many spheres. Advanced moral sentiment seeking to explain and support the idea and the feeling of brotherly love produced the monogenetic myth of the descent of all men from one pair of parents. Polygenism, is then thought to menace the myth. It becomes immoral. Though brotherly love might just as plausibly be founded upon the unity of species in a polygenetic mankind. The real explanation, however, is quite different: the development of human society.

The history of sectarianism presents the same spectacle under countless different forms. The simplest religious ceremonies are connected directly with certain moral ideas and an attack on the former is denounced as an attack on the latter, when in truth they do not need to stand in any connection whatever. Every new system of philosophy, every hard won scientific acquisition, has the same contest against the alleged "guardians of morals."

When the intellectual revolution and the materialist philosophy of the eighteenth century overthrew some of the prevailing prejudices, the jesuitical cry of alarm was everywhere raised that morals were being undermined. Because in a certain age the stock of moral ideas corresponded to a certain degree of scientific knowledge, because at a given time the opinion was universal that the soul is a temporary occupant of the human body and after its decay will rise straight to heaven and begin a new life there, the whole moral and ethical code was thought to depend upon the maintenance of this belief. Whoever dared to doubt the immortality of the soul was thought to have sinned against morality and virtue as though immortality and the dualism of soul and body were the only conditions on which they could thrive. Many a time indeed have men sought to uphold the existing moral order by this fable, and when no one knew better, the effort was praiseworthy. But every such prop is ready to fall the moment advanced knowledge lays bare its distortions. However it by no means follows that morality is undermined and threatened by the removal of the alleged prop. For the basis of morals is truth and not fiction. All of these pious fictions have not prevented the grossest immoralities, the horrors of the inquisition and trials for witchcraft, the greatest crimes mankind has ever committed.

The alleged descent of man from lower animals is denounced by the church as undermining the whole ethical and moral code; as if this had some connection with the alleged creation of man by a god or was indeed the result of it.

Following natural and necessary tendencies the human State has grown up and has become in civilized regions what it is today, the guardian of right and custom, the promoter of welfare and culture. Corresponding to this fact a moral theory of the State has been produced in the human mind, a pretty myth, according to which the State sprang from a social contract which the citizens once made for protecting rights and securing justice and it gives adequate expression to the ideas which the actual evolution of the State has produced.

But when it is announced, as the result of modern objective investigation, that the State arose by violence and owes its existence to the superiority of some over others, the "moral" heresy-hunters (*Angstmeier*) and hypocrites raise the alarm that the normal idea of the State is undermined, right is uprooted and public morals corrupted. It is the policy of stupid parents, who expect to inculcate morals and a sense of obligation in a child by telling him all sorts of ghost stories. Science should not be misled by such ungenerous and narrow views. Morals are the ripened fruit of the acutal development of civilization and cannot be harmed by the scientific investigation of its real foundation. On the contrary the truth will certainly be much more wholesome for its promotion than the stupid lie upon which it has hitherto been sought with little success.

As the origin of moral ideas is a very difficult problem and a dark region in human knowledge, it has always been easier to explain it in poems and fairy tales. Nevertheless it is not difficult to see that every progress in the perception of truth, and especially of nature, must promote morals.

For as nature's sway and the acts of man go to make up the

events of life, human action is reasonable when they correspond to natural tendencies and complement them; and unreasonable if they mistake these tendencies and oppose them.

There can be but one principle of human rationality and of human morals and ethics: to be governed by the import and tendency of nature's sway. Hence knowledge of nature, natural science in its full scope, embracing every department of human life, is the only and the necessary basis of the science of morals and ethics.

Without natural science there is no moral science. Hence the low state of morals where natural science is neglected, and the higher and purer morality with greater progress in the knowledge of nature's sway.

The explanation is simple. Nature has all the characteristics which oriental monotheism ascribes to its god: omnipresence and omnipotence. Everything everywhere happens as nature wills, according to nature. Indeed at bottom the idea of god is only a symbol of nature, perhaps unconscious and poetical at first, later misunderstood and misinterpreted.

As man himself is subject to nature, is constrained by its demands, must satisfy its needs, lives according to the measure of the strength and capacity nature has given him to follow its commands, so his mind is deeply impressed by its omnipotence and the resulting course of events. He can scarcely conceive another mode of existence—and this one seems right and just, reasonable and moral (*sittlich*). He has no other standard for the events of life than the assumed will, *i.e.*, the visible tendency, of nature; while "unnatural" is synonymous with unreasonable and immoral. Man's ethical sense has been grafted onto nature's sway. Its norms, even in social life, have been transformed and condensed in his mind into moral ideas. By nature the parents and elders assume direction of the rising generation—and the honor and respect which the younger pay the elder accords with our moral ideas. Whatever is natural is moral. Therein lies the eternal, fixed and unchangeable basis of all ethics and morals.

Hence there is really but one code of ethics and morals. It has been and always will be as fixed and unchangeable as the forces of nature. But if nevertheless there have been temporary and local differences in ethical views it is, first, because knowledge of nature

has not everywhere reached the same stage of advancement and men
often yield to the grossest self-deceptions in respect to it. Second,
because there are whole spheres of human life, like the social sphere,
which on account of meager knowledge are not considered natural,
in which the sway of nature is not conjectured or presupposed, in
which therefore a correction of inherited moral conceptions in accord
with the recognized "will of nature," or a concession to nature's
tendencies is entirely out of the question.

By searching for truth, therefore, and by investigating nature
and her rhythm, in the social sphere as elsewhere, science labors
in the service of morals and breaks the pathway for its progress—
although incidentally old and cherished idols may be overthrown
and the wail of the "moralists" aroused.

6. Rights

Heretofore rights have always been treated from the standpoint
either of individualism or of a very indefinite collectivism. As these
two extremes contended with each other, progress swayed from one
to the other in literature. But since neither was true, it ought not to
be surprising that neither the philosophy of rights nor the prevailing
scientific treatment of them is satisfactory. The various schools of
the philosophers have produced nothing but disgust and rancor
after centuries of labor.

Let us briefly review the dreary maze. The original rules of
human conduct receive their sanction in part from precedent and
custom and in part by reference to the will of the gods. Belief and
custom are the earliest sources of right, of what sets the standard of
conduct. As reflection awakens it distinguishes between these precepts of religion and morals and the laws which rulers arrange.
Consequently the earliest jurisprudence could consider political law
alone to be the source of right. Upon further scientific investigation
this naive conception was found unsatisfactory. Then began the
argumentation in a circle. Some sought the source of right in man
immediately, in his nature, in his social instincts or in similar
characteristics which were ascribed to him. Others believed that they
had found the source in the community, the folk, in society and its
"common will" (Gumplowicz, 1877: sec. 4, 21; 1881: I: 4 et seq.).

The truth lies between the two, as we have shown (Gumplowicz,

1881: Pt. iv: sec. I). Rights are not the product of the individual and his nature and constitution. Nor are they the creation of the folk or of a common will or national spirit invented *ad hoc*. Rights are a social creation, a form of communal life produced by the conflict (*Zusammenstoss*) of unlike social groups of unequal power. Such unlikeness and inequality is the necessary precondition of all rights. In the primitive horde, a homogeneous, simple, undifferentiated group, there are no rights, nor are they necessary. Complete equality prevails. It is not the soil in which rights are able to grow. There are neither family rights (promiscuity prevails) nor property rights —hence no rights of inheritance; nor any sort of rights in personality where there is no trade and commerce. Life is not regulated by published ordinances; whatever is, is holy. Forms of life produced in the course of time to satisfy wants, which we call custom, are fully sufficient to regulate the life of the primitive horde. No one marks their gradual rise and they are generally ascribed to the will of the gods. Custom and a few religious precepts suffice for men in such a condition.

But when unlike groups come together and different ethnic elements have to live side by side, the custom of neither is sufficient, for it is not recognized by the other. One subjects the other, sovereignty is organized, and the superior power of the stronger makes existence side by side possible by regulating the manner of life. The regulations thus built up for the existence of unlike elements side by side are reduced by practice to rules and principles which create rights.

Thus, as we have seen, the first family rights arose through the rape of women from another tribe—the right of the man over his wife. Thus also by reducing the foreign element to servitude arose the right of the lord over his slave. From this resulting distinction between the lord to whom the fruits of the soil belong, and the slave who cultivates the soil for his master, arose the right of property. The soil together with the acquired sovereignty passed from father to son in the father-family—hence the right of inheritance arose. If an alien trading element invaded this primitive sovereign organization, the exchange of goods produced other property rights. First of all the rights of debtor and creditor with all the complications to which the development of trade and commerce give rise.

Rights are always due to the contact of unlike social elements and every right bears evidence of such an origin. There is not one which does not express inequality, for each is the mediation between unlike social elements, the reconciliation of conflicting interests which was originaly enforced by compulsion but has through usage and familiarity acquired the sanction of a new custom.

Thus family right subjects the wife and children to the control of the father and compels the reconciliation of opposing interests until usage and familiarity substitute new customs and new morals for the original constraint. Property rights regulate the inequality between owner and non-owner in respect to the thing owned. The rights of inheritance regulate the inequality between the heir and the non-heir in respect to the inheritance. The rights of debtor and creditor regulate the inequality between them with respect to the object of the obligation. In short, every right arises from an inequality and aims to maintain and establish it through the sovereignty of the stronger over the weaker. In this respect every right is a true reflection of the State to which it owes its existence and which also aims only at the maintenance and regulation of the life of unlike elements side by side through the sovereignty of one over the other. And since the maintenance of inequality is the sole and real principle of every law, corresponding to each there is a duty. Corresponding to each one entitled to receive there are one or more obligated to give. Similarly in the State by its nature there are rulers and ruled.

7. Rights and the State

Thus it is plain that rights can arise only in the State and nowhere else. They are eminently political institutions, substance of the State's substance and blood of its blood, containing as it were a particle of political sovereignty. From where comes the grain of sovereignty in every right if not from the great reservoir of sovereignty which we call the State's power? From this great reservoir political sovereignty flows like water through an aquaduct into a network of rights. It is only necessary to turn the tap of execution, and political sovereignty. The State's power, is there. In civilized States a small fee is paid, generally in the form of a stamp tax for the privilege of drawing upon political sovereignty. Rights can no more be conceived without the State than an aquaduct without a reservoir, pipes and taps.

Nevertheless scholasticism succeeded in building up countless systems of "natural rights" which were alleged to exist without the State, beyond its borders and superior to its authority. Fortunately they are all overthrown, dead and buried. But their spirit hovers over the sea of jurisprudence where "innate" human rights are still spoken of. In addition to those "proclaimed by the French revolution," such as freedom and equality, other "inalienable rights" are also put forth—such as the right to live, to work, etc. They are deduced either from the "conception of man" as a "free, sentient and reasonable" being or more generally from the "conception of justice." We have elsewhere shown the arbitrariness and insipidity of these deductions (Gumplowicz, 1877: sec. 21-23; 1881: sec. 33 et seq.). They are simply deductions from natural rights though every premise is false and the whole system is buried in its grave. That man is a "free" being is pure imagination. Still less is he a "reasonable" being, if by "reason" we mean the peculiarity that a person is led in his action by reason and not by blind impulse.

The premises of "inalienable human rights" rest upon the most unreasonable self-deification of man; an overestimation of the value of human life, and upon complete misconception of the only possible basis of the existence of the State. This fancied freedom and equality is incompatible with the State and is a direct negation of it. The only choice for mortal men is between the State with its necessary servitude and inequality, and—anarchy.

There is much unavoidable evil in the former. But on the other hand it promotes and protects the greatest good that man can experience on earth. Anarchy raises to infinity the evil which is unavoidable in the State without affording even the least of its advantages. The greatest human evil is stupidity and baseness. Scarcely can the State hold it in check. In a condition of anarchy it rages without restraint heaping horror on horror. There is no third choice.[3] It is

---

[3] Engels, in his *Ursprung der Familie, des Privateigenthums und des Staats* and Marx too, has in mind such a return to the "gentile constitution." It takes a great naivete to conceive of the return to forms of social existence long since surmounted. It is as though an old man were to become a youth again.

impossible to return to the primitive horde. And between these two modes of social existence: the state and anarchy, it is not hard to choose.

It is no less an error to deduce rights from "justice" or a "feeling of justice," to place them above the State and to propose their realization in the State. This procedure rests on an optical illusion. For what is justice? Whence do we derive our conception of it? It is created only by the actual rights as they exist in the State. Our conception of justice attaches itself to political rights; our receptivity, our sense and feeling of it have no other source. It is no contradiction that occasionally we have reason to acknowledge that a political right is wrong and violates justice. For the development of our sense of justice, which takes place under the influence of political rights, may apparently exhaust itself since institutional rights exist only by virtue of written law or deep-rooted usage and tradition, while political relations together with our sense of justice continue developing. In such a case our yearning for justice is only the forerunner of a new statutory right which has been previously grounded in the conditions and in the degree of the State's development, and which might be said to be already recognized though as yet unwritten. In a word we must distinguish between justifiable reform movements based in the nature of the State, and mere Utopias. The former spring of themselves from the whole previous development of the State. The latter are separated from the State and stand upon ground on which no political institution has ever stood such as freedom, equality and absolute justice, apart from the State, and based on "natural rights."

What "justice" in this sense is and how it is found we do not and cannot know. To us justice is the simple abstraction of political rights and it stands and falls with them. If we imagine our past apart from political development and political rights the conception of justice vanishes utterly from mind. Plato recognized this, and as he attempted to explain in the *Republic* what a "just man" and what "justice" were, he began by describing the founding of the State out of heterogeneous and disparate elements. Presupposing that each part would assume the most fitting role that befell it in the State he called this organization of the State and of political sovereignty just. Hence, this normal condition of the State, in which each accommodates himself to the role that befalls him, is Plato's type of justice. By this shift, starting from the State, which is really the only possible way, Plato reaches his conception of justice which he then applies as a standard to the individual.[4]

The words of Thrasymachus in the same dialogue: "My doctrine is that justice is the interest of the stronger," might be applied to justice in the State. For in fact the weaker must accommodate himself to the stronger. The State can be regulated by no other rights than such as are most agreeable to the stronger. Indeed this is relatively best for the weaker and in this sense political order presents the only conceivable idea of justice, the only source from which we can draw conceptions of the just and justice. But it is universally the very contrary of freedom and equality and indeed naturally must be. In fact justice has universally been the real expression of the relative power of the social elements in the State. With changing conditions and especially with progressive development of the State in agriculture and industry, in science and art, relations gradually became more humane and lenient. Rights and legal regulations are humanized and the idea of justice in the abstract grows more perfect. Today no less than in Plato's time the State is the only standard of justice. The necessary conditions of its perpetuation determine the concept. What the State must do is right, and that can never be "justice" which the State cannot do.

8. Rights and Morals

We have seen that rights arise at the point where the new entity composed of unlike social elements can no longer be held together merely by customs and morals since the customs and morals of one party are not the same as those of the other. Into this discord in moral views, with which social unity is incompatible, rights first entered in the form of the commands of the rulers. But in time, as we said, they are transformed into customs and morals so that, being

---

[4] "Let us complete the investigation which we undertook in the belief that, if we first endeavored to contemplate justice in some larger object which contains it, we should find it easier to discern its nature in the individual man." (Plato, 1892: Bk. IV, 434). This greater object was wisely chosen. Only by starting from the State was it possible to arrive at a conception of justice.

rights, they become the substance of new moral ideas. The apparent contradiction between morals that precede rights and morals that in turn are produced by them needs some elucidation.

The customs and morals of the primitive horde come from the necessities of life and the common wants of primitive social unity. Needs change in the new social whole composed of two or more unlike elements. At first indeed because there are no common customs and morals, force, compulsion and political rights must bind the new whole together. But usage, habit and all the forces which led to fixed customs and morals in the primitive horde will not fail of their effect in the new social unity also.

The new rights only indicated the line along which the forms of life necessary to the new social unit must be developed. In time they will enter into the moral consciousness, for plainly the new social unity will consolidate. In one way or another certain modes of peaceable communal existence will be discovered. People will adapt themselves to necessities and by recognizing and accepting them create new customs and morals to which rights gave the first impulse.

The old morals of the respective social elements must necessarily be subordinated to the new morals of the complex whole, for while the former insures the existence of the simple group only the latter preserves the complex community.

For example, to a primitive horde and an unmixed stock, alien and enemy are synonymous terms. Its morals command the sparing of fellow members and the ruthless destruction of aliens. But as soon as any foreigners become a part of the community, whether received as slaves or allies or to serve some other interest of the new whole (the relation will be determined by a treaty from which rights will arise), instantly the interest of the new community which produces the new right begins to set aside the old morals which made "alien and enemy" equal and prepares the way for new ones which give the slave, the ally and whoever else has been taken into the social union a claim to protection and respect. However long rudiments of the old morals may persist in opinions and sentiments the new interest of the new whole has framed new morals which prove victorious over the old.

Wherever there are rights the process is the same. Although in primitive times, or even in the feudal State of Medieval Europe, the wealth of tolerated classes such as the traveling merchants may have provided lucrative booty for ruling classes and robber knights, (the theft of which did not offend against the old morals or detract from knightly honor). Yet the new rights which protected the property of the burghers in the interest of all prepared the way gradually for the new morals which today forbid the nobility to seize the property of other classes. With difficulty and after centuries of trial, but with final success, political rights have provided new morals concerning property and it is now inconceivable that in the Middle Ages knights and noblemen, who made so much of honor, did not scruple to surprise a city and rob its citizens of their hard-earned goods.

The displacement of the old morals by new rights due to the wants and interests of the new classes is seen most plainly in the development of patriotism. The original tribal consciousness of the respective social elements of the State is changed in time into a folk or national consciousness. While the old morals recognized only the duty of the individual to sacrifice himself for the narrowest syngenetic group the common interests of the new whole have created new morals which demand his unconditional sacrifice for a whole which is ethnically and socially complex.

If we must cite examples at least we do not need to go far afield for them. What was the nature of that patriotism to which every German was morally bound not many decades ago? If we characterize it in one word as "particularism" we shall at the same time have indicated the powerful change through which morals have passed in this respect as the result of events and new rights. The Rhenish Union was commensurate with the older morals. However, the same thing today by the same people in the same land would be called the height of immorality, treason and infamy. These moral changes have taken place since the events of Jena and the war for freedom, since the rights of the German Union and the new German Empire. The former morality of "parts" must yield to the new morals of a new "whole" which the creation of new laws gave impulse towards. As new rights paved the way for new morals, so now new morals will continue to be the strongest prop of the new system of rights—until in the perpetual change of earthly things new events and circumstances create new rights again to which existing morals must be sacrificed.

The objections that can be made to our presentation of the relation between rights and morals are easily foreseen, for frequently the relation is apparently reversed. Even in the present century how often have we seen decayed rights swept away by the powerful current of "public morals." And yet it was only apparently so. For in fact every such right was merely a screen behind which other conditions came into existence peremptorily demanding recognition as rights. Although existing written rights seemed to prevent the realization of the demand nevertheless moral ideas were created which, exerting a powerful influence and taking possession of the consciousness of the masses, suddenly rose like a tornado overthrowing the old rights as though they were paper; whereupon the rights which the conditions had long since demanded and which had already entered the moral consciousness gained legal expression and validity.

If I might use a somewhat questionable metaphor to illustrate this point: behind regular rights legitimately wedded to the nation and known as such, there appeared secretly, from the force of circumstances, illegitimate rights which shunned the light and in illicit intercourse with the nation begat morals. As these, still illegitimate, came into the world and grew up they helped to set the betrayed old rights, which had lost their force and justification, violently aside; whereupon the legitimation of the new morals followed by subsequent marriage, *per subsequens matrimonium*.

"So there was an unwritten natural right based in reason," cries some supporter of natural rights triumphantly. Not so fast. It is true that in such moments of development rights emerged through hard birth pains from the dark womb of actual conditions into the light of existence. But they are not natural rights, based on reason and independent of time and conditions. On the contrary, they are always conditioned in the actual circumstances. In the sense that they correspond to the conditions from which they spring they are natural and reasonable, but not in the sense that their source is in a natural consciousness of right or in reason and that they always remain the same. The requirements which arise from actual conditions according to time and place, which correspond to them and are therefore natural and reasonable, being formulated into laws, become rights after having struck deep root in moral consciousness.

Thus the objection that the source of rights is moral is based on a misconception of actual forces. Equally unfounded also is the doctrine of natural rights. But there is another objection which seems to be supported by the facts. Political rights do not always enter into the moral consciousness of the community. However long they may endure they have public morals against them and eventually must succumb. This frequently occurs and though it seems to establish the moral source of rights, in truth it does not.

We often see valid political rights stand like dead machines in spite of the application of the entire power of the State; never operating without the display of political force, disliked and repudiated by public morals, unable to create new morals and finally ending their burdensome existence somehow unregretted. Upon closely examining what sort of rights these are which cannot produce a moral ground into which they may strike firm root, we observe that there was no pressing need for them, that they arose from the momentary caprice of one party, from false ideas and theories, from misconceptions of actual conditions, etc. Such rights hang in mid-air without footing. They are powerless, valid only through external support and protection, without internal living force, a stranger and an enemy to public morals, unable to create new morals and hence from the start ordained to perish. Such rights are not rights at all. They have no vital force, they are still born.

All that has been said of the mutual relation of rights and morals applies to private as well as to public rights and morals. The former generate their own atmosphere as well as the latter, and are equally dependent on it for existence.

For example, take the changes in interest (usury laws) during the last three decades in certain States of Europe, especially Austria. First, the severe old usury laws according to the intent of canonical law (*Recht*), date from the period of industrial servitude and guilds. Overstepping the minimum rate of five or six per cent was not only made punishable by the State, but was held contrary to public morals. The industrial conditions, the restraints upon trade, commerce and agriculture fully justified the laws of usury. The severe laws were the outcome of actual conditions and produced in public opinion a moral consciousness of the objectionable character of usury. Meanwhile industrial development moved ceaselessly forward. Economic barriers fell. Trade, commerce and land became free. Productive industry felt an expansion hitherto unknown. Productivity far exceeded former limits. The old laws of interest were felt to be oppressively narrow. Behind the screen of this written law, the need for a new one more commensurate with the conditions made itself felt and began to undermine the morals based on the old. The latter lost its footing and was overthrown and a new right—complete freedom—was proclaimed, which soon did away with the old morals and created a new morality which saw nothing unnatural in the free contract of the parties about rates so long as no other immoral factor was involved such as taking advantage of youth, inexperience, unavoidable predicament and the like. Then the State permitted and even instigated the creation of institutions of credit which, even when lawfully managed, brought rates of interest which two decades before had been repudiated and denounced in both laws and morals, while prominent men of spotless character (who highly esteemed honor and morals) competed for their management.

Meanwhile the industrial boom wore itself out. For according to economic laws a relapse must come. Trade, commerce, industry, agriculture again declined and their productivity fell off. Again safety was sought in erecting old barriers and returning to the former narrow restraints. But above all else the new right of unlimited freedom in interest rates contrasted with the industrial decline and lost footing in the actual conditions which demanded something else. The need of change became manifest. The new morals wavered. The new rights had to fall and the old restrictions on the rate of interest became statutory law again. At first the newly resurrected rights struggled with the vanishing remnants of the morals which were based on the fallen rights. But they were victorious, "for only the living is right," and soon morals will be completely tranformed, especially as political power and criminal courts pave the way for new standards in public morality.

In every phase of private rights, examples may be multiplied at will of rights arising from actual conditions and shaping morals. Permit us further to point to the many changes in the law (*Recht*) of marriage and the resulting change in morals. Due to the long number of centuries the marriage tie has been held legally indissoluble, a taint of immorality is attached to divorce. If the law is compelled by actual conditions and the freer development of modern society to sanction the dissolution of marriage, as recently in France, the new rights have still to struggle a long while with the old morals. A recent article in the Paris *Figaro* occasioned by the new law read somewhat as follows: "Divorce—well; but remarriage? Public morals will not endure that in France(!)" *Figaro* need not worry. In Europe and even in France public morals have at times endured worse things than those of marital claims; for example the *jus prima noctis*. They will soon, if they have not already, come to terms with the new rights, divorce and remarriage, which supposing they last, are reasonable because they take account of existing needs and conditions.

One more question in conclusion. If morals are constantly changing and follow almost slavishly the rights which originate in actual conditions, why do men always conceive of law as changeless in the midst of change, as the unvarying source of rights and the eternal idea throned high above all transitory things of earth? Why do they thus appeal to law and regard law as the standard of rights and political institutions?

The explanation is very simple. The variability of rights and political institutions is visible and appreciable. They cannot possibly pass as changeless. Official announcements annul today the laws of yesterday. A ministerial ordinance suspends an existing political institution and substitutes another. But the change in morals is slow and unmarked as the progress of the hour hand of a clock. A generation is often but a minute on the moral dial—who can detect such a slight progression! Generations later the historian and the philosopher notice that the pointer has moved. The average man "hears it told indeed but lacks believing faith." Naturally so, for in the flowing stream of events man must lay hold on something fixed and unchanging or lose his bearings. Until Copernicus, the earth at least stood fast under his feet. Since then it moves in a circle and not even the sun stands still. No wonder that men grow dizzy and look hither and thither for some fixed point by which to direct their unsteady course in the ocean of life! It is an absolute necessity of human temperament to have such fixed points, like stars on the horizon. To it all the "eternal powers" which men worship owe their existence.

Nor will they pass away while man lives on earth. Among them are found moral ideas. For in them man seeks and hopes to find a firm point of support for all his actions, a guiding star by which to regulate all his acts and undertakings, a fixed standard by which to judge between good and bad, noble and ignoble. Indeed, he finds this in the moral idea he seeks. It is really a basal point and a guiding star for the whole of life. The error lies in each believing his morality the only one, changeless, the same for all times and peoples. It is no more true than that the earth is a fixed point in the universe. But just as the earth in spite of its ceaseless revolutions affords a firm enough ground for human efforts, so the individual's moral ideas afford him solid support upon which to base his character, his efforts and his will. What do the landlord or the homeowner care that the soil he tills or the ground on which he builds revolves with the whole globe! It is just as little concern to the individual that his morals will seem immoral to future generations. To him it is the one possible fixed ground which he can cultivate and build upon.

For the individual, however transient he himself is, ultimately finds in himself the firm support to which he can cling in the wild tumult of life for protection—and woe to him if he does not find it! It is only shortsightedness and pardonable weakness in man to believe that it is external to himself, for he seeks it there in vain. "It is not from without that it comes, thine inner self creates it." Thus whether it be purely personal feelings like real love and friendship which accompany men through life, or true faith to which pious temperaments devote themselves, or higher ideas like enthusiasm for folk and fatherland, for truth and science, to which the individual unselfishly sacrifices himself, every feeling and every idea is a "fixed pole-star in the flood of events" which shines before him, consoles and comforts him and ennoble him. Even though this is purely subjective and passes away with him. So it is with morals.

Thus, although philosopher and sociologist inquire how morals arose, what changes they have undergone, whether they are justified or not, the individual finds it sufficient for his life that he has them. But whether he has any and what they are depends upon the degree of development of his social group: upon the family in which he was born and brought up, upon his environment, upon the impressions received in tender years, upon the experiences he has passed through, perhaps also upon the knowledge he has gathered, but certainly to a high degree upon the laws which the State has maintained and to which he has had to conform.

9. Individual Efforts and Social Necessities

Thus by observing the social world and its phenomena we come to perceive that there is a necessity immanent in the condition of things according to which they move, by which they act and which sooner or later reaches fulfillment. It is not in man's power to suspend or check it. He is himself a part of that world and an element in those phenomena and all his actions are subject to this all-embracing and universally immanent necessity. His alleged and apparent freedom cannot alter or prevent its fulfillment.

The common understanding recognizes indeed that the so-called "natural laws" are fulfilled on a grand scale. But in specific instances, microscopic details of individual action are not easily apparent.

Concede for a moment the beautiful illusion that the individual acts "freely," and consider what significance it has in view of the fulfillment of necessity in individual life and human society. All of man's "free acts" may be reduced to a universal concept and a common denominator: preservation. Likewise all the processes in nature and human life which take place of immanent necessity may be reduced to a universal concept and common denominator: change and decay. In the realm of nature all is perishable. Man would preserve everything.

This fundamental antithesis lies like a curse on all of man's "free acts," which are condemned to exhaustion in fruitless struggle against nature's necessities. Human "freedom" is but the freedom of the captive lion, to run to and fro in his cage and to follow the menagerie, cage and all, hither and thither through city and country.

But the general perception that human freedom accomplishes nothing against external necessity, that it dashes like waves against a rock-bound coast only to be broken and scattered in spray, is of little worth. It is more important from the universal relation between human freedom and necessity to gain some insight into the essence and character of human actions.

We said that the whole tendency of man's so-called free activity

was to preserve what is by nature perishable and must pass away
to make room for the new. We try to preserve our health while
nature works quietly and incessantly for its decline. We try to pro-
long our life as long as possible even when nature has made its
destruction necessary. And as it is with these private values, so
it is with all the rest of life's goods. Men try to preserve economic
goods beyond the end of their lives for their descendants, and under
favorable circumstances their efforts are successful for generations.
Nevertheless the wealth of the Croesus of antiquity has fallen victim
to the all-powerful law of natural decay and perpetual change.
The Rothschilds of our century will leave as little trace in the future.

Man tries also with his whole being to preserve "forever" all
the social institutions which he, the blind instrument and means of
natural impulses and inclinations, creates; along with cultural products for making life tolerable, beautiful and noble—while natural and
necessary decay labors to overthrow them, undermines them, gnaws
at and devours them. We would preserve the social community in
which we are well off; but it must end as surely as the life of the
individual. We would preserve our language, religion, customs,
nationality and do not notice how they daily waste away like rocks
under dripping water.

Self-sacrifice to preserve what is inevitably destined to fall is
considered noble and heroic. Yet it is cowardly and ignoble to submit
to necessity. To oppose natural impulses is asceticism, for which men
exhibit their admiration. To follow natural impulses and necessities is
generally considered low "materialism." Fanatics who have neither
eye nor mind for the omnipotence of natural conditions are our
heroes in art in whom we delight. The more fanatical, the "greater"
they are. The founders of universal empires, the Cyruses, Alexanders,
Caesars and Napoleons won our admiration because they perished
trying to accomplish the impossible and unnatural. The simple man
who adapts himself to the natural and necessary conditions of his
environment is not worth consideration.

Our freedom of action and heroism may make the inevitable
fulfillment more painful for us, but it cannot prevent it or delay it a
single moment. The necessity immanent in things and natural conditions is fulfilled however much we oppose it. It is quite proper to
picture human life as a perpetual struggle against nature. However,

it is false to believe that man could ever at any point be victorious. What is fulfilled is always and exclusively necessity, never man's "free will." Man's efforts vacillate from side to side until finally they fall into the line of necessity—that is decisive for fulfillment. If we may be allowed to use a trivial illustration, let us suppose that from a number of stoppers of different sizes we have to select one for an open bottle. The relation between the open bottle and the pile of stoppers is controlled by an immanent necessity in consequence of which only one stopper, of suitable size, will fit it. This necessity will be fulfilled if we cork the bottle from the supply of stoppers at hand. And it will be filled in spite of our "free acts," which consist in applying a number of stoppers, some too small, some too large, to the mouth of the bottle and convincing ourselves that they do not fit. Eventually one will fit, the one of proper size, and when we find it we cork the bottle with satisfaction, proud of our "free action." A trivial illustration to be sure, in which other openings might be found besides the one in the bottle. Let us pass to a more serious example, better suited to scientific investigation.

Probably human freedom seems under less restraint in the sphere of scientific and philosophical thought than anywhere else. "Thoughts are free" and the field, not subject to censorship nor made unsafe by the State's attorney, is large enough. Free man may gambol there at will and enjoy his freedom, and he has always done so to the fullest extent. But the object of intellectual labor is the discovery of truth or knowledge. What has been the result of these "free" efforts for thousands of years? It is the old story of the bottle and the stoppers. After thousands of failures somebody makes a lucky grab and seizes the right stopper for the philosophical hole. But is that the work of a free mind or of meritorious intellectual labor? The necessity immanent in things and conditions was simply fulfilled. Groping in the dark we hit upon a truth.

Scientific and philosophical investigation, that noblest occupation of "free minds," is a pure game of chance. Philosophical and scientific truths stand like rare prizes among thousands of blanks in a wheel of fortune revolving about us. We "free thinkers," so proud of our "intellectual labors," grab awkwardly like innocent children and lo! among a million blanks someone draws a prize. This makes him a thinker of great renown whose "merits" are praised. Yet he is not at all accountable for the result of his intellectual labor. He is no more and no less meritorious than the "dunces," scorned and ridiculed, who had the misfortune to draw nothing but scientific and philosophical errors. No more meritorious, we say! Indeed "the great philosopher" who appears once in "thousands of years" is less meritorious than the crowd of little philosophers who by drawing countless blanks made it possible for him to win the great prize.

Let us go to another field of "free" human actions, legislation. Let us there see what relation freedom bears to the necessity immanent in things and conditions. How proud and self-conscious the gentlemen of the majority are, whether of the parliamentary right or left. They make the laws for the State today. They stake their best knowledge, they would apply all their wisdom, they appoint their best minds on the committees and entrust their shrewdest jurists with the drafting of the bills; and then the amendments by sections! Every one bestirs himself to furnish the great acumen his cranium can supply—and what is the result of all this application of "mind" and "free" thought?

For the most part we have a miserable botch which the real conditions of life and the necessity immanent in them must correct in order to meet the demands of the case and be endurable. Savigny labeled it ineptness (*Mangelan Beruf*) at legislation and ascribed it to "our times." As to the ineptness he was right. But no period has been or ever will be better than our own in this respect. Only by adapting themselves to immediate demands and taking account of real interests, in short by bending to social necessities, can lawgivers make useful laws—and it has always been so. But as soon as they mount the high horse of theory, set up ideal principles and deduce laws to bring about ideal right and justice; when instead of submitting to social necessity they enter the sphere of free intellectual activity in order to make laws in accordance with ideas and not in accordance with real needs and interests, the incapacity is clearly demonstrated.

This inaptitude for "free" origination is manifested in a still higher degree in politics. Every institution "freely" made is a wretched experiment which must be thoroughly transformed by the powerful currents of real interests and needs in order to answer to social necessities and gain any permanence at all. Human freedom in diplomacy exhibits the worst sort of bungling and must be forced into the right course by social necessity. What makes the institutions of human freedom especially frail in the sphere of politics is the fact that the fundamental tendency of all free human action, preservation and acquisition, is considered most applicable where the inexorable necessity of external change and decay holds most complete sway.

The aspirations of statesmen are directed toward political and national preservation and expansion. The necessity to perish and decay can go on only by violently overthrowing every free human institution. Hence, no new political institution can come to light without gore and destruction, struggle and bloodshed. Here human freedom, bent on preservation and acquisition, plays a most lamentable part; and social necessity, tending to change and decay, is revealed in its most awful sublimity.

There is still another important question to be decided. What is the relation of this pernicious human freedom to man's happiness in life? Can a better insight into its nothingness and vanity help him in avoiding evil and promoting happiness?

Certainly if men always recognized inevitable necessity in advance they might escape most ill-fated consequences by quietly resigning to it. But this is impossible, first because such knowledge is never vouch-safed to mankind as a whole, at most to exceptional individuals, and again, because human freedom, that oscillation back and forth on both sides of the line of necessity, is based on human nature and is therefore a necessity.

Although it is thus impossible for mankind as a whole to avoid disappointments, and escape the evil results of the opposition of individual freedom and social necessity, still it is worthwhile to inquire whether a more correct knowledge of necessity does not in many relations of life and spheres of human activity decrease the misfortunes that befall man, or better, whether through such knowledge much superfluous evil due to human freedom might not be avoided.

It has already been pointed out that we can never conceive of man as an isolated being; for he never has existed and never can exist in isolation. If then we conceive of him as having always been a member of a swarm or horde — and we cannot reasonably do otherwise—his life and well being depend upon his environment and is conditioned by it. Now the impulse of self-preservation, the source of the most powerful motive of human efforts and "free" activities, is by origin not simply individual but social. It finds expression in attachment for one's own and desire to subdue others.

This social impulse of self-preservation, the reverse side of which is the necessary desire to subdue and exploit the alien, opens new fields for human desires and activities, for example, the economic and the political, the technical, the scientific and even the artistic. In most cases, individual desires come into conflict with social necessities. Since, as is self-evident, the latter assert themselves over the former there is a preponderance of "misfortune" and "evil" in human life. If now man could know the necessities immanent in things and conditions and had strength to reduce his desires to their measure, his life would surely be much happier. Generally this is impossible for reasons both subjective and objective. However let us consider in what spheres it is possible to subordinate individual desires to social necessities, to adapt and accommodate one's self to circumstances.

Now the sphere of human efforts best adapted for this will be the one in which knowledge of inherent necessity is farthest advanced, the sphere of personal life. Here men are least deceived and have long since learned to subordinate their efforts. Every half-way reasonable man suppresses the desire to preserve his life beyond the limits set by nature and submits to the necessity of death.

One thing, however, many people have not yet learned, or perhaps an artificially cultivated trend of thought has made them forget: the low value of life. Its overvaluation leads to great personal misfortune. Especially is it an unfortunate conceit of the "civilized" nations to place too high a value upon the "good" life.

Yet if man would measure the "natural" worth of human life by the productivity and multiplicity which nature yields in this realm, how low the value would seem to be. A subterranean quake and thousands of human lives are sent to destruction. Thousands perish in every storm at sea. A plague here today and there tomorrow and hundreds of thousands fall victim. A bad summer, the failure of harvest, and hunger frequently snatches off millions in overpopulated regions.

But on the other hand nature can indulge in lighter play with human life—millions of children see the light daily and nature has shrewdly provided for this phenomenon not to cease.

Considering these natural conditions is there any sense or justification in overestimating the worth of an individual life as civilized nations do? How much misfortune and evil men might be spared if all the social, political and juridical institutions which follow from such an exaggerated estimation of human life should fall away.

Next to the preservation of life the satisfaction of natural wants is the most important content of human endeavors. Here too the wants produced by man's freedom are directly opposed to natural necessities and fill the life of civilized man especially with useless torment and strife. Nature directs man to an unhampered satisfaction of these material wants according to his physical powers. An unnatural trend of thought produces forms of life which increase the sum of evils incident to life and run counter to natural necessity without being able to check it.

The impulse to satisfy wants forces man into economic organization. How hard his struggle with nature is needs no lengthy explanation. Necessities press him hard and close. He endeavors to head-off the discomforts. Apparently he frequently succeeds, but at last succumbs. His efforts are expended in two chief directions. He strives greedily for possessions which he must ultimately leave behind, and he endeavors to get still more in order to compete with greater opulence, whereas economic inequality is a genuine necessity.

Economic wants lead men to politics. The State is expected to furnish to some the means of satisfying their higher economic and cultural wants at the expense, though not the harm, of others. But the State, like all human institutions is perishable, and the older, already in decline, must give place to the new, developing in power. Yet how much energy will be devoted to checking the uncheckable, to preserving the life of what is doomed to perish.

In the internal organization of States human freedom overshoots the limit of necessity either to force the natural development of social relations prematurely or to suppress it unduly and cause stagnation. Hence comes that perpetual oscillation in the inner life of a State which Comte supposed to be the result of two opposing principles, the theological and the metaphysical; and which he expected would disappear with the dawn of positive political science. But we consider it simply the natural process of "human freedom."

But human freedom celebrates its greatest triumphs in the sphere of technics, science and art. For the simple reason that it is only a question of discovering what are the real necessities, the actual facts and the laws of nature or (in art) of reproducing her products. Men need only sniff about in technics or science until they discover how, or to experiment in art until they strike it right, and this they do with great patience and with assurance of ultimate success.

Technics and science have no higher task than to discover nature and learn its laws. Since it is always the same, and the stream of mankind flows ceaselessly and man's thirst for knowledge is always the same, he must eventually succeed in wresting secrets from nature. The whole of man's freedom here consists in submitting to nature's necessity—his great success is in recognizing what it is, in adapting himself to it in technics and learning it in science. Thus human endeavors are in no wise opposed to natural necessities. Their greatest success and man's greatest good lie in this sphere. Likewise in art. Free reproduction is the highest aim. The impulse thereto lies in human nature and hence its satisfaction, like that of every other impulse, yields human pleasure. But the better he succeeds in reproducing, the more faithfully he clings to nature and its necessities. The truer the expression, so much the greater his triumph and his good fortune. He meets with success all the more because he does not act contrary to nature but rather takes it for his prime example and teacher.

The result of our investigations is indeed not very flattering to mankind in general. For since the sum of human ill increases to the degree that "free" human endeavors are shattered fruitlessly on necessity it follows from what precedes that real success and good fortune can be found only in the domains of technics, science and art. This is accessible to only a small minority of mankind. Whereas in the sphere of economic and political life, where these endeavors run powerlessly to waste against necessity, very little real happiness is to be obtained, and in the sphere of personal life only discreet resignation can ameliorate the necessary evil at all.

10. Positive Ethics

The statements in this section on social philosophy have frequently touched the domain of ethics. It is to the credit of Ratzenhofer (1901) to have placed the study of ethics upon a sociological basis. In order to characterize the way in which he sets about and accomplishes this task, we would like to herein outline the primary tenets of his *Positive Ethik*.

The "drive of the dominant original impulse causes man to satisfy his material needs without restraint, then to vigorously satisfy these needs at the expense of more profound organic needs. This in order to complete his physical individuality. Then he turns to a struggle for existence against hostile creatures as a whole, and also against his fellow-creatures in order to secure his existence to the limit of vitality." At this point "human sexual relations intervene to pacify this conflict of individuals, whereupon both sexes come together for propagation of the species and unite in society to satisfy their group needs. In this way, disturbances due to individual antagonisms are decreased in intimate contact. Stimulated by this mating drive, man transmits the desire of developing his individuality further through a group of blood relations. This is the origin of ethical perception whose meaning is individual renunciation in favor of the species" (1901: 36). With this, we stand on the threshold of an ethics based upon facts.

In the primitive horde people learn "to harmonize the urge for individuality with the conflicting needs of social intercourse and the struggle for existence" (1901: 37). The forms of this correspondence are manners and customs. Its content is the "awakening morality." But the individual always remains the starting point and agency of it. "Communities are neither carriers of consciousness nor of perception." Therefore one cannot speak of ethical perception or morality between two communities. But it is this condition, the "absolute hostility" which prevails among various primitive hordes (*Abstammungsgenossenschaften*) and the ensuing constant threatening of one group by the other that contributes enormously to developing in each individual an ethical principle moving from individual utility to general utility. From an inherent physiological interest there develops the individual interest. From this evolves the interest of the species which has its roots in the relations between married people and children and finally the social interest. The latter "includes those social structures in which one lives in a community of interest (*interessengemein*) (1901:67).

While the moralists now like to operate with the category of "altruism," Ratzenhofer only recognizes the community of feeling and behavior and defines any altruism as "impossible" (1901:67).

Man is an egotistical creature like any other living being. The ever popular notion of altruism belongs to the sphere of slogans. Nevertheless, Ratzenhofer shows how the individual interest not only develops into social interest but how the latter in turn expands toward wider circles, even toward mankind as a whole. But in general, it is scientifically and sociologically known, that man "can never feel and act other than according to interest, *e.g.* in the strict sense, selfishly. Furthermore, that an ethical perception can only be derived from a felt interest. All assumptions of moral qualities beyond this all-comprehensive community of interest are unsuitable in the formation of a proper estimate of man, society, mankind. It is improper to attribute to mankind a volition of which men are incapable by natural law" (1901:79). As a sociologist and a positivist, Ratzenhofer went on to prove how all ethical perception is actually based on selfishness. "An ethic" he says, "which considers the egoism of moral judgments to be unimportant, generates that sort of hypocrisy, trains those hypocrites which we despise so deeply in clericalism; where all words are full of resignation and all deeds full of selfishness lacking any refining interest in the species" (1901:81).

Ratzenhofer advances an incontestable argument against these "hypocrites." Man "because he is the product of his inherited interest, cannot desire anything that does not lie within his range of interests" (1901:82). Through this insight "all subterfuges in human behavior present themselves openly, naturally, and clearly before us. But because individual interest has been given a bad name—like a deviation from the path of virtue—by the ecclesiastical ethic (and also add by the philosophical ethic), the present world bears witness to an abyss of untruthfulness" (1901:83). Nonetheless, it is "the most important goal of practical wisdom to combine self-restraint (*Seinsollende*) with the full maintenance of individuality."

For this purpose he first of all takes into consideration the ethical development of social interest. "As the most highly developed organism, Man is already born with a natural tendency to extend his interest unto other individuals. These natural tendencies give direction to social interest as soon as the stimuli of other people are present" (1901:84). Man receives such stimuli in the progress of civilization. "Any socializing tendencies which need association to be able to arise and fulfill themselves, are the product of experiencing the value of certain individual renunciations on behalf of the specie or for a social structure to which one belongs." Such renunciations mutually exercised now become "norms for self-restraint to the extent that experience teaches that they fulfill common needs" (1901:86). "The experienced public need leads to moral habits" which become general ethical perceptions within civilized nations. This provides an enormous support to self-restraint, and at the same time also develops the respective physiological and natural tendencies towards socialization. Among such habits of socialization are: avoidance of open hostilities, respect for the rights of private property, consideration for the aged, the sick, women and children, etc. As cultures advance some of these moral traits find themselves "in the custody of political power in order to secure its realization through compulsion."

Social interest is susceptible of progressive development. Within civilized nations it develops from an interest in the horde, family, tribe and people into a national interest. This "is founded far more on the affinity of ideas, customs and culture than on that of blood" (1901:94). A parallel development leads to the creation of transcendental interests whose objects are the enigma of existence. In this transcendental interest lies that surrender of personal interests which promotes "religiousity." This transcendentalism is necessary for most people since the social bond is often too weak to guarantee ethical self-restraint. (1901:97). However, this generalized "ethical perception" cannot guarantee complete stability because the egotistical drive always evokes an egotistical interpretation of the divine commandment. Hence hypocrisy, sanctimoniousness, external charity, etc. remain with us.

Transcendental interest can also degenerate under the influence of self-interest. "The most extreme disintegration of this generalized transcendental interest is found most often in the self-proclaimed agents of revealed interests." (1901:99). Pantheism, "which main-

tains the principle of the uniformity of all existence, and hence the
belief that morality is a characteristic of nature" (1901:103), exercises a wholesome reaction against sin remissions based on a dualism
of God and the world.

But "the most important breach in the dualistic *Weltanschauung*
is made by sociological research. This leads to a positive monism
which replaces egotistical interest with the "transcendental interest
of the unity of consciousness in its original force." The deeper this
change in the *Weltanschauung* affects people, the more certain it
is that ethical perception will be reliably supported by transcendental
interest. Transcendental egotism will give way to unselfish transcendental socialization. Instead of renunciation for others, which
only amounts to a remission of sin, unadulterated renunciation will
become the human ideal" (1901:109). However, this transformation
of the entire *Weltanschauung* and consequently of "moral characteristics" will not be accomplished soon and probably never universally: "for a full understanding of the monistic principle will remain out of the reach of man in society for a long time to come. At
present, it primarily needs adherents among the thinkers of all
nations in a form suitable to mass understanding." The strength of
such a positive monistic *Weltanschauung* is that its ethic is based
upon "the biological and physical demands for the protection of
society against either those who are unable to submit to moral self-
restraint or to those who expect to find salvation from all the evils
of individualism through a merger with some universal omniscience"
(1901:113).

A warmth, such as the enthusiasm of a prophet, overtakes us
from these discussions by Ratzenhofer. A new world is rising in
front of our eyes, an "Empire of God" that is an empire of truth
based on the perception of the lawfulness of nature and its events.
A universe in which the individual "is an integral part, feels at one
with it and its harmonic consciousness" (1901:112). Egoism is
transcended by means of an ethnic of community interests. But is it
possible that such a community of interests can exist among people?
Ratzenhofer gives a vigorous "yes" to this question. However, "the
Christian ethic with its neglect of the egoistic dimension in ethical
perception, and utilitarianism, with its ignorance of social necessities and its neglect of an extended ethical perception (for others)

are not suitable to prove this community of interests." A socialized ethic can develop from sociological perception as a consequence of positive monism, wherefore "man feels happy in the regular operation of natural forces, and dissatisfied, if this is interrupted through his own or alien factors" (1901:114). A great deal is contributed by such a community of interests other than the insight into lawfulness of natural events, namely the "acquired conviction of the value of morality." "The ethical significance of the monistic *Weltanschauung*" inheres in its suggestion of "the harmony of personal interests and public welfare in its positive conception of human nature" (1901: 115).

This community of interests and the overcoming of egoistic interests on behalf of public need is formed by self-restraint. "The characteristic of ethics can only be understood if we consider the individual as a member of a union. For moral norms have their roots in the obligation which is imposed upon social relationships by conditions essential to life" (1901:116). Since this obligation is an outgrowth of laws of nature, "moral self-restraint is given through laws of nature and these become an ethical force in human relations." The conception of moral self-restraint ultimately depends on the perception of the lawfulness of nature and its events. For "lawfulness of law itself is an absolute self-restraint; but more generally useful for human nature is moral self-restraint, which is identical to the recognition by mankind of the lawfulness of nature" (1901:118). Since, however, the latter varies according to time and individuality of people: "each historical period and each people have a morality." This objective morality which has its roots in the law of nature awakens those restraints which lead to ethical perception.

Generally, man has those restraints for which the conditions essential to life have trained him" (1901:122). Consequently social development changes the quality of these restraints. "To the extent to which these restraints serve public utility, they become the social conscience" (1901:123). This conscience is therefore "a product of the development" of interests, from individual interest to social interest. The highly developed conscience "is the ethical strength in a man, which is all the more reliable the deeper it lies in the natural tendencies of people and if it has attained through continued application the force of habit over several generations" (1901:124). At that point it becomes the "kinetic foundation of all good will" (1901: 125). The consequence of conscious self-restraint is that man feels responsible for moral beliefs. However, man "only has that feeling of responsibility which is conveyed to him by his inherited and acquired abilities . . . This extremely important item in sociological perception overthrows the scientific foundation of the penology of our times. For how can one ethically justify the punishment of people who by their very actions reveal an absence of any feeling of moral responsibility or valid self-restraint? In the absence of restraint their natural tendencies hold sway. And these society considers to be evil. Indeed, the present situation of penal law is in a state of lamentable disorder because of an awakening realization of the untenability of its principles" (1901:126). Today, "the encouragement of penal law belongs to the most profligated institutions of the State. It is nearly useless, does a great deal of harm and brings immense distress and misery to people. This can only be changed when individualism in science is replaced by a science based on sociological understanding. This science rejects punishment as a corrective technique because man only acts unscrupulously owing to his natural tendencies. Therefore criminals have to be considered sick when they are induced by these tendencies to dangerous behavior. Thus condemned persons must not be punished but treated or cured. As everyone knows, the prisons are not sanitoriums but tormenting establishments of crime. If an individual is both incurable and dangerous then protection of society demands that he be removed or painlessly destroyed. Naturally, the latter practice demands that sort of legal protection so that it remains congruent with moral self-restraint" (1901:127).

Ratzenhofer has constructed his ethic on inherited and long standing interests which develop from individual to social values. His ethical theory "serves a purpose derived from the needs of living beings, which at the same time is subject to nature but whose events it still wants to influence to some extent through the instrument of intelligent behavior" (1901:35). With this he has not only affirmatively answered the skeptical question of the opponents of sociology (whether there is a place for ethics within a social system) but proven this affirmation with his thorough going work, *Positive Ethik*. In this book, Ratzenhofer has not only removed all fictitious foundations of moral beliefs and in a scientific and monistic way based them on social development, but he also has disproven the popular objection that "positive monism" ruins moral beliefs and makes an ethic impossible. On the contrary, he proves that positive ethics are based on much stronger foundations then all hitherto existing theological and metaphysical moral systems.

By so doing, Ratzenhofer has rendered a priceless service to sociology, because he has deprived the opponents of sociology of their sharpest and most effective weapon. The reproach that "positive monism" and the sociological theories which are based on it are the negation of all ethics and morals, must now perish. For Ratzenhofer has proven that ethics are an integral part of sociology and that its deepest roots lie in the social order. The contribution that Ratzenhofer has made to sociology—compared with Comte and Spencer —consists of the fact that while they tried to establish an equal position for sociology alongside the other moral and political sciences, Ratzenhofer proved that these social sciences are dependent on sociology.

11. Might and Right

There are several omissions in the *Outlines* before us. For example I have not treated the psycho-social phenomena of language and religion because I discussed them at length in my *Rassenkampf*, to which I must refer the reader, especially as I should like to have the "sociological investigations" appearing under that title considered preliminary in part, and in part also supplementary to these *Outlines*. For a similar reason I have given no space here to the special question concerning the relation of might and right, because in the first place I treated it at great length in my *Rechtsstaat und Socialismus* and so would have had to repeat. Besides, the criticism made from many quarters failed to make me alter my views. Further, my position on the question is sufficiently characterized in the present *Outlines* by the thorough treatment of the origin and development of rights and also in the examination of the essence of the State and the social struggle.

Nevertheless I should consider it a serious omission if I failed at this point to consider the criticism made of my position on this question by a highly esteemed scholar and juristic philosopher, Professor Merkel, of Strausberg, who reviewed my book in *Schmoller's Jahrbuch* (Merkel, 1881:IV:301).

This review refers me to an article by my honored critic on "Right and Might" in the preceding issue of the same magazine. And I am probably not wrong in assuming that article was written after he knew the contents of my book, *Rechtsstaat und Socialismus*. Therefore I am justified in considering it an integral part of the review.[5] in fact Merkel has so divided his critical material as to enumerate concisely in the fourth part of his review doubts about my position. This greatly facilitates my reply to the objections made.

First of all I notice with satisfaction that Merkel's position is in fact not so far from mine as it might seem from his review. For between my discussions and his "article" I can discover no essential difference. I shall therefore confine myself to showing that the objections which are made in his *review* are considerably weakened if not entirely removed by the concessions made in his previous *article*.

The first objection is that I assert an "essential" difference between political and private rights whereby "the differences really existing between these subdivisions of rights are in part expressed correctly, though generally with exaggerations;" but that I do not recognize "what they have in common."

[5] *Rechtsstaat und Socialismus* appeared in the summer of 1880 and shortly after a copy was sent to *Schmoller's Jahrbuch* for review. A year later, in the summer of 1881, appeared a double number (2 and 3) of the *Jahrbuch* with Merkel's article on "Right and Might" at the head. At the same time my book was mentioned among the "books received" with the remark that the "next number would contain a notice of it from the pen of Professor Merkel." Thus, plainly, he had knowledge of the contents of my book at that time. Besides I find in the article unambiguous allusions to it: for example, page 16, where it reads: "Scholars of former and of quite recent time have thought that they could prove that the sovereign power in the State could not be surrounded with effectual barriers and restraints." Again, on page 18: "The arguments just recently urged with especial emphasis against the possibility of such progress (in the sphere of international law)," and so forth. The attempts and the arguments mentioned are in fact contained in *Rechtsstaat und Socialismus* which Professor Merkel undoubtedly had in hand some time before this number of the *Jahrbuch* appeared.

The objection is correct in so far as the entire plan and economy of my work aimed at proving the essential difference, *toto genere*, between public and private rights; to which end I was, in that context, only interested in emphasizing the prevailing differences. I have not denied "what they have in common" and it would be hard "not to recognize" it after the whole juridical literature had based the identity of the two "rights" upon it. But it could not fall into my scheme of work to enumerate it for yet the hundredth time because it would be superfluous. However, that the really essential differences which I asserted exist, in spite of what there is in common between these two subdivisions of rights, can be proven from Merkel's article on "Right and Might" by showing, in particular, that the statements and assertions concerning rights therein contained are inexact and incorrect just because the author does not make the distinction which I demand, but rather formulates his propositions upon "rights" in general. Consequently it happens that he asserts something false about the one subdivision every time that he states something true about the other. Thus, for example, at the very beginning of the article cited, Merkel says: "Rights in their origin, their stability and their changes, as witnessed by history, appear to be dependent upon might in many respects and questions of right not infrequently find their solution in the guise of decisions by might which combine the effects of the proof of the better right with the proof of the greater strength. Events of that sort are difficult to harmonize with the prevalent ideas of right." What Merkel says here is only true of public rights, for whenever "private rights" are settled by the "decision of might," we speak not of "rights" but of caprice and wrong. Public rights alone may be settled in this way without sacrificing their character.

In view of such an assertion as this, intended to characterize both "subdivisions of rights," but really true of only one, shall I withdraw my proposition that the difference between private and public rights is fundamental? I think not. So much the less as I see my honored reviewer, in consequence of falsely grouping two fundamentally different things in one concept, ensnared in a net of doubts and contradictions from which he tries very hard to escape without success. In my humble opinion they disappear upon holding fast to the essential distinction between public and private rights as I form-

ulated it in *Rechtsstaat und Socialismus*—possibly with somewhat
too much bias but correctly in the main. Thus, let us hear Merkel's
lament over the impossibility of reconciling the concept of "rights"
with the solution of questions of right by appeals to might.

"It is hard to bring such events into consonance with the prevailing ideas of right. Right is here determined by factors which seem
foreign and even contradictory to our ideas of its nature, since
according to them questions of right are not questions concerning
the relative power of the contending parties but rather concerning the
truth and merits of their assertions and the value of their claims before a higher forum."

What Merkel here says of "rights" applies only to private
rights. For only questions of private rights concern "the truth and
merits of the assertions of the contending parties and the value of
their claims before a higher forum" and not rather "their relative
power."

But questions of public right are different, even though they
are often put in this form. One example among many: Shall the
Duke of Cumberland succeed his uncle in the government of Bruns-
wick? Is that a question "of the truth and merits of the assertions of
the contending parties and the value of their claims before a higher
forum?" Of course not! It is not a question of private rights. It
therefore does not depend upon the "truth and merits of the assertions." There is here in fact no "higher forum." For the German
Empire is at once party and judge. Thus it is in fact, a question of
public rights, a question which will undoubtedly be determined by
factors which are foreign to the nature of "rights" (political interests) ; a question undoubtedly "of the relative power of the contending parties," one of whom, the German Empire, does not need
to recognize a higher forum over it, because within the sphere of its
operations it is itself the highest forum. Whoever insists upon grouping public and private rights together under one general concept will
never escape from doubts and obscurities and is necessarily forced
into the delicate situation of setting himself, for the sake of "rights,"
in opposition to the most vital interests of his folk and State on
questions of public rights. Now I consider this false doctrinairism,
and see the occasion of the error in the incomplete distinction between public laws and private rights. Though they have much in

common it is only in form. In principle they are fundamentally different. But Merkel's whole argument rests on their identity. And he acquires the appearance of confirmation for his view by alluding to private rights (which of course do not withstand the criterion of might) to proving the inadmissibility of that criterion, and then appealing from the arbitrary vacillation of decisions of might to the higher idea of right— which unfortunately avails nothing in questions of public right.

The consistent disregard of this essential difference runs through the entire article and even leads to absolutely incorrect statements of fact. When, for example, it is said that "statesmen have always shown an inclination, seldom unreservedly confessed however, to treat questions of right as questions of might . . . ," the statement is incorrect when referred to private rights. It is correct only when applied to public and international law.

They would be strange "statesmen" who threw the weight of their influence and power on the side of private rights. I should not be able to name a single one, and they would certainly not deserve the title. But even Merkel is not thinking of such meddling with private rights for he immediately adds as example that these statesmen "generally stand in the position of the Athenians of old whom Thucydides makes to say in a dispute with the Medians: 'As to the Gods we believe and as to me we know that of necessity every one lords it over whomsoever he has power. . . ' "

Thus "rights" in the broader sense, including private rights, are not brought in question here, only public laws. Sovereignty (*Herrschen*) alone is spoken of, not performing justice or acting the judge. If, as Merkel says later on, "theory in the greater number of its advocates affirms the independence of rights and the essential difference between right and might." Then theory has been largely and chiefly occupied with private rights, a field in which the State has left it full authority (juristic rights, *responsa prudentum*, etc.). And if there are isolated cases in which it has drawn public law into the scope of its discussion it was still only theory—and we know what that signifies in relation to public rights, for whose advocates, the statesmen have no more bitter reproach than the charge of dogmatism.

Thus after all, there has never been any contradiction within the several subdivisions of law. For the statesmen never troubled themselves about private rights and their assertions, like those the Athenians of Thucydides, applied to public rights. But the jurists have always been up to their ears in the latter and still have the most narrow views of the State. Thus, their opinions and assertions are serviceable only for private rights. For public law they have never offered anything but "theory," "precious material for the wastebasket." In fact there is no real contradiction because people did not have the same thing in mind.

I find that there is no real contradiction after all between what I said in *Rechtsstaat und Socialismus* on public right and law and what Merkel says in his article on the same subject. Though, where he speaks of "rights" in general without distinguishing public and private rights, our statements appear indeed to contradict but only in so far as they do not apply to the same thing.

If Merkel makes the essential distinction between public and private rights a reproach against me, it would be easy for me to show that his discussion would have gained much in clarity and verity had he maintained the same distinction throughout. He would not have been forced to limit every proposition about "rights" in general as soon as it was expressed and to restrict it with respect to public law and then private rights. For example when he says:

> "Where this might [of objective right] is appealed to in the struggle over subjective right, it is presupposed that its activity will issue from a position lying outside the conflicting claims and interests and appearing to hold a neutral relation to them" (Merkel, 1881: 5).

This statement holds good of private, but not at all of public rights. For of the latter he himself concedes that:

> "the conditions for establishing and extending the sovereignty of the neutral factor [that 'neutral position'] are less favorable . . . in public rights. That very factor [objective right as neutral might]," he says further on, "finds itself confronted with more powerful forces in the struggle for sovereignty in the State and for limiting or extending it while the sources of its own might flow more sparingly. Far greater hindrances stand opposed to the development of its organs than in the sphere just considered. The question

here is to surround the supporters of sovereign power, whom right itself furnishes with superior weapons, with barriers and hinder the misuse of its weapons. To many this appears a self-contradictory problem which must therefore simply be abandoned. Scholars formerly and in quite recent times have thought they could show that the supreme power in the State could not be surrounded with barriers because, as they say, there can be but one supreme power within one and the same sphere" (1881: 16).

The last expression seems to imply that Merkel does not share their view. Is it really so? We would not venture to say so. If there is any difference between his view and theirs it is certainly not fundamental. We will show from his article presently that he is not so very far from those "scholars" and that there is only a slight shade not so much of opinion as of scientific tendency separating him from their position and ours.

Merkel is wrong in charging the opposite view with overlooking the fact: "that the force of the neutral factor itself, rooted in common and deep-seated convictions and usages, as for example in the form of traditional constitutional law supported by a feeling of right and a sense of need in all classes, may conceivably be the highest force within a community."

Without overlooking this and other considerations enumerated by him, it is possible to maintain that all these substitutes for the "neutral factor" will not suffice in a given case of public rights to replace that higher might which stands neutral above party. Even Merkel himself, who overlooks none of these factors, speaks of a "remnant which no progress [in the development of rights] can overpower"— and more than that I have not asserted. I merely located it unequivocally where it always has and always must appear, that is, in the highest sphere of public and national rights. It is plain from more than one statement in his article that even he, though reluctantly and with evident regret, makes the unconditional sovereignty of rights cease in that sphere where we, without circumlocution and with well-founded resignation, substituted might for law. He freely concedes that:

"in the field of International law, down to the present, the original connection between subjective rights and subjective might" has been retained "in respect not only of the acquisition but also of the enforcement of the former in its broadest scope. In this field," it is again said, "in consequence of the weakness and slight development of the neutral factor the competition for more favorable conditions of life still maintains in part its primitive form. Still the frequency associated with clear-cut decisions of might made in the existence of the former is manifested even here in many ways that will be referred to later, among others, in the mutual recognition of rights between civilized nations. But this is frequently associated with plain decisions of might made in the post-primitive way and does not prevent the contest for rights from finding its solution, in the most important cases even in the form or upon the basis of elementary decisions by might."

"Acquisition through power here takes the form of acquisition by laws, in so far as this is affirmed, without the necessity for a direct genealogical line between he who 'has taken possession' [playing on Goethe's words: "Whence did grandpapa get them? He took them!"] and he who establishes the right to possession. War here proves to be a continual and abundant source of new rights, the rule for whose creation is not to be sought in some higher principle but in the result of the test of strength which war imposes upon the struggling parties."

Thus there is no disagreement between our position and Merkel's in reference to international law. With reference to national (State) laws, likewise, he concedes, as stated above, that "the conditions for founding and developing the sovereignty of the neutral factor are little favorable." And he does not allow himself to be led astray by the favorite formula of public rights which speaks of "sovereignty in virtue of one's own right." He says explicitly: "Whenever sovereignty over another or any right of decision in public affairs is exercised 'in virtue of one's own right' we have to do in truth with the principle of might."

Thereby he too strikes "rights" from the supreme position in the State. We expressed the same thought by saying that between public and private rights there is an essential difference. He objects to the form of expression but plainly agrees to the fact. For however much he points to progress toward a nation of law, with which the neutral factor acquires an ever higher and more dominant position in the State, which we do not deny, he has to concede at last that "the problem of saving right from its dependence on might through progressive devolpment will continually present itself anew as still unsolved in spite of all progress" (Merkel, 1881: 20).

Will Merkel in spite of this concession reproach me further because I grant the possibility of "limiting the State's power through judicial decisions" only to a very limited degree and certain extent? Does he mean that what I say "still remains a simple assertion?" But if such a limitation of the State's power through "constitutions and judicial decisions" were possible as Merkel asserts in the review, would not the problem of "saving law from its dependence on might" be solved? Which he elsewhere says "will continually present itself as insoluble in spite of all progress."

Merkel should not have referred me to his article. For in it he takes away grounds for the criticisms which he levels at me in the review. Moreover he concedes, even in the review, that "it is true that the dependence of right upon might appears more palpable, intensive and direct in the sphere of public law than in that of private rights." Only he considers that "no ground for denying the existence and even the possibility of the existence of real rights in the former sphere."

That depends entirely upon the view that a man has formed of "rights." Whoever regards law as objective, throned high above the strife of parties, proclaiming its will in the form of statutory norms, must deny its existence and even the possibility of its existence where, even as Merkel concedes "the problem of saving right from its dependence on might presents itself as unsolved."

As I hold the view mentioned I must of necessity draw the conclusion that public rights are entirely different from private rights. Whoever on the contrary holds fast to the conception of "rights" even when "dependent on might" may, of course, discard my distinction.

I think it has been proven in the foregoing that there is at bottom no difference between the actual conception of the matter itself in Merkel's mind and in mine; between his conviction as to the real state of the case and mine. Throughout, the difference between

us is not one of cognition but of tendency, in consequence of which
Merkel lays more stress upon the fact that rights must tend to complete "release" (*Erlösung*) from might, while in my book, *Rechtsstaat und Socialismus*, emphasis was put on the fact that "release"
was impossible and that we must come to terms with the dependence
of national law on might.

Yet from where, I ask myself, considering the similarity in the
knowledge and conception of the matter itself, derives the difference
of standpoint and emphasis, right in Merkel's case, might in mine?
I don't think I am wrong in referring simply to the difference in the
political situations of Germany and Austria in the seventh decade
of the present century. Ultimately every political writer unavoidably
reflects the political situation surrounding him however objectively
he wishes to be and proposes to proceed.

No German of the seventies and eighties of this century needed
to be anxious about might under the régime of the Iron Chancellor.
On the other hand he has no doubt had some apprehension about
"rights." What is more natural than that both teachers of public law
and philosophers in Germany have emphasized the pre-eminence of
right over might postulating the independence of the former over
the latter.

Not so in Austria. We did not need to worry over "rights." They
thrived like intruding weeds in every path even where the direction
"reserved for might" was to have been expected. At the helm sat a
party calling itself constitutionalist and fancying that the entire
State could be subjected to the "rule of law." In particular it
expected to be able to attain this objective by holding ready the
universal remedy, a special tribunal constituted *ad hoc* for every
possible political crime. It was content with this—for indeed the
"eye of the law" in the form of a court of justice watched over the
State. Recently this party has even proposed to submit certain actions
of parliament, *e. g.*, those relating to election cases, to the jurisdiction
of a particular court of justice created *ad hoc*.

This effort, which is certainly well meant, proceeds from the
erroneous assumption, rather is controlled by the delusion, that an
ordinary mortal at once becomes an angel or at least an infallible
pope upon sticking a judge's commission in his pocket. It needs but
little experience, however, to learn that every judge above all else

is and remains a man. And in spite of all the conscious objectivity which he industriously cultivates (and that not always) he is quite as much the slave of blind impulses, prejudices and efforts which have their source in his social, political, religious and natural position as every other mortal and certainly not less than any representative of the people.

It must not be ignored that at some point in the State, law must cease and might begin. The creation of a court for constitutional cases would only transfer the point from the representative body to the court. Would this be better?

The so-called constitutionalists, who ought really to be called the "national rights" party (*Rechtsstaatliche*), because from the first they have labored under the delusion that the whole State could be represented in a juristic formula, have deeply atoned for their error. Power suddenly fell from their hands for mere right's sake. Nothing else could have happened, for the State belongs to might and not to right, although it creates, forms, develops and promotes "rights." This latter thought I have discussed in *Rechtsstaat und Socialismus.*

It is possible that this witches' Sabbath of "national rights," which raged in Austria in the same decade that Germany got a taste of the "might before right" theory of the Iron Chancellor, has a share in the Austrian's somewhat different standpoint on the question of might and right. The German reacts perhaps unconsciously against the all too powerful interposition of might. The Austrian, because legality has been so emphasized, may have become a little anxious for national might. I can see no other difference between Merkel's standpoint and mine.

Part V

History of Mankind
as the Life of the Species

1. Sociology and the Philosophy of History

The relation between sociology and the philosophy of history is similar to that between statistics and history. The former has been called a cross section of the latter. That is to say, statistics is occupied with a given condition, while history would embrace the entire course of human destiny (*Geschick*) as a whole. But it is very plain that this is an impossible task. So far as accomplishment is concerned, statistics have a great advantage in the temporal and local limitations which it assumes.

So with sociology and the philosophy of history. The latter would give us the idea of human history in its entirety, would set forth the theory of the whole course and hence it must fail through inability to survey it all, for the idea of a part conceived to be the whole always falsifies the idea of the whole.

On the other hand, the task of sociology is more capable of solution because of the limitations which it assumes. It disclaims embracing the entire history of mankind. It is content with investigating the process of human group-making, the constant repetition of which makes up the content of all history. Without inquiring as to the import of the whole course of history, which it does not know, it is content to show its conformity to law, to investigate the manner of social evolution, in a word to describe the processes which regularly arise from a certain contact of human societies and the mutual effects displayed. We would treat the principal questions of sociology: conformity to law in the course of political history, the way societies develop, and the problem of whether in historical periods of considerable length we meet with certain ideas, general tendencies

298

(like progress, improvement, and so on), or even general forms of social process.

2. Conformity to Law in Development

Conformity to law in the events and developments of political history has often been suspected, much discussed and even positively asserted. But, as we have pointed out elsewhere (Gumplowicz, 1883:6 *et seq.*), no one has succeeded, so far as we know, in demonstrating it concretely and clearly. While, on the contrary, the shallow objections of antagonists who denied its existence and spoke of free will and the guidance of Providence seemed to be growing more formidable.

It is a most interesting fact that in spheres which are very near to political and social life and which, though not identical, are connected with it by an intimate bond of causal relation, such conformity is so plain and apparent that it cannot be questioned by even the most zealous adherents of free will and of the guidance of Divine Providence. Yet they have never realized that by conceding development according to law, independent of the will of the individual, in art and science for example, they concede it *eo ipso* in these deeper, fundamental domains.

Let us therefore consider those spheres in which conformity to law is doubted by no one in order next to show the intimate connection between this conformity to law and that in the social and political sphere upon which this depends.

Is it not a scientific commonplace to speak of the evolution of a people's art, science and philosophy? What do the modern historians do but demonstrate their lawful development in each nation; an evolution in which plainly the individual must, unconsciously and involuntarily does, accommodate himself to the laws of the whole and the movements of the community. What does it signify that for example the connoisseur can tell almost exactly when a work of art was created, the school to which it belonged and almost the place whence it must have come, without knowing the artist? It is not the individual fashioning according to his own arbitrary will but the community and its evolution, whose slave he is born to be, as whose slave he works and creates. The individual does not compose. It is the poetic mood of his age and social group.

The individual does not think. It is the spirit of his age and social group. Otherwise the connoisseur could not tell whether the picture exhibited belonged to the school of Tintoretto or Rubens; whether a rediscovered Latin poem is classic or post-classic; whether a philosophical fragment belongs to the Aristotelian or Alexandrian age. That the connoisseur can identify is the best proof that the individual's thoughts, feelings and actions are influenced and determined by his age and social environment.

Thus we recognize these facts generally and without contradiction, while refusing to draw the necessary conclusions from them elsewhere. But we have seen that the pattern of a man's feeling, thought and action simply result from the stage of social and political development in which he happens at the time to be (Gumplowicz, 1883: Pt. iv: sec. 2). Can it still be doubted that the social and political situation exercises a determining, constructive influence on the mental constitution and endowments of men which are on the whole always equal?

The peasant boy with artistic talents will draw rude figures in the sand or carve in wood with a pocket knife his entire life. Raised upon a higher social plane, educated in an art school in a cultivated community, he will become a representative of his time and people, that is, of the educated classes that stand at the peak of the historical development of the nation. What he has become is due not only to his natural endowments but especially to the social environment in which he was educated and its level of development. But he cannot arbitrarily be anything. He can be only one stone more in the mental structure which the community and its grade of development necessarily determine, a stone whose place is assigned to it by the development of the whole.

There is therefore no doubt and it will be generally conceded that coordinated mental development, or, as it is also called, the development of the human mind or of the mind of mankind, follows fixed laws and that the individual so far as he participates in it, actively or passively, must patiently endure, doing nothing, thinking nothing which does not of necessity follow from given historical premises of evolution. There is therefore no individual freedom of will. Only omnipotent law here exists.

But how is this mental evolution related to evolution in the social sphere? That the former is not possible or even conceivable without the latter conclusively follows from the close causal connection between mental development and social, political and economic conditions which we have elsewhere demonstrated. (Gumplowicz, 1883: 23 *et seq.*).

Man's psychological character, his mental evolution and so also his mental activity is conditioned by the stage of his political and social evolution. The nomad wandering about with his horde has one set of thoughts; the hunter pursuing game in the forests has another; the subjected slave has another; the townsman living by trade and commerce another; the member of the ruling caste another; and the priest whose power lies in the mysterious charm of religion another. Their thinking is determined by the place which they occupy in society and by the degree of its evolution.

But though we can comprehend how collective mental life is connected in a general way with the stage of social evolution, we lack the microscopic insight to see how each individual is connected with it and how his thought, feelings and behavior are influenced by it.

Similarly the physicist is able to explain the appearance of the rainbow from the position of the sun and the stratification of the clouds but he has not the means to show how each atom of steam and water acts in relation to each ray of sunlight, nor how the refraction of prismatic colors arises from the action of each ray of sunlight on each atom and drop. Nevertheless after the general demonstration of the necessity of the phenomenon who would doubt that the same necessity which sways the collective whole constrains each little part to take its appropriate place.

We see and know the whole mental evolution to be, like the rainbow in the heavens, a matter of necessity. We know that a condition of society, like a particular position of the sun, must deflect culture and civilization just so and not otherwise, and that with a given degree of social evolution we must meet with one set of mental colors in art and science and not another, although we lack the means to show microscopically, so to speak, the necessary influence and effect of the passing social conditions upon each individual's acts, thoughts and feelings. Can we consider the necessary total effect and doubt that it is the sum of necessary individual influences and effects which no man can escape?

Intermediate between the individuals and the general mental effect are social structures whose inherent lawful evolution must be assumed from the necessity and the lawfulness of the total effects despite there being no more direct or immediate indications of it.

Thus whoever concedes conformity to law in the evolution of art and literature, science and philosophy (and who will deny it?) must grant the same conformity to law in the evolution of social structures and the consequent restraints upon the individual.

3. The Evolution of Mankind

We have learned that social evolution is always partial, local and limited in time. It has been especially emphasized that we can form no conception of the evolution of mankind as a unitary whole because we have no comprehensive conception of mankind as a whole. But, let us ask, can we not form a conception, broader than the evolution of individual groups and social communities, of mankind so far as known to us. If so how should we have to conceive this relative whole (relative, i. e., to our knowledge)?

For we know that Biblical naivete, corresponding to a "theological way of looking at things," to quote Comte, likened the evolution of man to a genealogical tree springing from Adam and Eve. It has been repeatedly pointed out that the same view still prevails in the domain of social science, in which Comte rightly recognizes the persistence of the theological phase down to the present.

The polygenetic view which prevails quite generally at present necessarily does away with the conception of unitary genealogical evolution. But the change only involves assuming several or innumerable starting points. Precisely speaking, it is a change of form only, or rather of number, that is, there is the evolution of several genealogical trees instead of one. There is assumed to be a steady progression along a line of evolution from the simple to complex, from rudimentary leaf to full grown tree, from primitive to refined and, what is decisive in evolution, from some given original point of incipiency to our time "of great progress, the summit and climax" of all.

It is plain that such a conception is irreconcilable with a duration of life upon the earth that surpasses comprehension. Starting from the idea, which the results of modern investigation of nature make clearer and clearer we dare not liken the social evolution described above to any such single or even multiple genealogical scheme. For such a scheme proceeds only from our inclination to investigate beginnings above all else, while in the nature of the case we are only capable of knowing the becoming.

True science, or, again to quote Comte, "positivism" begins only when we overcome the desire to know the beginning of things and are content with a knowledge of their becoming. If we keep in mind the two ideas of the eternality of life upon the earth and our inability to know the origin of things, we shall obtain an entirely different scheme of social evolution. We have a conception of its emergence based upon facts. If now we banish all thought of the unity and the origin evolution, we have left, as concrete remnant, a process of evolution going on at different times and in different places but always according to the same laws. Thus those transitions which we described above, from the primitive horde with promiscuity and the mother-family to woman-stealing and marriage by capture and then to a simple organization of sovereignty, to property, state and "society," must not be conceived to be processes which befall mankind developing, as it were, from a certain point of beginning onward whether along single or multiple lines, but processes which are always being completed and renewed wherever the requisite antecedents occur. With such a conception only, and in no wise with the contrary one referred to, can we reconcile the fact that the primitive stages of this process are still observable in distant parts of the world as fresh and original as they must once have been in our own past.

Evolution as we have presented it is no chronological or local verity and applies to no particular subject. It is a typical truth—in so far as it presents a process which is always true of human species wherever groups of men are found in the proper social condition.

It is erroneous and entirely false to speak of the "evolution of mankind" (*le développement de l'humanité*) as Comte does. For we can speak only of social evolution within the compass of the human species. It always begins wherever and as soon as suitable social conditions are at hand. And it moves lawfully to a culminating

point, dying out and disappearing when there is no further manifestation of necessary social energy. It is impossible to doubt that
evolution really dies out and becomes extinct in view of the countless
sites of exhausted culture and sweeping social activity which now lie
waste and barren. There are many examples in Asia, America and
Africa of extensive regions from which all life has now disappeared,
yet from whose development once issued forth the most magnificent
fruits of civilization.

These facts are calculated to support the idea of a cyclical
course of social development in general, an idea which gains a foot-
hold just from the cyclical development of states. I have discussed
this point often and must here return to it again.

4. Cycle of Development

It sounds like Hegel or Schäffle to assert that the life of every
people runs in a cycle, that once it has arrived at its highest peak of
development it hastens to its decay and that the most able barbarians
will prepare its extinction. Sober minds are not inclined to take it
seriously.

Nevertheless it is not difficult to show the causes of this cyclical
motion in the natural, economic and social conditions of folk-life.
The causes are so plain, their operation so very powerful and general
and at the same time so obvious and indisputable that knowledge
of them ought to convince that their effects will neatly and necessarily follow; for they are economic and demographic and thus lie
in the region where man's limits and dependence on physical wants
are wholly undeniable; where irrefutably men must be reckoned
with as blind natural forces pursuing their courses in accordance
with law.

Men's wants and desires, as we have seen, cause them to raise
themselves by groups and societies from a primitive condition to a
condition of culture and civilization. Having once attained it,
so to conduct themselves that their fall necessarily follows through
other groups and societies in a progressive state.

In a primitive political body, which is economically poor, men
have only one want beyond the desire of self-preservation, the reproduction of the species. In this stage many children are begotten
and population grows with great rapidity. The wish, which emerges

on a higher level of culture, so far as is possible to insure a better material existence for the descendants, is not effective to check the increase of births for the reason that future members will be no worse off than the present with regard to property while every living human being represents one more unit of labor, which of itself may conduce to betterment of condition.

For this reason political bodies in the lower stages of culture and welfare increase rapidly and so make a great relative gain in numerical strength which can be sustained by increasing productivity and economic prosperity at home. A population in such a state of progressive development is very likely to lay the foundation for a body politic over which a highly civilized and cultivated minority will rule.

If, with the development of the political body, the lowest classes also rise to a higher degree of civilization and become prosperous. In truth, it cannot be otherwise, anxiety for the future welfare begins to exert a restraint upon the natural increase of the people. The former heedlessness, companion of poverty, gives way to a "wise care" and population begins to stagnate and finally to decline. Thus the collective body becomes numerically weaker than those which have not yet reached this degree of "refinement," and this further conduces to economic weakness and political decline. While the community that stands still lower in development, that still has a poor proletariat in process of development, carries off the victory through its numerical strength. There are the real, ever active causes which bring about the cyclic movement in the life of folk and State and which explain why it is always the highly cultivated State that is destroyed by "barbarian hordes."

But such hordes are not necessarily external, and if they were, they alone would not be able utterly to destroy powerful civilized states. Unfortunately every State conceals in its own bosom, and the higher it rises in the scale of civilization so much the more, barbarian hordes enough who only await the given signal, the critical moment of civil or foreign war, to begin the work of destruction. The fall of many a powerful civilized State under the assault of rather small barbarian hordes could not be comprehended if it were not known that domestic social enemies of the existing order let the secretly glimmering hatred of the propertied and ruling classes burst into bright flame at the moment of danger. This alone is often sufficient to turn the toilsome labor of centuries into dust and ashes. This inner enemy necessarily increases with the development of civilization. Thus, every center of civilization, apart from the danger threatening it from without, fosters the seeds of destruction within itself.

5. Progress and Innovation

But the fact of cyclical development in state and folk is also decisive to the question of "progress" in the sphere of human activity. Two assertions which I made in *Rassenkampf* have given considerable offense and provoked lively controversy, *viz.*, that there is no progress and that there can be nothing essentially new in the realm of intellectual knowledge.

That I of course, recognize progress in the development of an isolated center of civilization, each time beginning and running to its end, has been brought out conspicuously by the briefest of my reviewers in the English periodical *Mind*. The general conclusion to which he finally comes reads: "is that there is no such thing as either progression or retrogression of history as a whole. But it applies to the particular periods of a process that continues in an unending circle—to particular countries where the social process is forever recommencing." It is indeed remarkable that the English critic who reviewed my book in fourteen lines caught my thought correctly while so many German critics who made extended reviews of it are of the opinion that I deny all progress whatsoever.[1] However

---

[1] On the other hand Maurice Block, in the *Journal des Economistes* was inclined to accept the complete negation of progress (though I do not go so far) if I had made a reservation in respect to science and its technical application. The passage is so remarkable that I quote it. "One of the author's views," says Block in concluding his discussion of the *Rassenkampf*, "will meet with many objections: it is the negation of progress. Things change apparently but not in reality. The vesture changes, so to speak, but not the body nor the spirit. And yet there is some truth in the proposition. If the author had taken the oratorical precaution to exempt science and its industrial applications I should have been persuaded that he was right, for I have asked myself more than once whether it could be proven that there were in Memphis, Babylon and Nineveh less good men in proportion to the whole population than in Paris, London or Berlin." I readily assent to the reservation in favor of science

I see from this circumstance that I could not have expressed myself clearly enough on this point and therefore feel bound to pursue the matter further or rather to express myself more decisively.

As I consider man to be a permanent type not only physically, as with Kollman, but mentally (Gumplowicz, 1883: Pt. ii: sec. 4). I am of the opinion that there is a fixed upper limit to his mental activity also, to which individual natures fortunately endowed have always been able to attain, but which no man can ever exceed.

Man's physical strength in the nature of the case can never exceed a certain maximum, which of course various individuals have at all times attained to. In morals there have always been good and noble creatures everywhere, as well as low and bestial ones in a profusion of gradations. It is recognized that a real improvement in men is scarcely noticeable and that an apparent improvement is brought about locally and temporarily only by conditions, institutions and

---

and art which Block requests, only however with the counter reservation set forth in the text above respecting the uninterrupted development of human civilization. Who will guarantee that it's thread, and even the thread of mental development, will not be completely sundered from time to time, so that for later generations trying to rise again nothing will remain of all the former achievements? What profit did the entire European Middle Ages draw from the astronomical knowledge of the Chaldeans and old Egyptians, thorough as it doubtless was? Was not the thread completely sundered? If we compare the grotesque sculpture of Christian Europe in the Middle Ages with the works of Greek art must we not confirm that fact that the stream of development of human civilization from time to time disappears on the earth without trace, only to reappear after a long while in some far distant place, working its way laboriously up through rifts and fissures? Or is the opinion justified perhaps that such catastrophes, suddenly destroying results of civilization hundreds of years old, and causing them to disappear utterly, were only possible in "earlier times" —but that we, armed with the printing press and the steam engine, are entirely free from them and that our mental labor will not perish? We would gladly share this opinion if only the authorities will set us at rest upon one point, the cosmic stability of our planet. For to judge from some very recent indications the forces seething under our feet in the interior of our planet seem to have very little respect for our mental and artistic productions. And they care as little for laws of the development of human civilization. Indeed human civilization is threatened by two distinct anarchistic forces: social and cosmic. The former we may indeed resist—may gracious destiny long preserve us from the latter. Then would we be assured of endless progress in science, art and technology.

measures introduced from the outside. It is quite the same in intellectual matters.

Man's intellect is ever the same—it moves in a sphere having a fixed and unexpanding upper limit which has been reached from time to time by individual geniuses. But there is an apparent progress arising from the fact that from place to place and time to time an intellect of equal power finds footing upon the total accomplishments of his predecessors and uses them as the starting point for further successes. Not that later generations work with higher or more complete intellects, but with larger means accumulated by earlier generations and with better instruments. In this way they obtain greater results.[2] So it is of course impossible to deny progress in the field of invention and discovery. But it would be a mistake to explain it from the greater perfection, or the progress of the human intellect. An inventive Greek of ancient times, if he had followed Watt, would have invented the locomotive—and if he could have known the arrangement of the electrical telegraph, it certainly might have occurred to him to construct a telephone.

Between human intellect four thousand years ago and today there is no qualitative difference nor any greater development or perfection—only the completed labor of all intervening generations insures the advantage of the modern intellect, which with this accumulated supply today apparently accomplishes greater "miracles" than the like intellect four thousand years ago did without it. But in fact, laying aside the temporal advantages of the former, the latter accomplished no less wonderful things.

Fortified with this, one could object to my assertion that progress is relative and appears only in separate periods of development by saying that it only needs such continuity of mental labor to lead mankind into unsuspected and indefinitely prolonged progress.

The conclusion would be impregnable if the premise, the uninter-

---

[2] "Newton deprived of all the resources of science would still have had the same intellectual strength and would still have been a man of many eminent qualities, in particular, accurate judgment and imagination. If only a part of science, greater or less, had been put within his reach he would have been a Pythagoras, and Archimedes or a Kepler. But with all the resources which his century presented to him he was, and he had to be, a Newton." (Quetelet, 1835a: II; 393).

rupted development of human civilization in general, were equally certain. But this is doubtful. First, we find proof in well-known history of the continual recurrence of catastrophes which send centers of civilization precipitately to destruction. What happened in India, Babylon, Egypt, Greece and Rome may sometime happen in modern Europe. European civilization may yet perish, overrun by barbaric tribes.

If any one believes that we are safe from such catastrophes he is perhaps yielding to an all too optimistic delusion. There are no barbaric tribes in our vicinity to be sure—but let no one be deceived. Their instincts lie latent in the populace of European States. The deeds of anarchists are only scattered flashes of lightning—who will guarantee that the storm will not some time break? The barbarians do not live so far from Europe as appears to be generally assumed. And the insurance of Europe against these infernal powers would not be entirely free from risk.

Thus the proposition that the development of civilization is perpetual and uninterrupted, as premise to the conclusion that progress may be indefinitely prolonged, could have only a potential value.

It must also be considered a proof of the stability of the human intellect that in spheres which have no connection with invention and the discovery of natural forces, i.e., in moral and social philosophy, not only is there no indication of progress, but nothing new whatever has been said for thousands of years. "There is nothing new under the sun" and nothing new can be "invented." Our insight respecting virtue and custom, human happiness and social relations, are no more mature than those of the oldest people of antiquity. On the contrary, we often become aware that we are behind them in many things. Though brotherly love has been taught at different times to very different peoples by individual law-givers and founders of religions, our attitude toward relatives and kinsfolk is just as different from our attitude toward strangers as ever. To make war upon strangers and overpower them is a virtue. To betray one's fellow citizens is a crime. Respecting the value of life, the mutual relation of the sexes, the institution of marriage and the like, the individual centers of civilization continue to revolve in the same vicious circle. The opposite view from our particular vantage point seems the

lower. Whatever strikes us as new and original is only a new combination of very old thoughts and opinions—a combination springing of course from a new individual conception. For only in nature
is individuality endlessly varied.

Individuality is always producing new combinations from the
ancient store of human thought, and if it were possible for a man
to know all the thoughts of past ages, if he could even know all the
philosophers and thinkers of olden times and peoples, he could
easily reproduce his own most original systems and his most characteristic conceptions of the world merely by citing from his predecessors. In fact Bastian does something similar. We often find his
phenomenal mind working out entirely original ideas with simple
citations from other authors. The whole is the most original product
of his individuality. But his remarkably comprehensive memory enabled him to gather up the ready cut stones for his system from the
works of thinkers of all ages and peoples.

The individual conception is new, but the material is exclusively
old. Consciously or unconsciously it is constantly repeated, never
newly created. For here where no invention or discovery in the field
of natural forces is involved the human intellect has from the first
traversed the whole sphere of perception possible in the nature of its
organization and can never rise beyond.

The conceptions of the human mind in this sphere are just like
kaleidoscopic views. Philosophers and thinkers have been turning
the kaleidoscope for ages, and it is impossible but that particular
portions have often been exactly repeated though probably the whole
picture never will be, since the combinations are infinite. The difference in the picture we ascribe to the difference in individuals, and
perhaps correctly.

6. Justice in History

Nothing so shakes the conception of a "just providence" in
simple devout souls as the perception of the "world's injustice"
obtruding itself at every step in human life. In spite of toilsome
theological explanations and justifications, simple faith in God is
disturbed and pious hearts are stung by the doubt whether all the
injustice with which human life overflows can be the work of a good
and just God? It is the necessary and inevitable consequence of an
anthropomorphism which conceives of God in the likeness of man

and hence ascribes to him human "justice." But that which comes to pass in the world and in life, or properly, in life and history is in no sense human justice. It is rather historical justice which to man's mind must seem to be harsh injustice. Although here again the fault is due to that false individual standard which man applies to the events of life. They come to pass according to an entirely different scheme, so to say, a great social standard by which they must be judged. If we measure them with individual human rulers we suffer.

What is commonly meant by justice? A certain standard in the distribution of material goods and moral responsibilities. In fact there are two conceptions of justice. One starts from the complete equality of all men and hence requires an equal measure of rights and possessions for each individual. The other takes into consideration the unequal value of individuals and their powers and doings, and is content with a proportional distribution. Both take the individual as the object and standard in exercising justice, and in every transaction having man for its object, ask whether it is commensurate with the value of the object. If so it is pronounced just; if not, unjust. There is no opportunity for variety of judgment save as difference of opinion prevails concerning the value of the object or the proper conception of justice.

These conceptions of justice start from the consideration of man's conduct toward man to construct their criteria of judgment, which have a certain justification in themselves. But men are not content to apply them to human conduct alone, transferring them to historical events and even to natural events in general.

In the case of historical events the transference is due to the false hypothesis that they are brought about by men through their free will. In the case of natural events it is due to an anthropomorphism which represents God as acting after the manner of men and brings them about.

No elaborate proof is necessary to show how incongruous such an idea is. Historical events are not brought about by men any more than natural events by God. If they have no author whose conduct can be regulated according to the value of the objects affected nothing can be said about justice or injustice in connection with them.

In a somewhat different sense, however, without regard to the

subject's action, the question could be raised whether the course of
history and of natural events strikes individuals according to their
merits, *i.e.*, whether the good are spared or rewarded, the bad fallen
upon and punished; hence whether there be justice or not in history
and nature. But even in this form such a question is inadmissible
because the individual is never the object of history or nature.
Nothing depends upon him and we have no criteria of his worth
even if we should conceive him to be the subject of the historical and the natural process.

History and nature are visible and recognizable only through
their effects on masses—indeed they may be said to occupy themselves only with certain natural groups and quantities consisting of
a number of individuals—that is with communities or families existing either together or in relation to successive generations. The
only possible relation which is perceptible between the effects and
the existence of the objects is that of causality, the connection between their natural constitution and the fate that befalls them.

In other words, these human groups in the current of history and nature play precisely the part of any other cluster of natural
objects exposed to the workings of nature. Natural forces will
produce effects upon them according to their character—rotten
limestone will yield to the process of weathering quicker than hard
granite. Rain will change a treeless declivity into a bare rock, while
a wooded slope will gain fresh strength and luxuriance from it. In
this interplay of cause and effect, of occasion in the objects and
action by natural forces we cannot speak of justice and injustice.
No more can we talk in terms of the destinies of a folk or an individual. They are the results of causes lying partly in the object,
partly in the natural forces of history and nature. Hence there is no
justice in history unless we wish to apply this category to the conformity of results to causes. Such justice as this we always find
realized with inexorable rigor.

In life and in history every man suffers whatever fate is conditioned by his natural constitution. Yet his natural constitution depends not on him, but, as we have seen, upon the social milieu from
which he emerges. This is to blame if individual fates are so seldom
proportional to individual merits. For fate strikes the individual in
proportion to the merits of the species, so to speak. His own merits

may be different. Historical development cares nothing for that.

Hence the individual often suffers wrongs which he does not deserve, but which derive directly from causes buried within the past of his social medium, as when childen atone for the "sins" of their ancestors of which there are numerous examples. It is quite natural for the development of the inherent forces of history depends upon the character and the conditions of its subjects. The subjects are, as we have seen, not individuals, but the social media in which individuals are produced as an outcome.

The course and the events of history are commensurate with the character and conditions of the social media and this we must recognize as historical justice. There is no other in history or even in nature.

Hence the alpha and omega of sociology, its highest perception and final word, is: human history, a natural process. And even thought one may be shortsighted and captivated by traditional views of human freedom and self-determination, one should not believe that this knowledge derogates morals and undermines them. It is on the contrary the crown of all human morals because it preaches most impressively man's renunciatory subordination to the laws of nature which alone rule history. By contributing to the knowledge of these laws sociology lays the foundation for a morality of reasonable resignation, higher than that resting on imaginary freedom and self-determination and resulting in the inordinate overestimation of the individual and his unreasonable aspirations which find expression in horrible crimes against the natural law of order.

7. Designs of Philosophical History

The human spirit is admirable for the indefatigable way in which it tries to trap the known history of manhood into a locked system. All these systems of philosophical history have in common the fact that they see the solemn final resolution of world history in the present. At the most they prophesize a coming future world order wherein all dreams of mankind will be realized. The factual events and developments unfold rather uniformly in such systems. These systems of philosophical history differentiate themselves only in their ascriptions of causal agents of change. In them, the individual thinkers seek and believe they have located the cause of the entire cycle of history in the various fields of nature and society.

Arnold Fischer (1897) for example describes the cycle of the social history of mankind as a succession of "constant decrease of intensity in the organic process of life," which in its first stages is dominated by instincts. This decreasing biological intensity is augmented and supported by "spiritual power," that is, sensations, consciousness, empirical reason and logical reason. Into such a scheme of natural law Fischer structures the course of written history starting with the "maternal-family," then moving through all the known phases of "paternal-rule," the fusion of gens, etc., up to the most modern formations—social democratic trade unions. The German working class appears to him as a popular expression of logical reason; the last word of world history. What a great waste of knowledge and effort is entailed in building a design of philosophical history which seeks to place the entire structure of world history on so weak a foundation. This design of philosophical history is handed down to the present through some ephemeral causative agency. This is the old Hegelian method.

The Frenchman Adolphe Coste (1899; and 1900), although he proceeds more intelligently and interestingly, does not improve upon the situation. He also describes, though in a very fascinating and pleasant manner, the course of written history. But unlike Arnold Fischer, he does not terminate history with the workers' trade unions, but with joint-stock companies and business syndicates (*anonymen Aktiengesellschaften*) as the fullest bloom of human culture. Coste thinks that these joint-stock companies originated in the absolute regime (*ancien regime*) but could only fully develop their impersonal character within a parliamentary system. Corporate "anonymity" will achieve that which the socialists of all tendencies will not be able to, namely, the abolition of capitalism. Coste appeals to the socialist agitators: "Calm down, soon there will no longer be any more capitalists. All great accumulated wealth will automatically be redistributed into a number of smaller units which will be entrusted to various investors. Thus, there will be neither primitive accumulation nor feudalism . . . The domination of billionaires will vanish." That is the joyous ultimate resolution of Coste's "objective sociology" which by any true measurement is nothing other than an intellectual design of philosophical history. It overestimates a momentary social and economic phenomenon and considers it to be the ripe fruit of world history and the remedy for all social evils.

Lamprecht's volume on *Geshichtsphilosophie,* which I have dealt with in my *Soziologische Staatsidee* (1902: 175), belongs to the same categorical design of philosophical history. In this connection, we should mention the writings of Breysig (1900) and Lindner (1901). with which Goldfriedrich deals in his recent work (1902). We also have to take into account the work of Chamberlain (1900), the writings of "race theoreticians" such as Woltmann (1903), Ploetz (1884), Reibmayer (1897), Wilser (1904), Driesmans (1902). They all see the course of history as only the outer shell of certain psychological and generative events. They maintain that if one wants to reach a proper understanding and thus the proper mastery of historical development, the psychology of history must be viewed as the core of the human sciences.

It is now realized that designs of philosophical history, as well as modern race theory, are more pretentious than sociology. Human understanding is said to move through the following three stages: (1) knowledge of facts, (2) pre-determination of the future which is based on the facts, and (3) application of the aforementioned two stages with a view to improving the species—which means the mastery of evolution. From the vantage-point of the last of these three stages, the philosophy of history attempts to overpower the first two. Whereas racial theories pretend to have even this third element within their control and deals with the second stage doubtfully and hesitantly. Sociology does not claim to have any power over the third stage at all. Sociology is satisfied to note the legality of social events. In the meantime it does not dare utter any apodeitic statements as to whether these same laws will obtain in the future.

My standpoint, as outlined above, was developed in the first edition of the *Grundriss der Soziologie* twenty years ago. Such a reserved attitude was adopted for two distinct reasons: first in consideration of the poor results which were obtained with the propheticism of older sociologies such as those of Comte and Spencer. They both deceived themselves by their prophesies about the course of future social history and thus they lost any justification for a *bona fide* sociological theory or an applied sociology. Second, a cautious attitude seemed to be justified on the grounds of the primitive stage

of the new science of sociology, which distinguished itself so markedly from preceding sciences. As a consequence, moving into the second
and third "stages" of historical prediction seemed to me to be too
ambitious. This was proceeding into an area of uncertainty.
While laying the foundation for the new sociological science I restricted myself to uncovering the factual bases of social evolution.
This task never permitted me to move beyond knowledge of the
facts of evolution.

Now I have to confess that today after twenty years (despite
the fact that my theory has not experienced a widespread or many-
sided recognition, nor for that matter any critical attempts at dis-
proving what I have written), I still do not yet dare to move beyond
by position as have the American sociologists, Ward (1903) and Giddings (1894, 1899) as well as Gustav Ratzenhofer (1901). These
younger members of the sociological fraternity (I have to consider
myself older in deference to the priority of my publications) are
proceeding in a more daring way with their statements and do not
even hesitate to proceed to the third stage, the application of human
knowledge for practical ends. They not only draw conclusions enthus-
iastically from the facts of the past, but they also speculate about
the future from such evidence as they have available to them. They
do not doubt that today one can move towards an applied sociology.
As Ratzenhofer expresses it: "Out of naive empiricism we have
evolved a more sophisticated consciousness of facts" (1901:89).
Ward who announces an "Applied Sociology" has the same position.
I have to confess that I do not share this confidence of the younger
sociologists because I still am not clear on this one point: is it indeed
granted to all sciences to move through the aforementioned three
stages of knowledge? Here I want to stipulate my doubts.

If biology describes the actual conditions of the growth of
organisms, then even if a single individual violates these conditions
it can forecast its destruction. But it can also give each individual
advice on how to provide himself with the prosperous conditions
for its growth. There is no doubt that the biological sciences entail
each of these three stages of human knowledge within themselves.

I doubt however if the same situation holds for all sciences, and
especially if it is possible for sociology to dominate the second and
third stages of knowledge in a similar fashion. For already the

course of future social development depends on so many uncalculated variables and unpredictable conditions that one cannot speak of any degree of safety in a social prediction. If it is already this difficult to move beyond this second stage of knowledge, how is sociology to reach the third stage of knowledge which has included within itself a knowledge of the determination of the future? But as I said these are my personal doubts, which are only valid for myself in my own work. It is not impossible that the progress of scientific sociology will invalidate my doubts and justify the hopes of Ratzenhofer, Ward, and others who are taking an optimistic view of the possibilities of sociology (Oppenheimer, 1898; and Stein, 1905). For my part, I choose to remain within the first stage of social science speculation, which only deals with the facts of social development and the laws of society which impress themselves on consciousness. I must therefore accept (with satisfaction) the reproach that this is the exclusive level of my sociological work.

BIBLIOGRAPHY

Achelis, Thomas
 1881 Ethnologie und Geschichte, *Ausland*. vol. 4, no. 2.
 1889 *Die Entwicklung der modernen Ethnologie*. Berlin: E. S. Mittler & Sohn.

Ahrens, Heinrich
 1889 *Naturrecht oder Philosophie des Rechts* (second edition, in 2 vols). Vienna, 1870-71.

Allievo, Giuseppe
 1899 *Saggio di una introduzione alle scienze sociali*. Torino: Unione.

Bachofen, Johann Jakob
 1861 *Das Mutterrecht. Eine Untersuchung über die Gynaikokratie der alten Welt nach ihrer religiösen und rechtlichen Natur*. Stuttgart: Krais und Hoffman.

Bärenbach, Friedrich von
 1882 *Die Sozialwissenschaften*. Leipzig: Brockhaus.

Bastian, Adolf
 1860 *Der Mensch in der Geschichte. Zur Begründung einer psychologischen Weltanschauung*. Leipzig: O. Wigand Verlag.
 1867 *Völker des östlichen Asien: Studien und Reisen*. Leipzig: O. Wigand.
 1871 *Ethnologische Forschungen und sammlung Material für dieselben*. Naumberg A. S. (printed) 1871-73.
 1872 *Die Rechtsverhältnisse bei verschiedenen Völkern der Erde. Ein Beitrag zur vergleichenden Ethnologie*. Berlin: G. Reimer Verlag.
 1881a *Der Völkergedanke im Aufbau einer Wissenschaft vom Menschen*. Leipzig: O. Wigand Verlag.

1881b *Die Vorgeschichte der Ethnologie. Deutschlands Denkfreunden gewidmet für eine Mussestunde.* Berlin: Harrwitz und Grossman.

1884 *Allgemeine Grundzüge der Ethnologie. Prologemena zur Begründung einer naturwissenschaftlichen Psychologie auf dem Material des Völkergedankens.* Berlin: G. Reimer Verlag.

Below, Eugen von
1903 Supplement, *Münchner Allgemeine Zeitung.* vol. 105, Jan. 15.

Bluntschli, Johann Kasper
1885 *The Theory of the State.* Oxford: The Clarendon Press.

Breysig, Kurt von
1900 *Kulturgeschichte der Neuzeit: Vergleichende Entwicklungsgeschichte der führenden Völker Europas und ihres sozialen und geistigen Lebens.* Berlin: G. Bondi.

Carey, Henry Charles
1858 *Principles of Social Science.* Philadelphia: J. B. Lippincott
1878 *Die Einheit des Gesetzes nachgewiesen in den Beziehungen der Natur, des Sozialgeistes, und der Moral wissenschaft.* Berlin: Expedition des Merkur.

Charms, Gabriel
1881 Voyage en Syrie, *Revue des deux Mondes.* Aug. 15.

Chamberlain, Houston Stewart
1900 *Die Grundlagen des neunzehnten Jahrhunderts.* Munich: F. Bruckmann.

Comte, Auguste
1839 *Cours de Philosophie positive* (4 vols.) Paris: Impr. Larousse, 1890-95.
1881 *La Philosophie positive* (condensé par Christian Cherfils, preface de Jules Rig). Paris: M. Girard & Brière, 1912.

Coste, Adolphe
1899 *Les principes d'une sociologie objective.* Paris: Felix Alcan.
1900 *L'experience des peuples et les prèvisions qu'elle autorise.* Paris: Felix Alcan.

Curtius, Ernst
1892   *The History of Greece* (trans. by A. W. Ward). New York: Charles Scribner's.

Dargun, Lothar
1883   *Mutterrecht und Raubehe und ihre Reste im Germanische Recht und Leben.* Breslau: W. Koebner.

Darwin, Charles
1871   *The Descent of Man, and Selection in Relation to Sex.* New York: D. Appleton and Company.

DeTocqueville, Alexis
1838   *Democracy in America* (trans. by Henry Reeve). New York: G. Dearborn & Co.

Driesmans, Heinrich
1902   *Rasse und Milieu.* Berlin: J. Räde Verlag.

Durkheim, Emile
1895   *Rules of Sociological Method.* Chicago: University of Chicago Press, 1938.

Engels, Frederick
1884   *Der Ursprung der Familie, des Privateigenthums und des Staats. Im Anschluss an Lewis H. Morgan's Forschungen.* Hottingen/Zurich: Schweizerische Völksbuchhandlung.

Fischer, Arnold
1897   *Die Entstehung des sozialen Problems.* Rostock I.M.: C. J. E. Volckmann.

Giddings, Franklin H.
1894   *The Theory of Sociology.* Philadelphia: American Academy of Political and Social Science.
1899   *The Principles of Sociology: An Analysis of the Phenomena of Association and of Social Organization.* New York: The Macmillan Co.

Goldfriedrich, Johann Adolf
1902   *Historische Ideenlehre.* Leipzig: O. Weber Verlag.

Gravière, Julien
1884   La fin d'une grande marine, *Revue des deux Mondes.* No. 1.

Gumplowicz, Ludwig
1875   *Rasse und Staat: eine üntersuchung über das Esetz der Staatenbildung.* Vienna: Manz.

1877 *Philosophisches Staatsrecht.* Vienna: Manz.
1881 *Rechtsstaat und Socialismus.* Innsbruck: Wagner'sche Univ-Buchhandlung.
1883 *Der Rassenkampf: Sociologische Untersuchungen.* Innsbruck: Wagner'sche Univ. Buchhandlung.
1885 *Grundriss der Sociologie.* Vienna: Manz.
1892a *Die soziologische Staatsidee.* Graz: Leuschner & Lubensky.
1892b *Soziologie und Politik.* Innsbruck: Wagner'sche Univ. Buchhandlung.
1897 *Allgemeines Staatsrecht.* Innsbruck: Wagner'sche Univ. Buchhandlung.
1899 *Soziologische Essays.* Innsbruck: Wagner'sche Univ. Buchhandlung.
1905a *Geschichte der Staatstheorien.* Innsbruck: Wagner'sche Univ. Buchhandlung.
1905b *Grundriss der Soziologie* (second augmented edition). Vienna: Manz'sche Hof-Verlags and Universitäts-Buchhandlung.

Hildebrand, Richard
1894 *Über das Problem einer allgemeinen Entwicklungsgeschichte des Rechts und der Sitte.* Graz: Leuschner & Lubensky.

Holbach, Paul Henri Thiery
1781 *The System of Nature; or the Laws of the Moral and Physical World* (with notes by Diderot), trans. by H. D. Robinson. Boston: J. P. Mendum, 1853.

Ihering, Rudolf von
1877 *Der Zweck im Recht* (two volumes). Leipzig: Breitkopf & Hartel, 1877-83.

Kollmann, Julius Konstantin Ernst
1881 Die statistischen Erhebungen über die Farbe der Augen und Haare in den Schulen der Schweiz, *Zeitschrift für Anthropologie.* vol. XII.
1883a Die Autochthonen Amerikas, *Zeitschrift für Anthropologie.* vol. XIV.
1883b Kraniologische Gräberfunde in der Schweiz, *Zeitschrift für Anthropologie.* vol. XIV.

1883c Über den Wert pithekoider Formen und die Wirkung der Korrelation auf dem Gesichtsschädel des Menschen, *Zeitschrift für Anthropologie.* vol. XIV.

Krauss, Friedrich Salomon
1903 *Die Volkskunde in den Jathren 1897-1902. Bericht über Neuerscheinungen.* Erlangen: F. Junge.

Lamprecht, Karl Gotthard
1902 *Soziologische Staatsidee.* Berlin: H. Heyfelder.

Le Bon, Gustave
1881 *L'homme et les societes, leurs origines et leur histoire.* Paris: E. Flammarion.

Lilienfeld, Paul von
1873 *Gedanken über die Sozialwissenschaft der Zukunft* (five vols.) Berlin: G. Reimer, 1873-81.
1898 *Zur Verteidigung der organischen Methode in der Soziologie.* Berlin: G. Reimer.

Lindner, Theodor
1901 *Geschichtsphilosophie. Weltgeschichte seit der Völkerwanderung* (five vols.). Stuttgart and Berlin: Cotta Verlag, 1901-05.

Lippert, Julius
1881a *Der Seelencult in seinen Reziehungen zur althebräischen Religion.* Berlin: T. Hofmann.
1881b *Die Religionen der europäischen Kulturvölker.* Berlin: T. Hofmann.
1883 *Allgemeine Geschichte des Priesterthums* (two vols.). Berlin: T. Hofmann.

Marx, Karl
1867 *Capital: A Critique of Political Economy* (three vols.). Chicago: Charles H. Kerr & Company, 1909.

McLennan, John Ferguson
1865 *Primitive Marriage: An Inquiry into the Origin of the Form of Capture in Marriage Ceremonies.* Edinburgh: A. & C. Black Ltd.
1866 Kinship in Ancient Greece, *Fortnightly Review,* vol. 4 (2 issues).

Merkel, Adolf
    1881   Right and Might, *Schmollers Jahrbuch für Gesetzgebung, Verwaltung und Volkswirtschaft im Deutschen Reich.* vol. 4.

Mill, John Stuart
    1848   *A System of Logic: Ratiocinative and Inductive.* New York: Harper & Bros.

Morgan, Lewis Henry
    1877   *Ancient Society: Researches in the Line of Human Progress from Savagery through Barbarism to Civilization.* New York: Henry Holt Co., 1907.

Mucke, Johann Richard
    1897   *Mitteilungen aus der historischen Literatur.* Greifswald: J. Abel Verlag.
    1898   *Urgeschichte des Ackerbaues und der Viehzucht.* Greifswald: J. Abel Verlag.

Oppenheimer, Franz
    1898   *Grossgrundeigentum und Soziale Frage. Versuch einer neuen Grundlegung der Gesellschaftswissenschaft.* Berlin: Vita Deutsches-Verlagshaus.

Pascal, Blasé
    1660   *Les Pensées.* London: J. M. Dent & Sons Ltd., 1913.

Pascot, Giovanni
    1896   *Origine delle religioni.* Pordenome: Gatti, 1900.

Passavant, Carl
    1884   *Craniologische Üntersuchungen der Neger und Negervölker, nebst einem Bericht über meine erste Reise nach Cameroons im Jahre* 1883. Basel: H. Georg.

Perty, Maximilian
    1874   *Die Anthropologie als die Wissenschaft von dem Körperlichen und geistigen Wesen des Menschen.* Leipzig and Heidelberg: C. F. Winter.

Plato
    1892   *The Republic* (trans. by Benjamin Jowett). New York: Random House, 1937.

Post, Albert Hermann
    1875   *Die Geschlechtsgenossenschaft der Urzeit und die Entstehung der Ehe. Ein Beitrag zu einer allgemeinen vergleichenden Staats und Rechtswissenschaft.* Oldenburg: Schulze.

1876 *Ursprung des Rechts.* Oldenburg: Schoulze.

1878 *Der Anfänge des Staats und Rechts lebens.* Oldenburg: Schulze (C. Berndt & A. Schwartz)

1880 *Bausteine für eine Allgemeine Rechtswissenschaft auf vergleichande ethnologische Basis.* Oldenburg: Schulze (C. Berndt & A. Schwartz)

1884 *Die Grundlagen des Rechts und die Grundzüge seiner Entwicklungsgeschichte.* Oldenberg: Schulze (A. Schwartz).

Ploetz, Karl Julius

1867 *Naturgeschichte des Rechts.*

1872 *Naturwissenschaft des Rechts.*

1884 *Auszug aus der alten, mittleren und neueren Geschichte.* Berlin: A. G. Ploetz.

Prichard, James Cowles

1855 *The Natural History of Man* (two vols.) London.

Quetelet, Lambert Adolphe Jacques

1835a *Sur l'homme et le developpement de ses facultés, ou de physique sociale.* Paris: Bachelier.

1835b *A Treatise on Man and the Development of his Faculties.* Edinburgh: W. and R. Chambers, 1842.

1848 *Du systéme social et des lois qui le régissent.* Paris: Guillaumin et Cie.

Ratzenhofer, Gustav

1901 *Positive Ethik. Die Verwirklichung des Sittlichseinsollenden.* Leipzig: F. A. Brockhaus.

1902 *Kritik des Intellekts.* Leipzig: F. A. Brockhaus.

Raumer, F. L. G. von

1883 *Historisches Taschenbuch.* Leipzig, 1830-1839.

Reibmayer, Albert

1897 *Inzucht und Vermischung beim Menschen.* Leipzig and Vienna: F. Deuticke.

Roberty, Eugène de

1881 *La sociologie, essai de philosophie sociologique.* Paris: G. Baillière.

Rocholl, Rudolf

1876 *Philosophie der Geschichte* (second edition). Berlin, 1881.

Rümelin, Gustave

1868a Über den Begriff eines socialen Gesetzes, *Tübinger Staatswissenschaftliche Abhandlungen.*

1868b *Über sociale Gesetze, Tübinger Staatswissenschaftliche abhandlungen.*

1875 *Reden und Aufsätze* (three vols.). Freiburg: J. P. B. Mohr, 1875-94.

1901 *Politics and the Moral Law* (trans. by Rudolf Tombo). New York: The Macmillan Co.

Rütimeyer, Ludwig

1866 *Über Art und Passe des zahmen europäischen Rindes.* Braunschweig: F. Vieweg, E. Sohn.

1868 *Versuch einer natürlichen Geschichte des Rindes, in seinen Beziehungen zu den Wieder Kävern in Allgemeinen.* Zurich: Druck von Zürther und Furrer (2 vols.).

Schäffle, Albert E. F.

1875 *Bau und Leben des sozialen Körpers. Encyklopädischer Entwurf einer realen Anatomie, Physiologie und Psychologie der menschlichen Gesellschaft, mit besonderer Rücksicht auf die Volkswirtschaft als sozialen Stoffwechsel.* Tübingen: Laupp'sche Buchhandlung, 1875-78.

1885 *Die formlosen Zusammenhänge oder Bindegewebe.* Tübingen: Laupp'sche Buchhandlung.

Spencer, Herbert

1864 *First Principles of a New System of Philosophy.* New York: D. Appleton Co.

1874 *The Study of Sociology.* New York: D. Appleton Co.

1880 *The Principles of Sociology* (three vols.). New York: D. Appleton Co., 1880-1896.

Stein, Ludwig

1897 *Die soziale Frage im Licht der Philosophie. Vorlesungen über Socialphilosophie und ihre Geschichte.* Stuttgart: Ferdinand Enke Verlag.

1898 *Wesen und Aufgabe der Sociologie. Eine Kritik der organischen Methode in der Sociologie.* Berlin: G. Reimer.

Steinmetz, S. Rudolf
   1901   Bedütung der Ethnologie für die Soziologie, *Barth Viertel-jahresschrift*, n.r. 21.
Thomas Aquinas
   1587   *On the Governance of Rulers (De regemine principum)*, trans. by Gerald B. Phelan. London and New York: Sheed & Ward, 1938.

Vico, Giambattista
   1725   *Principli di Scienza Nuova di Giambattista Vico. D'intorno alla commune Natura delle Nazioni* (second edition published with a note by Giuseppe Ferrari). Milan, 1836.
Virchow, Rudolf L. K.
   1877   *Beiträge zur physischen Anthropologie der Deutschen.* Berlin: Wiegandt, Hempel & Parey.
   1857   *Üntersuchungen über die Entwicklung es Schädelgrundes im gesunden und Krankhaften Zustande.* Berlin: G. Reimer.
Vogt, Karl Christoph
   1863   *Lectures on Man: His Place in Creation and in the History of the Earth.* London: Longman, Green, 1864.

Ward, Lester
   1903   *Pure Sociology: A Treatise on the Origin and Spontaneous Development of Society.* New York and London: The Macmillan Co.
Whewell, William
   1846   *Indications of the Creator: Extracts Bearing upon Theology from the History and the Philosophy of the Inductive Sciences.* London: J. W. Parker Ltd.
Wilser, Ludwig
   1904   *Die Germanenbeiträge zur Völkerkunde.* Eisenach and Leipzig: Thüringische Verlag.
Woltmann, Ludwig
   1903   *Politische Anthropologie: eine Üntersuchung über den Einfluss der Descendenztheorie auf die Lehre von der politischen Entwicklung der Völker.* Eisenach and Leipzig: Thüringische Verlag.

SUBJECT INDEX

adaptation, 41, 162, 216-17; to an obvious end, 155, 158

America, 14, 16, 32, 68, 174, 230

American Academy of Political Science, 72, 74

American Journal of Sociology, 11, 13, 61, 85

American sociology, *see also* sociology, 11-13, 57, 61, 64-66, 69-71, 90; and reception of Gumplowicz, 57-70

Ancient Society, 88f

Anomie, 23

Anthropology, 18-19, 24, 41, 46, 112, 135-36; 175-78

Anti-semitism, 15, 58

atomism, 26, 50, 109

Ausland, 165f

Austria, 12-13, 296-97

authority, 34, 37, 45, 51, 55-56, 67, 69, 232, 234, 236

autochthons, 111-12, 174

barbarism, 126-28

Basis of Rights and the History of Their Development, 132

Belief, behavior and the sociology of Knowledge, *see also* sociology, 48-57

Biblical theory of descent, *see also* descent, 110, 133

biology, 25-26, 48-49, 70, 96-97, 102

bi-variates, 21-22

bourgeoisie, 35, 231

causation, law of, 151-52

Chicago School, 65-66

Class, Status and Party, 47

class, 34-35, 44-45, 48, 50-52, 56, 59, 63-64, 69, 206, 213-15, 222-23, 228, 248; change, 60; civil, 248; formation, 60, 214; of phenomena, 141-150; theory of, 47

classes; the twofold origin of, 216-19

classification, 141-42, 223

collectivism, *see also* individualism, 238

communism, 239

complexity; law of, 153

conflict, 27, 32, 48, 51-52, 56, 64, 66, 100, 184; ideology, 35-36; policy, 35-36; sociology, 56; sociology of, 34-48; theory, 19, 34-37, 57, 63, 66, 68-69, 71

conformity to law; in development, *see also* development, 299-302

consensus, 20, 23, 31, 63-64, 66

conservatism, 36-37, 56, 70, 247

constitutionalism, 239, 297

corso, 54

custom, 124, 159, 222-23, 235, 260-61

cycle, *see also* development, 37; of development, 304-06; of social history, 314

Darwinism, 66, 100f, 168, 174f, 178f, 216

Darwinismus, 26, 62

descent, 111-12, 114, 157, 170-71, 223, 258

determinism, 29, 47, 54, 66, 71

Development of Sociology (The), 66

327

NAME INDEX

333

Date Due